THREE-QUARTER FACE

Also by PENELOPE GILLIATT

NOVELS
One By One
A State of Change
The Cutting Edge

SHORT STORIES
Come Back If It Doesn't Get Better
Nobody's Business
Splendid Lives

SCREENPLAY
Sunday Bloody Sunday

CRITICISM
Unholy Fools

BIOGRAPHIES
Renoir
Jacques Tati

Three-Quarter Face

Reports & Reflections

Penelope Gilliatt

Coward, McCann & Geoghegan, Inc.
New York

"Nabokov" was first published in *Vogue*. All other
pieces first appeared in *The New Yorker*.

Library of Congress Cataloging in Publication Data

Gilliatt, Penelope.
    Three-quarter face.

    A collection of movie reviews and profiles, chiefly
from The New Yorker.
    Includes index.
    1. Moving-pictures—Reviews. I. Title.
PN1995.G49   791.43'7   79-20607
ISBN 0-698-11015-3

Printed in the United States of America

To William Shawn, and to my daughter Nolan

Contents

THREE-QUARTER FACE

INTRODUCTION

A writer of fiction is often asked how that can marry with writing about the factual. I never see the conflict. A profile in the usual sense has to do with entering into someone else's temperament: which is a fictional process. Profiles proper and profiles extrapolated from observation of work are the matter of this book.

First, profiles proper. I believe—and *The New Yorker* has been good enough to recognize this (like *The Observer*, which I worked for over many years as film and theatre critic and still have a close connection with in the writing of pieces and of short stories)—that conventional reporting mechanics are rather off the point in reflecting someone's character and work. The mysteries of creativity are not to be found in misquoted gossip-press cuttings or even in verbatim public statements. The face is three-quarter turned to us in leisure and in friendship. But a vital quarter is always inexplicable except through paying attention to a man or woman's talk, small-talk, gestures, way of living, choice of intimates, and professional endeavors.

The essence of writing a profile proper, I believe, lies in spending convivial and discursive time with the person over weeks, sometimes spread out over years. There is not much truth to be found about something as complex as the creative temperament in the usual hastily confected question-and-answer method. To write of someone is not a matter for one morning. I don't believe it can be sagely done by the usual commonplace inquisition about what-are-your-hobbies and do-you-enjoy-good-conversation. The task is more inventive than that, more convivial, and more sober.

First of all, one has to love and admire and have pondered over the subject's work and cast of mind. This is why the writing of a profile is kin to creating a character in fiction. It can't be accomplished without affection, nor without taking a great many notes, even though the end result may seem pared down to the bone. Any writer who is any good will unconsciously reflect, in the prose of his report, the style of his subjects' own use of language, and some of them will talk sparsely: as Sam Beckett usually does, for one, except when he is playing pool late at night in Paris. Writing a profile proper can only work if there is underneath it an iceberg of the unreported. We all know that an unedited manuscript of every word one of us uttered in one day would convey nothing material, and I believe that the choice of what to quote and describe can only be taken by someone equipped not only with knowledge and interest but also with fellow-feeling. And perish the word "elliptical," which is often used pejoratively: there is more truth about character in a couple of lines of *King Lear*—say, about the intimacy between Lear and Fool in the majestically shortened "Never, never, never, never, never!", with its following "Pray you, undo this button"—than there often is in the "character studies" of the sort that celebrity-minded journalism so often wastes newsprint on now. They are not very nourishing. An equivalent of non-caloric artificially-flavored what-not soft drinks.

So what is a profile? It takes fiction, with its fugitive insights and heed, to tell us about the prevailing idiom of a character. The center of things lies in listening and watching at the living moment. To my mind, tape recorders tell very little. After a time—the length of time depending on whether the person is either shy or reassured by the sight of someone taking notes of talk in cars or at mealtimes, which Nanny said wasn't polite—my way of going about it is to make notes in one of my scores of black leather notebooks: records of real-life lines that are, in spirit, more like fictional lines of dialogue because, when they come to be quoted, they are compressed. The point of a profile is to record exact expressions of focussed and very particular minds. The truth lies, of course, not only in talk, but also in behavior. Sometimes one catches it as the character sees friends, plays word games, or goes walking with a dog. One can go shopping with people, or cook, as I did with the late, great Jean Renoir in Paris, or deal with pigeons on a terrace as I did with Woody Allen. I remember that Diane Keaton was rather startled at first when she noticed me hauling out a notebook in her gym class, but she saw the point later. Witty, brilliant woman.

And what moves one to write a profile? Essentially, devotion to the long track of a career. Sometimes, with a character engaged in non-solitary work—which rules out writers, of course, but applies very much to film and stage directors—it is crucial to watch them at work, rehearsing and shooting and editing. Impossible to write adequately of anyone who doesn't haunt the writer's thought. It follows that one has to speak the language of the person one is writing about. One can't do a profile through an interpreter. By "to speak his or her language," I mean something both literal and figurative. It is a joyful affair to report accurately on the inner vernacular of someone whose character and work one cherishes.

Second, profiles in the less exact sense: through reviews that are essays about the works that most precisely reflect the creator's intelligence. I suppose we all have a terror that the world is likely to blow up through stupidity or tantrum, but no one described in this book is guilty of the crisis of the receding brain-pan. Though we are certainly in the middle of an energy and food crisis, we are not yet in the over-touted McLuhan crisis of a decade ago in which no one in the near future was expected to read. It is moving, at what are considered to be universities in the backwoods rather than at Yale or Oxford or Harvard or wherever, to see the continuing capacity of undergraduates and dons to dwell in other centuries and continents—by reading, or going to see plays of other places and other times, or watching often subtitled films that don't reflect the immediate present of motorbikes and transistor radios. In doing a profile through reviewing someone's work, one needs to *evoke* it. Evocative criticism seems a better thing than analytic criticism. Analysis tends to be barren and overweening: it thinks itself the master of the thing criticised, not its servant. Such writing ties the English language into granny-knots. It forbids sentences that seek and anecdotes that expand. There is a world lost if we don't "waste" time. Jean Renoir said something of this sort to me in Paris when we were shopping for gigot of lamb. We were talking about bi-planes, and Mozart, and his maid's eyesight, and the word "sensass" above a nightclub. I suppose this was "wasting" time. But, as he said to me, most of the ideas that sustain civilization were born of loitering in the agora.

I

MASTERS

OF LUIS BUÑUEL

People often ask "How old is he?" about someone living who has made a long-ago landmark, and they tend to get ratty about a master who has ceased producing work. But that is his privilege, surely. Some artists have the prodigality of Mozart, some abide by a very few great works. There is a phrase in legal Latin that goes "stare decisis"; which means to "stand by decided matters." Morgan Forster, for instance, elected for the last decades of his life to publish no more novels. This didn't prevent him from being the most convivial company. I was once on a boat with him going around the Greek Islands. When we came to Mount Athos, where anything female—even a possibly female fly—is forbidden, we sat in deck chairs and talked. He, as a man, could have taken the climb, but he chose to refrain. It was his right, as I see it, as it was his right to stop novel-writing. The hell with hounders saying to great people "Where is the output?"

In the case of Luis Buñuel, he is still working at his peak in his old age. He survived exile from his beloved Spain, first in New York, where he was forced into demeaning jobs, then in Mexico, where he bravely went on making films on nearly impossibly low

17

budgets and with a lot of bad actors. His is a most moving case of genius surviving. He sat things out, and eventually, in his seventies, was able to work again in Spain. I have seldom seen such vivacity of intellect in the old. To watch him night-shooting in Seville was extraordinary. Every provision was made for his deafness and his comfort, but he raced about from his stolid director's chair like a twenty-year-old, enchanted to be at work, editing in his head with the conciseness of all the best filmmakers: think of Eisenstein, for instance, who never cluttered the cutting-room floor with waste footage, because he knew what he was going to do before he shot; or of Orson Welles.

I spent three years getting to know Buñuel and waiting for him to be ready to work on a film that has turned out to be one of the most innovative, funny, and intellectually complex works of his life, "That Obscure Object of Desire." He is a man of extraordinary stamina and courtesy. At the end of shooting the film, as I say in this piece about him, he left a party for the cast and the unit, and went into the restaurant garden without saying anything to the hordes who wanted to talk to him. He came back with an orange for me. We had spoken for three years of Surrealism, of which he is miraculously a working survivor. We were about to say goodbye and he guessed that I didn't fancy the restaurant's lunch of octopus much, any more than he did. This gaunt man, elated by work, took the time to bring me, decades younger, what he knew I would like.

People keep trying to make Luis Buñuel rest, like a sheepdog calming a recalcitrant sheep. "Do you think I'm growing old badly?" he asks me, and then dismisses the topic. More interesting things.

We are in Seville, where Buñuel is shooting a new version of Joseph von Sternberg's "The Devil Is a Woman," under the very Buñuel title of "That Obscure Object of Desire." He is seventy-seven now, this master; among the last of the Surrealists, and surely the only director from the silent days who is still making amazingly innovative pictures. "If I were a colonel, I'd have been on the retired list for years," he says to me one night during filming. "I always mean to stop, and then there is something else to say. I hate constraint. It's like the sight of blood. I have been accused sometimes of finding something yearning in odd people, of mocking the haplessness of their efforts, but their very unhappiness should surely be just one more reason to love such human beings. One of the things that appeals to me about the beautiful heroine of 'Belle de Jour,' which I started making in 1966, is her secret feeling that she deserves shame."

"That Obscure Object of Desire," which has nothing to do with von Sternberg's version and everything to do with the original book source, Pierre Louÿs's "La Femme et Le Pantin," and with Buñuel's poised and prodigal view of the world, is the first film that Buñuel has shot in his native Spain since "Tristana" (1969) and only the second since "Viridiana" (1961), which caused a hue and cry among the censors. They had seen the script, but they had no idea of the reflective antagonism to the regime which they would be countenancing. Buñuel swore after the Civil War never to make his home in his loved country while Franco was alive. His generation's roots are in the Civil War. "You won your war in 1945," he says to me sadly. "We lost ours in 1939." (In spite of the political changes that have recently taken place in Spain, he has still not returned.) He is wearing a black beret, as usual, and a cardigan done up on the wrong buttons. "I expect this will be a very small film," he says. "One needs just a hole to look out of, like a spider that has spun its web and is remembering what the world outside was like. This hole is the secret of things. An artist can provide an essential margin of alertness." Buñuel's films are full of genuinely Surreal elements, though they have often been misunderstood as simply the wisecracker's panoply of anti-bourgeois gags.

The old man is very deaf, and he prefers not to speak much English; he and I talk mostly in French. His French is as fluent as his Spanish. He is night-shooting a scene with his old friend Fernando Rey, the actor, in a balmy little square dripping with bougainvillea, just behind Seville Cathedral. It is 2 A.M. A postcard shop and a souvenir shop are staying open on account of the doings, the women who run the shops leaning against their open doors to watch and causing no disturbance. There is respect for work; the gossip about it can come later. Buñuel sits at a table in front of a monitor TV, with a hearing aid in one ear plugged through to the scene, so that he can hear the dialogue clearly. The seat is also to make him rest, but he is forever up and down with the actors and the continuity girl; the shots have long since been planned with the cameraman, Jean Harnois. Buñuel gets up in the middle of talking to me, makes his courtly little bow, and orders some coffee.

He starts to talk again while the cameraman works on the setup. "You see, I should like to make even the most ordinary spectator feel he is not living in the best of all possible worlds. We have to lean on this habit of affection. Don Jaime, in 'Viridiana,' takes pains to save the life of a bee. It is the falseness of society which interferes with the full concord of man. But there are many rebels. I am very fond of the priest in 'Nazarin,' which I made in 1958. He could as well be a hairdresser or a waiter. What interests us is that he stands by his ideas. Nazarin is a bastard heir to the great estate of the world." Buñuel watches the shot, and then says "Another," in French. He goes on about Nazarin. "It is left open to you to decide whether this unfrocked priest, with his disastrous struggles to deal with venality and suspicion, is meant to seem a good and simple Christian struggling with the Devil or a self-deceiving man gulled by an inadequate system." Buñuel's Mexico of 1900 is like a series of Goyas.

After getting up again, he remarks, "Octavio Paz said that all a chained man needs to make himself free is to close his eyes. Paraphrasing, I would add that if the white eyelid of the screen could disclose all that it has concealed the whole universe would jump."

"When your eyes flicker with the lids shut, it looks as if you are having a dream," I say.

"A dog in front of the fire. Are you warm enough?" he asks. "A film is the story of a dream. A dream recalled, because of the realistic nature of the cinema."

Buñuel makes the strange as normal as it often is. I tell him that in London I once saw a taxi drawn up facing the wrong way outside a house in a one-way street while the driver leaned up to dust the top with a yellow feather duster. He looks interested and amused, as he generally does, and I remember Francisco's valet in "El" (1952) polishing his bicycle in bed. Certain shapes seem to make Buñuel laugh: bicycles, cellos. In "L'Âge d'Or" (1930), fragments of Beethoven symphonies, Wagner operas are made startling and comic by being rescored for chamber orchestra. And who can forget the mysteriously funny solemn cellist in "The Discreet Charm of the Bourgeoisie" (1972). Buñuel sees life pencilled in with mystery. If he is inclined sometimes to show us the deformed or dwarfish, remember that these people are described in Spain as touched by the hand of God.

Henry Miller called this visionary man a passionate skeptic. I should call him a stoic optimist. His hopes for film are boundless. "Mystery is an essential element in any work of art," he says. "It's usually lacking in films, which should be the most mysterious of all. Most filmmakers are careful not to perturb us by opening the windows of the screen onto their world of poetry. Cinema is a marvellous weapon when it is handled by a free spirit. Of all the means of expression, it is the one that is most like the human imagination. What's the good of it if it apes everything conformist and sentimental in us? It's a curious thing that film can create such moments of compressed ritual. The raising of the everyday to the dramatic. I have wanted all my life to make this world visible to people: the world we can't read about in newspapers."

We move to another scene. There is a quarter of the usual filmmaker's fuss about new setups. We talk about Defoe: about "A Journal of the Plague Year," a book that is a favorite of his and mine—a piece of apparently on-the-spot reporting that was actually done fifty-eight years later—and about "The Adventures of Robinson Crusoe," which Buñuel made into a film in Mexico in 1952.

"The Robinson Crusoe idea interests us, doesn't it?" he says, his eyes, which are huge, staring into mine. "We are fascinated by the question of whether we could live alone." Of the film, he says, "At first, Robinson is full of superior airs about his situation, but then he discovers he is part of a great fraternity. He suddenly lets out a howl to the heavens for the sake of the company of his own voice. Is this Surrealism in the sense in which it's often used, to mean the unreal? I don't think so. It was Surrealism that taught me to suppose thought and sympathy are moral paths that men cannot refuse to take. It taught me that man isn't nature. A marvellous poetic stride forward."

Buñuel's work is born of the humor of a sad man distressed by his own vision of the world but with a fond eye for the mass of self-deceptions that make life bearable. He is one of the most mannerly men I have ever met. The only thing that stirs him to impatience is the sort of charity that is seen as a virtue by people who don't question the anguish that makes charity necessary. "I'm not a Christian, but I'm not an atheist, either," he says. "I'm weary of hearing that accidental old aphorism of mine, 'I'm not an atheist, thank God.' It's outworn. Dead leaves. In 1951, I made a small film called 'Mexican Bus Ride,' about a village too poor to support a church and a priest. The place was serene, because no one suffered from guilt. It's guilt we must escape from, not God."

He pauses to watch Fernando Rey. "In spite of what you hear, the films my collaborators and I have made are not in the least ambiguous in practice. Only in theory, as an element of struggle or violence. The crisis of drama comes at the moment of doubt. In the case of Robert Bresson's work, something very strange happens. Everything seems quietist. Yet one has the strongest possible presentiment that something is going to happen. This is what could be called violence in film: this powerful state of doubt."

The extremely nonviolent Buñuel has a wife, whom he dotes on, and two sons—one French, one American—whom he adores. He has a blithe sense of humor. One day, over coffee, he remarks solemnly to me, "To the Devil in disguise I say, 'I believe in God, but regarding His only son there is a lot to be discussed.'" At Buñuel's home in Mexico City, if you ask for tea he says that his house specializes in liquor but that he keeps Hungarian wine for tea eccentrics.

Buñuel was born into a patrician family in Calanda, a small town near Saragossa, on February 22, 1900, and went to Jesuit college in Saragossa, where he took a passionate interest in insects. At the University of Madrid, he read Freud and wrote film reviews (including one on Keaton, who is an idol of his). His father, before marrying, had spent years in Cuba, where, as a wholesale merchant, he amassed something of a fortune. As a young child, Luis sang in the church choir, with a very good voice, and learned to serve at Mass. He devised entertainments. Belonging to a family of seven children, he tended to make fun happen within the confines of the household. His sister Conchita remembers one evening when Luis recited what she translates as:

> With this pair of scissors
> And will to fight, it's plain
> We'll have a revolution
> And capture all of Spain.

After a time in Madrid, where he reluctantly studied agricultural engineering at the university and later, at the Natural History Museum, became absorbed in helping to classify insects, he went to Paris and explored Dadaism. "Dada was made up of refugees from all the countries of Europe," he says. "As the old world crumbled, man could begin again. That was our hope. Our wish was to honor the claims of the unconscious, and I suppose Freud was our patron saint." He made Surrealist films, financed by his mother, by the Vicomte de Noailles, and by a friend's lottery winnings. He also worked with Dali, but the collaboration was short-lived. It amounted to "Un Chien Andalou" (1928) and a few days on "L'Âge d'Or" before they had a row. No wonder. Buñuel is the least publicity-seeking man in the world; Dali thrived on publicity.

Frenchmen and Spaniards find a clear difference between the tracks that Surrealism took in their two countries. The French, say the Spanish, are more fanciful; the Spanish, say the French, are more concrete. A French Surrealist of the time might have shown a tree growing out of the ground upside down; a Spaniard would always have shown the tree the right way up, however great an element of the fantastic he gave to it. Buñuel, this great Spanish Surrealist, spent formative years in France but has never lost the Spanishness of his angle of mind.

After he had done some dubbing work in France and Spain and had made four films in Spain, the Civil War broke out. Buñuel offered his services as a film man to the Spanish Republican government in Paris. "In 1938, I was sent on a 'diplomatic mission' to America," he says in Seville one morning. "Suddenly, the war was over, and I had no friends, no job, no country. I got work at the Museum of Modern Art, thanks to Miss Iris Barry. I was employed to dub films for Latin America, because of my fine speaking voice." As he speaks the last phrase, he lowers his voice to a deep bell chime. "Then Dali published an attack on me for being anticlericalist. The trustees seem to have been alarmed by Dali's information that I was a member of the French Communist Party." In 1942, he sadly left the museum. "I thought the end of the world had come." He wrote and spoke the Spanish narration of Army Intelligence films and worked in Hollywood as a dubbing expert. In 1946, he went into exile in Mexico, where there were years of semi-obscurity, of making potboilers on low budgets with melodramatic actors. It should be said that some of these potboilers are invigorating pieces of work. "Illusion Travels by Streetcar" (1953) is a reckless low comedy about a streetcar driver and a conductor who get drunk one night, steal a streetcar, and then spend a frenetic time trying to return it. Instead of passengers, butchers' sides of beef hang from the handstraps in the streetcar. An American woman tourist gets scared when she is told she can ride the streetcar free. She thinks it is a Communist plot. In "Tristana," many years later, the same Buñuel voice sounds when Fernando Rey, as an obstreperous rationalist, shouts at a funeral party, "Long live the living!"

In 1950 came "Los Olvidados," which was greeted with a furor of welcome at Cannes. The film is a strictly unsentimental view of a teen-age gang in a Mexican slum. "I made a version of 'Wuthering Heights' in 1953," Buñuel said. "It's no good. A great book. In

24

the old Paris days, it was the one we most admired. But while I was away they overlaid a huge Wagnerian sound track on the print. Nobody can even say 'Thank you' without its sounding like the 'Liebestod.'" He spoke of "The Young One" (1960). "The Mexicans' inability to perform with the faintest hint of naturalism meant that I had to ask Zachary Scott to overplay drastically, so as to impose some unity on the style."

Since 1958, there has been one masterpiece after another: "Diary of a Chambermaid" (1964), "Simon of the Desert" (1965), "Belle de Jour," "The Milky Way" (1968), "Tristana," "The Discreet Charm of the Bourgeoisie," "Le Fantôme de la Liberté" (1974). He always says that he is never going to make another film, and his current producer, a staunch and witty Polish Parisian named Serge Silberman, is prepared to fly to Mexico City again and again to rouse Buñuel from his quiet life with his many dictionaries, his books on insects, his siesta, and his evening drink. He likes going to sleep with piano music being played on the record-player. He says to me that he would prefer to have lived in the Middle Ages: "More introspective, more spiritual, and more rebellious."

Silberman and Buñuel first met in 1963. Silberman asked him for a loan of ten dollars. "Never repaid," said Buñuel cheerfully in the Oak Room of the Plaza, in New York in the summer, en route between Mexico City and pre-production in Paris on "That Obscure Object of Desire." "That's a producer for you." Mr. Silberman was at the table. Buñuel firmly ordered Irish stew for Silberman, "so that Serge won't exchange it for something else, because it's already a mélange." Buñuel wore a brown linen jacket, which made his eyes burn more brilliantly than ever under his noble forehead. He and Silberman fool around together like a couple of boys. Buñuel's eccentricity and love of the bizarre are legendary. There is a story, for instance, that as a child he ate ant sandwiches. Not a word of truth in it, he says. The passion of his childhood was for putting on shadow shows. The little boy was already an original. With Surreal effect, he introduced a real actor into a puppet show.

After Silberman had read fifty pages of "Diary of a Chambermaid," he decided to make it. At the end of the night shooting of

"That Obscure Object of Desire," Buñuel, recalling this, puts his hand on my shoulder. "The writer and I worked in a monastery, you see. I pretended to humor Serge, and told him, 'We're going to take you to a nice house in the country. The people will be dressed in loose uniforms but won't do you any harm.' Serge really thought he was going to a lunatic asylum."

Six of Buñuel's last eight films have been written in collaboration with Jean-Claude Carrière, a French dramatist, who played a curé for Buñuel in "Diary of a Chambermaid." Carrière, too, went to Jesuit college. He told me, "Buñuel says it's getting more and more difficult to find an actor who can speak correct Latin." Carrière says that Buñuel's unwillingness to talk about himself is matched by genuine humility when he talks about his films. Above all, he wants them to be absolutely simple, direct, unaffected. He is hurt when he is accused of making films that are warped or profane. He believes that works of art begin in the unknowable. A true Spaniard, preoccupied with the inward, he is antipathetic to the French legacy of Descartes and Voltaire which holds that everything can be explained. He sometimes gives actors startlingly un-French directions.

Francisco Rabal overdid coming out of an elevator in "Belle de Jour," and looked around nervously. "What shall I think about?" he asked Buñuel.

"Oh, think about your aunt," said Buñuel.

On the set in Seville, an autograph hunter comes up to Buñuel and asks for his signature. "Dali would be jealous," he murmurs.

At lunch for the crew, Buñuel and I sit apart from the racket. "When Jean-Claude and I work together, we work always from a key word. 'The Milky Way' was 'heresy.' 'Discreet Charm' was 'repetition.' 'Le Fantôme de la Liberté' was 'hazard.'" He goes on, "I find myself disliking very few things. I am fond of the hotel where I stay in Paris. It overlooks a beautiful cemetery. So much is beautiful and striking."

26

He begins to laugh, and I say, "What is it?"

"I was remembering an actress with two lovers, both filmmakers, who both made her swear never to make a film with Fellini. Two filmmakers not jealous of one another but jealous of someone else, whom they'd never even met. Sophisticated people sometimes have truly Surreal worries."

"There is a difference between Surrealism and grotesquerie, but most people don't understand it, don't you find?" I say.

"We won't find the difference in Roget's Thesaurus or in Larousse, but it is there, I see, in your head. I wish I were back in Paris with André Breton and could tell him about our conversation. We could have a fine time. Unfortunately, you are the wrong age." He looks at me severely, this genius whose vivacity of intellect is a young man's. "However, it can't be helped. Mostly, things have a tendency to happen at the right time."

"Did Surrealism?"

"It was absolutely necessary. This territory of trapdoor fantasies had to be explored. I wish we had some music."

"'I beg of you, something from Scarlatti,'" I say, quoting from "The Exterminating Angel" (1962) one of the meaningless remarks that the party dialogue warms up to in its absurdity.

He nods and grins; he has a true grin. I speak again of "The Exterminating Angel," in which a group of smart people at a dinner party inexplicably find themselves unable to leave, and slowly disintegrate. "Hell is not oneself. Hell is a lot of people who won't go," says Buñuel. "I've always liked the idea of people separated from the rest of society." He admires Kafka, "Lord of the Flies," and many Latin-American authors who have never been translated into English. He reads a lot and travels little: two reasons for the lack of clutter in his mind.

"We are living in the best of times and the worst of times," he says. "Greece was more international; Rome was more materialistic; the modern world is a place where we can do anything. Incidentally, what is the word for *métis* in English? I have always been interested in the idea." He commits the English word "mongrel" to memory, almost visibly printing it on some slate in his head.

27

"There is everything to be hoped for from mongrels. Often it's the purebred who have caused such bigotry, who have becalmed the spirit of man."

He speaks about Freud. "The influence of post-Freudian attitudes in America has sometimes made my films slow to be accepted there. The hack inheritors of Freudian theory have made a certain class rather literal-minded. Of course, the paradox is that Freud himself was immensely important to the Surrealists. A great prophet. Though I still don't want to be told who my mother is, who my father is. I know this. I prefer to dream about who might be my sister. Otherwise, I am a very isolated man. I don't like crowds. I like my friends. I can't understand producers in Hollywood." He rapidly and skillfully mimes a man talking on two telephones at once. "They took me out to Hollywood. Dubbing Latin-American films. They asked me what I would like to see. A script conference? A studio scene? A cutting room? I said a studio. There was this beautiful woman speaking an unknown language and then yelling at me to get out. They told me she happened to be Greta Garbo, and the language she was speaking happened to be English."

He gets up and walks off, and comes back with an orange for me, picked from a tree. "You weren't lonely?" he says.

"I was thinking."

"Film is the complement of conversation. As a cat is. I keep a cat in the half-open drawer of my workroom in Mexico. Many a tale we have spun together. Insects are one thing, cats another."

We go on talking, and then he abruptly gets up and asks me to forgive him if he has a siesta. As he says this, straight-backed, leaning forward from the hips, he looks like a sail in the wind.

Buñuel is famous for his speed of working. He edits a film in his head before shooting. This way of filmmaking is natural to him, and not just the result of working in Mexico, where his average shooting schedule is fifteen days and other filmmakers' even less. He and Silberman have a long-standing argument about whether it took a day or a day and a half to edit "The Discreet Charm of the Bourgeoisie." He wears a viewfinder constantly: "Not because I ever use it but to remind myself that I am a film director. American films show the triumph of the will. I make films about the failure of the will. Not maudlin but serious. The sentimental is the immoral." When Nazarin, the failed Christ figure, is on the road and is offered a pineapple, a symbol of help and charity, one feels a flash of hope for the loosening of human bondage. Buñuel's love for everything human is not exhausted at the end of the bitter "Viridiana," when, after beggars have stormed the novice Viridiana's house, and even raped her, life is left with peace apparently restored: cards being played, and Viridiana trying to go back to her life of prayer. His admirers include Carlos Fuentes, whose mistrust of sentimentality and renown he shares. "The credits in a film should be done away with," Buñuel says. "Films should become anonymous, like Chartres." Henri Langlois, the film archivist, once said to me of Buñuel that the way he shoots everyday objects gives them the dignity of isolation. He photographs things in a way that makes their essence seem more actual and more potent than ever before.

Buñuel looks grave when he approaches the subject of censors. "They are like nannies sitting on our shoulders, inhibiting calm and destroying our phantoms. 'Viridiana' was shown to them in pieces. They asked for only one slight change, in the ending. I felt that it was actually an improvement over what I had thought of. Trade agreements were invoked to prevent the film from being shown in France. I don't see why people objected. It's the story of the progress of an innocent and her discovery of the world, in all its carnality and greed. The beggars and thieves with whom she surrounds herself after her Candide life are not up to her innocence. They can only complain that the string beans are a little tough today."

Jeane-Claude Carrière, in Paris, described their way of writing: "Working together means living together. Buñuel is a man of habit. He can't write in a city. We go to the country in Mexico, or to our monastery in Spain. We work in each other's presence, talking about the film. Then, in the evening, I write a scene, with two copies. At six-thirty, he goes to have a drink. When I come at seven, he is obliged to tell me a story. He is absolutely sure that the imagination has to be trained, like a sportsman. He has such a fantastic universe of his own, so peculiar and so rich, that the effort to get it all into the script is doomed. Most of the time, what he needs is for me to choose. In our monastery, once, when we were writing, some Mexican journalists arrived and said, 'Do you think you will get the Academy Award?' Luis said with a very upright look, 'I have already paid twenty-five thousand dollars for it.' They were appalled. Not what they expected of a great man."

At a break in the shooting in Seville, Buñuel says, "I have a horror of unusual angles. I sometimes work out a marvellously clever shot, and then the cameraman and I laugh and we scrap the whole thing and shoot quite straightforwardly. I'm interested in repetitions. We used them a lot in 'The Exterminating Angel.' In life, we repeat ourselves every day. How many times has it happened at a party that we say hello to someone and an hour later we shake hands again, say hello, and then exclaim 'O, what are we doing? We just said hello a while ago.' "

When I arranged to see Buñuel at his house in Mexico City, while he was equivocating about making "That Obscure Object of Desire," he insisted, with typical courtliness, on coming to pick me up. I was ready five minutes early, but he was earlier. He plans the coming day as exactly as he plans his films. "We shall have a conversation and something to drink, and then lunch, and we shall find out what interests us both," he said when we met. "Then if you'll excuse me, I shall have a short nap. Then more conversation and another something to drink." I remembered Geneviève Page in "Belle de Jour," and her war on torpor. If ever a man has vanquished the stupefying by sheer quality of mind, it is Buñuel. He is fascinated by almost everything. He has no need of newspapers to be as scholarly as any filmmaker I know.

His house is a pale-pink brick, with white-painted gates, a dog called Tristana, and a pretty courtyard. The drawing room leading into the dining room is dominated by a Dali portrait of him, which he said he had just brought himself to hang. "Thirty-five years is too long for a fight." The word "fight" made me remember hearing that he had been a boxer in his youth.

30

Mme. Buñuel sat quietly on the sofa doing needlework. She met her husband in Paris, in 1926, when she was a eurythmics teacher.

"Mexican actors don't seem to be teachable, but did you ever manage to train a crew?" I asked.

We sat down in the dining room. "There can be dignity in technical shortcomings," said Buñuel. "But to work with Catherine Deneuve or Fernando Rey: what a reprieve."

"Yes."

He looked at my fingers. "You are playing the piano in your head."

"Yes."

"I like to think of instruments as having personalities. The piccolo is an ants' nest of sound. The violin is the carpenter of sound, sawing away contentedly. The clarinet is a poor thing: to be a sheep's baa transformed to wood is humiliating. Bass drum: prophetic, stubborn, slightly rude."

"Does Freud still interest you?" I asked.

"The cinema is an involuntary imitation of dreams. It might have been invented to express the life of the unconscious, whose roots go so deep into poetry."

"Characters in your films often have the look of a Zurbarán," I said. "That gaze inward."

"You saw the Zurbaráns in Seville? I often think of them."

"Your films make one wonder what's going on in people's minds."

"Dreams, and also the most everyday questions. 'What time is it?' 'Do you want to eat?' That sort of thing interests us all very much. When I am back in Spain, I shall need my strategy and my accomplices to stop my mind from wandering. We shall be shooting near my family home in Calanda. The town has three thousand inhabitants. It is savage and illiterate, with a foundation of elegance. On feast days, there are hunts with packs of dogs. Goya was born nearby. At Easter, there is a beating of drums for two days and two nights. It is an unforgettable example of the Catholic Church's capacity for assimilating pagan ritual into the Resurrection story. One can't get the sound of the drums out of one's ears. I often think of it.

31

"My father was a volatile man. He emigrated to Cuba. He came back to Spain, at forty-seven, in 1899, and married a beauty. I tell you this because one day, who knows"—solemnly—"you may want to write an encyclopedia and put it in. My childhood slipped by in an almost medieval atmosphere. The two basic elements of that atmosphere were a profound eroticism—perhaps I should say intensity; certainly not blasphemy, which is to be distinguished from heresy—and a profound consciousness of death. These are very Spanish characteristics, and our art is impregnated with them. The Civil War, ferocious as no other has been, exposed them only too clearly. At Calanda, we lived in a beautiful house, with cypress trees running down to the river; I have put it into my films."

We had lunch. Mexican chairs, Mexican sideboard, Mme. Buñuel in a yellow smock. Chairs grated. "I like natural sound," said Buñuel. "A zipper, a glass on a table. I can't bear music put onto a film any longer. Perhaps it's because I am deaf."

A pile of dictionaries rose beside his plate as we talked. "I like to find things out." He was tracking down something from Joyce. He is attuned to Melville. The atmosphere was convivial and inquiring. Jeanne Moreau, whom he worships as an actress, once said that her ideal life would be to live as Buñuel's pupil in a house run by him, and take a cold shower every morning, and talk, and go to bed at sundown.

I asked Buñuel about his sons. A friend of mine had once found him crying for joy at the news that one son, whom he hadn't seen for nearly a year, was coming to see him. "They are both very content," he said. "Their school days were happy, and I think they never felt a sense of injustice, which is the most corrosive emotion, apart from jealousy." I could see his mind going back to some past injustice done to him; he saw my eyes following his mind, and he said, "The only cure is to cleave to the truth. One day at the Jesuit college, there was an undervest in my soup. 'Please, sir, there's an undervest in my soup,' I said. I was sent out of the room, but I said as I went, 'But there is an undervest in my soup.' I suppose some boy put it there. The same thing has often happened to me with my films. People don't believe it, but there *is* an undervest in the soup."

"The revolution of Surrealism has been won. What's the sediment? What would be your greatest hope for film now?"

He replied instantly. "To give us the ease of a quest for pleasure and inquiry which isn't followed by the pounding hooves of guilt. It should be possible. Imagination will do the work."

DECEMBER 5, 1977

OF JOHN FORD

He pretended to be right-wing, he seemed by the evidence of his
public countenance to be right-wing, but he was entirely left-wing
in his attitude to the virtual repertory company of actors he drew
up. He valued their communality as much as any theatrical Com-
munist writing furious tracts in libraries could ever hope to do. He
was deeply and importantly American in his sense of the frontier
mood and in his feeling, one that abides in the American continent,
that much remains to be discovered. It is this sense of inquiry, far
more than the "streets paved with gold" myth, that I believe draws
so many foreigners of seriousness to America. This is not to say
that New York City—the immediate entrance to America for so
many people from Europe, the Caribbean, Puerto Rico—is not
packed with drunks, resentful bus-drivers who pull away from bus
stops just as scuttling old ladies burdened with shopping-bags are
within hope of catching the thing, and youngsters with knives
who will stab an Orthodox Jew, carrying no money because it is an
Orthodox holiday, in the hope of robbing him of twenty-five cents.
But John Ford's films celebrate the stamina and decorum that char-

acterize the America that is seldom written about, seldom visited
by foreigners. We owe his work a debt.

John Ford occupies a unique place in American cinema. Though
he was born of two strongly Irish immigrants, in 1895, his films set
in Ireland seem diluted compared with his films set in America, in
which his sensibility about the sweep of the country's history
reflects the exceptionally American fact that his parents chose to
inhabit this land instead of being its citizens by accident of birth.
Even some of his earliest films are clear predecessors temperamen-
tally of great later works like "Stagecoach" (1939), "The Grapes of
Wrath" (1940), "My Darling Clementine" (1946), and "She Wore
a Yellow Ribbon" (1949). All his films may be large-scale, but they
have a warm intimacy of observation. Ford always had an intense
talent for dailiness, and his films about America's past exude a
strong feeling for the household zone of history. For all the vitality
of his narrative technique, character was of more consequence to
him than plot. Ford was urgently interested in the matter of how
an individual behaves when he is pushed to the limit—which is to
say that Ford's nature was theatrical, since all drama, whether
tragedy, comedy, romance, or farce, catches people at moments of
extremity. But the events of a Ford film unfurl in no hurry. There
is always time for the establishment of a mood belonging to a
character, or for Ford's view of a piece of behavior. He was much
stirred by moments of mourning and moments of forgiveness. The
elegances of sexual intrigue were of no interest to him. There was a
deep chivalry at work here, and a presiding interest in the tri-
umphs achieved by people who are themselves ultimately defeated: one thinks of the vanquished heroes of "The Long Gray Line"
(1955), "The Searchers" (1956), "The Wings of Eagles" (1957),
"The Last Hurrah" (1958). It is significant that the first film he

35

made after the Second World War was "They Were Expendable" (1945), which was about the First Philippine Campaign, for Bataan and Corregidor, in 1942, one of America's most afflicting losses among remembered battles.

Ford's pictures create a stratified moral structure in which ethical truths can be trusted to prove themselves even if the proving costs the exponents damage. Men and women—though there are not many interesting women in Ford's pictures—exist as models for others and as promontories of divine goodness. They are individuals only incidentally. Ford's Catholicism affects the nature of his films to a notable degree, considering how subordinate a hand he generally credited himself with in his scripts. He liked to think of himself as a jobster, and made much too little of the idea that he stamped his work indelibly with his beliefs. It could be said, though, that his films are anti-intellectual, and that this accounts for the sticky muddle he made in "The Fugitive" (1947) of the graceful dubieties of Graham Greene's "The Power and the Glory." The flickering verve of his films lies in their concreteness. We are in a laconic, fraternal, high-spirited, freebooting world, which is seen always from the point of view of the infantryman, and in which the infantryman stands for the group. In Ford's Westerns, there are remarkably few of the solitary shoot-outs that have made the standardized Western hero's lone swagger down Main Street represent such a shrivelled idea of courage. Ford was concerned not with conflicts through saloon doors but with conflicts of interest: migrant workers at odds with droughts, upstart officers at war with the West Point brass. For him, contact with the open air leads to virtue. He bestows on the American past a mixture of meditativeness and awe, and it is part of his achievement that he tells us more about our feelings for history than about the record. He summons up the America of Lee, Lincoln, Twain. A poignantly adhered-to state of order reigns over the moments of convulsive historical development which so many of his movies recount. There are visible annexes of this feeling for the regulated and concordant in his scenes about families, in the number of men who wear uniforms, and in the proportion of his characters who are doctors (in "The Hurricane," of 1937, for instance; in "Stage-coach;" in "The Horse Soldiers," of 1959).

A Beethoven-musicologist friend who has learned to read Beethoven's musical shorthand has deciphered long-buried evidence of ideas that Beethoven was later to develop or reconsider in writing the matchless quartets. Equivalent scholarship and love of art have gone into the Museum of Modern Art's patient preservation program of films of John Ford made between 1917 and 1937. To quote Eileen Bowser, an associate curator of film at the museum, "A few years ago, Twentieth Century-Fox agreed to make available its surviving nitrate studio prints and negatives for the museum to copy on acetate stock, insuring that these films would continue to live long after the nitrate has turned to powder." The museum is in the midst of showing us its rescue work. As far as it can, and where the decay of the nitrate print does not prohibit projection, it is screening the original nitrate prints rather than the copies. The nitrate prints are beautiful, with the peculiarly sharp, silvery quality of black-and-white which has been lost since the coming of acetate, and which all the technological accomplishments of later cinema have never compensated us for. John Ford himself had little use for the novelty of the wide screen, which gave him what he called "a lot of real estate" on each side of the people he wanted to show; and until the end of his life, in 1973, he continued to prefer black-and-white to color. "Why?" asked the American film director Burt Kennedy once, in a published dialogue. Ford said, "You like spinach? It's all a matter of taste."

Ford's special reverence for doctors is plain among the films at the museum in "The Prisoner of Shark Island" (1936). The plot is based on the true story of Dr. Samuel Alexander Mudd, who set John Wilkes Booth's fractured leg after Booth had killed Lincoln. Mudd was arrested for doing his job as a physician, and sentenced to life imprisonment in Fort Jefferson, the disease-riddled Civil War prison on Shark Island, off the Florida coast. After a racking and unsuccessful attempt to escape, he won executive pardon for his bravery during an outbreak of yellow fever. Ford's Dr. Mudd (Warner Baxter)—the script is by Nunnally Johnson—is typically

37

untriumphant both in escaping and in doctoring. He is simply an ordinary physician whom crisis amplifies.

To extend the terms of the profession, there is also the benign medicine man played by Will Rogers in "Steamboat Round the Bend" (1935, and also at the museum). The Doc is the proprietor of a rickety steamboat that goes in for a race with the handicap of seeming to be made of scrap iron and old boots. Will Rogers gives a tender comic performance that takes its own sweet time. Among other things, the character has to deal with a hypocritical preacher, dressed in a flowing white robe and a silk hat, who is vehemently teetotal as he gives a sermon to a boatload of swiggers. Later, there is a fine pause in which the Doc considers the case of a truculent, scared runaway girl who is trying to shout herself into feeling grownup. "I got some hot coffee," he says after looking at her with careful concern.

Ford's talent for a particular kind of luminous, mischievous gangster comedy is not to be underrated in favor of his more obviously serious pictures (though I don't care much for a flappy Moss Hart comedy, in the current showings, starring Wallace Beery and named "Flesh," which was made in 1932). This talent is represented at the museum in a splendid example called "Up the River" (1930), with Humphrey Bogart and Spencer Tracy: Bogart's second film, Tracy's first. Bogart's job in prison is to take down the details of incoming criminals' biographies. He questions a gentle girl who seems destined to be his first love; after she had finished telling fortunes, she says, looking fragile, she would recommend certain oil stocks. Spencer Tracy, already exhibiting the stoic energy onscreen that made audiences assume he wasn't doing anything (a quality that often defines great film acting, including Brando's), asks the girl if she's really stuck on the Bogart character or if there's a chance for him to muscle in. He seems to have an attachment to impossible aspirations. On arriving at the jail, he asks for a cell with a double bed and a southern exposure. Bogart gets out of prison and back to an iron-bar mother who supposes him to have been in China. To have to reply "Coming, Mother" every time she shouts for him obviously strikes him as worse than jail. Spencer

Tracy and another escaped convict—after aiding Bogart—break back into prison, because they want to play on the convicts' baseball team. The film is laxly funny, terse, idiosyncratic; made from a screenplay by Maurine Watkins, it has some of the flavor of a movie by Preston Sturges.

If one had to begin to make up a "typical" Ford film, I suppose it would include John Wayne, scenes in Monument Valley, a dance, a fight, a funeral, a train, the steaming breath of horses. It would have his comedy, his intense and sustained gravity, his feeling for theatricality in landscape. It would have his particular use of light: something on fire at night, scenes in bright sun seen through the frames of windows or of openings in darkness. It would have an ideal Ford stock cast: to give us, perhaps, Hank Worden's bad jokes, Ward Bond's blunt candor, Jack Pennick's agreeable dopiness, Victor McLaglen's air of an Irish bouncer, and Henry Fonda's look of being the President we need. There would be no lechers, and few cardinal sins; instead there would be pugnacity and boozing to stand for the hedonist vices that Ford's Irish soul permitted. The period would be one in which society is on trial: during a war, or amid popular crisis, or winning some sort of Pyrrhic victory. Events would take place in a succession as easygoing as Ford's attitude toward his own past, and the nation recorded would be the America that died in the Civil War, if it ever existed. (John Ford used to recall that his father had four brothers who fought in the Civil War: one on the Confederate side, two on the Union side, and one on both—"He got *two* pensions.") At the end, the central figure would characteristically fend off society's endearments and soft comforts; a Ford hero exemplifies an ideal of self-sacrifice that is as convinced as Abraham Lincoln's renunciation of his law practice to change American history. But even including all this, would one arrive anywhere near, say, "Young Mr. Lincoln" (1939), with its detail and veracity about small-town myth? With its Independence Day log-splitting contest, its tug-of-war won by hitching a rope to a mule cart, its adjudicator of a pie contest who chooses between apple and peach with the gravity of a Supreme Court judge? Its performance by Henry Fonda of a young Mr. Lincoln whose impulse not to respond overfast seems the product of country stock? Its wonderful sequence about two country brothers caught up in a murder of which each is accused of being guilty, and about their mother, who, in a Solomon situation, refuses to save one child at the expense of the other? Everything in this sequence is opacity and muffled sound; would anyone but Ford have shot it so?

"Young Mr. Lincoln" is too well known and comes slightly too late in Ford's career to be in the museum's program, but at least two films that are in it are just as typical, startling, and deeply affectionate about the on-running of American history. One is "The Iron Horse" (1924), about the building of the Union Pacific Railroad. The element of profit-making cynicism that must have gone into the building of the railroad is here veiled in a feeling of idyll. Though we are watching something in the movement of history which must have been rushing and harsh, Ford makes it seem lyric. Davy Brandon (George O'Brien) and his father want to pioneer the wilderness. The father is killed by a two-fingered renegade in an Indian raid. An evil creature named Bauman, jockeying to make a mint, fails in maneuvers to get the tracks to run through his property, but he persuades the Indians to attack the railroad that is being built with such fierce difficulty. Many of the workers are Chinese. ("Say, boss, there's no getting on with these furriners. I knocked five of them down and even then they wouldn't work," remarks someone in a subtitle. This is an example of Ford's raucous sense of irony, I believe, not of his occasional bigotry.) The film is full of shots packed with differentiated, expressive faces: faces of people watching a scrap in a saloon, fighting Indians, lugging heavy railroad ties, being nearly mowed down by stampeding buffalo. There is a battle characteristically shot in the doorframe of a semi-built log cabin. The cabin is a place hardly begun, like the lives of the pioneers. The train represents the force of events; the figures seem small, and they are either swept along or left behind. A white man is killed in railroad festivities, and his widow falls on his grave as the train chugs on. An Indian is killed in an attack on the railroad, and a dog sniffs his body as the train heaves its way

40

across the continent to link up with the tracks from the East. Ford was only twenty-nine when he made "The Iron Horse," but it already bears his marks. A powerful humor, camaraderie, and respect for courage are active in this reverie about endeavor, which was partly shot in no circumstances for dreaming: in a temperature of twenty degrees below zero.

The Museum is also showing "Three Bad Men" (1926), which is better still. This one was written by Ford and John Stone from a novel by Herman Whitaker, and beautifully photographed by Ford's great colleague George Schneiderman (co-photographer of "The Iron Horse"). It is 1876 in the West. Gold-rush time, land-rush time. In an iris shot we see a tree being felled. We open up to a wilderness. Three rakish bad men (George O'Brien, J. Farrell MacDonald, Tom Santschi), who are furtively heroic but decline to see their heroism at all seriously, take over the marrying-off arrangements of a flower-faced but spunky girl. One of the trio wears a battered stovepipe hat. Another, Mike, is a mess. Every frame of the crowd sequences has the sort of ardent vivacity that so often makes Ford remind one of Griffith. The great land-rush is first shown in a pan shot of thousands of wagons and horses waiting in line for the stroke of noon. Then the stampede begins. A wheel comes off a cart. Wagons spill and splinter. A baby is dropped, and it is then picked up by someone at full gallop who has nothing to do with it. A high-wheel bicycle is dragged by a horse. One tired nag won't move above a walk, though the hordes of others go pell-mell. There are characteristic Ford scenes to do with the use of light: a prospector's tent lit up with gunpowder, burning wagons sent pelting toward a church in order to set it on fire, people in the church being rescued by men with flares. This is a major film, and an especially important one for the museum to have rescued. Its comedy, self-amusement, and poetry are rare. So is the direction of the acting. We are in an epic world warmed by domestic detail and by teasing, protective insights into the characters of men under stress. The members of the cast play together like a company of Russians. In the end, after saving their girl, Ford's three musketeers meet tragedy one by one. But Ford himself would not have

41

approved of the word "tragedy." He once said, "Tragedy is never wholly tragic. Sometimes tragedy is ridiculous." In "Three Bad Men" he directed as serious a tragedy as could be imagined, yet also made it blithe.

SEPTEMBER 8, 1975

OF HITCHCOCK

The great Hitch has carried his country with him. His voice remains prewar, Punch-magazine Cockney. He adores seeing the English, and he has remained English to the core in his dottily immaculate, gadgety house on a golf course in Bel Air, Los Angeles. It is a house that I suspect to be concocted much in alliance with Jacques Tati's prissy women and impractical architects ("Mon Oncle," "Les Vacances de Monsieur Hulot," "Playtime," for instance). Hitch likes to seem sepulchral but he is a most kind-hearted man. His devotion to his wife and to the country of his birth is total. It is not at all surprising that François Truffaut studied his work so seriously and that he should have written a long book of interviews with him, translated by Helen Scott.

Alfred Hitchcock, ex-Londoner, whose prewar work in England is going to be better known here now that it is showing at the

Museum of Modern Art and available to campuses, lives on the edge of a golf course in Bel Air. The prim grass, eerily green in the eerily affable climate, looks about as convincingly vegetable as the paper grass that French butchers use in window displays of steaks and lamb cutlets. A few years back, Hitchcock was standing at the window of his living room and looking out at the golf course; he said that a rich man had recently had a heart attack and died at the ninth hole in his motorized golf cart, and the people the dead man had been with, though probably stricken, had decided they might as well finish the round, as they were halfway there. The first part of the situation sounded actual; perhaps the second part was a Hitchcock elaboration, the barren fancy of an émigré who has never really brought himself to be seriously rooted in America. He told me that his reason for liking Hollywood is that it leaves him alone. But when he was making films in England his Englishness had a powerful grip, and it gave his pictures a pungency and warm rapidity that he has never been able to muster in Hollywood. The work he did then has a wonderful fighting humor and sense of social detail. It was the time between the two world wars, and he came of tough stock. His wife, much like him in bearing and humor, whom he met in his early twenties, was the script girl and editor on his films; the jobs then were combined. The Hitchcocks now, cordial and devoted, are old-time Cockneys in a vacuum. The English they speak is the English of *Punch* captions in the twenties, with dropped "g"s at the ends of words. They have a shining gadget kitchen, which Hitchcock seems as pleased by as some English girl in the war would have been by G.I. nylons. He showed me an enormous freezer locker, opening the door onto a blast of nether chill and gesturing me in first. Courtliness? Of course. I looked back, though. He was wearing the famous Hitchcock-character's flat expression, like some murderous prospective mother-in-law inspecting her victim: more chill than the air. A Hitchcock script? Image of me in some future plot slowly icing between sides of beef. The mannerliness of the drama would have tickled him, probably. But I think one makes too much of the apparent ghoulishness of his humor. There is some rawness of spirit underneath it. It's true that there has been, for a time, a fanged cheekiness in his work, but he isn't a mere exploiter of terror; he couldn't exploit it if he didn't know very well what it is to be terrified. The minute of claustrophobia about the freezer locker, which I think he saw and was nice enough to obscure, recalled a story about his childhood when his father sent him, aged four or five, to the police station with a note asking the sergeant to lock him into a cell for five or ten minutes. The boy hadn't an idea what he had done wrong, but he was locked up all the same. This is what happens to naughty boys, thunders the voice of Them to Us. Punishment in Hitchcock's films comes from the sky. The blameless are always being mistaken for the guilty; it is one of the abiding themes of his movies. Jesuit-trained, a pupil of St. Ignatius College in London, Hitchcock in his best films describes a determinist system of fiendish cleverness inhabited by people who are superstitious but not deistic and who become transgressors by chance. Later in his career, his appetite for what it is to be morally quite nonplussed can seem gluttonous, but not in the early films that he made in England. Some of them will be showing from now on in a two-month season of British cinema at the Museum of Modern Art that starts with fragments of Frank Benson's 1911 Richard III, Herbert Tree in "Trilby" in 1914, and the 1913 Hamlet of Johnston Forbes-Robertson, whom Shaw congratulated upon playing into the hands of "the wily William" by actually doing something very close to the well-known drama of the same name, unlike Henry Irving at the Lyceum, who had been blithely cutting out Fortinbras and bulldozing William's every defence.

Hitchcock is represented by "The Lodger," "The Ring," "Blackmail," "Juno and the Paycock" (he doesn't think much of it), the rather absurd "Waltzes from Vienna," "The 39 Steps," "Sabotage," and "Young and Innocent." The fine-grained moments in the best of these films are very local and entirely recognizable: they are about Londoners of the working class between the wars, intimate, quick-witted, looting interludes of fun, scared of losing their jobs, and pursued by some uncomprehended Nemesis that may well, for all they know, be something as ignoble as fear of the boss. The child locked up in a prison cell for no understood reason is very much present in them. So is Hitchcock's intensity of feeling

45

for London and for an English period when class hurt. It was only after he began to work in America that it became visible that the master entertainer was wanting in the sense of great events, of something that would associate him deeply with people's needs and with their inner lives in society. England in the twenties and thirties gave that link to him automatically, and he was a subtle and fierce reporter.

As a schoolboy, he was trained in mechanics, electricity, acoustics and navigation. But he also had a bent for storytelling and generalship, and it led him to the cinema. His visual sense was passionate. He had always admired American film photography for using backlighting in shots where the standard English technique flattened the foreground into the background. At the beginning of his career, with Famous Players-Lasky and then with Gainsborough Pictures, he did practically everything except act; in spite of his truculent, abashed trademark-appearances in his films, he is one of life's voyeurs, not one of its performers. He wrote silent-film subtitles, and that gave him a long-lasting terseness and sense of narrative geometry; he did drawings for the titles (endearing, succinct, plump sketches in black ink); he was assistant director; he wrote scenarios; he was the cameraman. Later, he was one of the first directors to use the camera as if it were itself a character, not a trickster gadget able to stare up from impossible positions under steering wheels or from the depths of the waste pipe of a washbasin, as happens in films now, and also not the representative of someone in the stalls behind the proscenium arch, which was the convention then. Faces lunge at you in some of his early films. He had been on location in Berlin, and Murnau and Fritz Lang much interested him.

"The Lodger," which he made in 1926, is the first obviously Hitchcockian film. It is subtitled, promisingly, "A Story of the London Fog." The story opens with a closeup of a drowned girl—murdered? Hitchcock did the emphatic shot of the girl with her blond hair spread out on sheet glass lit from behind. The look of the closeup is very like the best of German cinema at the time and not at all like anything in English cinema. There are cuts to a policeman, and to a reporter, and to people gossiping in a pub. A cloaked

46

figure with a hat appears behind the pub window glass and goes. A teletype taps out the news about a woman witness who describes the murderer as having a scarf "COVERING THE LOWER HALF OF HIS FAC [slight pause in the machine's diction] E." More blondes are killed, brunettes look smug, and the fair-haired tuck dark curls under their hats before going out at night. The difficulty in the film is that the Jack the Ripper part is played by Ivor Novello, who has the bottom half of his perfect face hidden with a cloak but still signals with absolute recognizability to any audience that he is a matinée idol who couldn't conceivably be a villain. Hitchcock has since become more canny about casting stars to serve only his own purposes. The virtue of "The Lodger," which matures in "Blackmail"—much like it—is its wonderful vivacity of social report. The family takes in the lodger because they need money and because they reckon the man is a gent. All the characters are down on their luck, and everyone scrutinizes everyone—not because they are creatures of the later Hitchcock's prankishness, which was to become a mannerism, but because he saw their lives as depending on it. The prospective son-in-law in "The Lodger" is faintly better dressed than the older generation, with a faintly higher ceiling on his ambitions; perhaps one of the definitions of being working class is that one hopes for only a limited amount for one's children, instead of taking the right to an empire or the White House for granted. Like "Blackmail" (with Cyril Ritchard, and an inventive, rich film, which bridged the year to the talkies, existing both in a semi-talkie version and in a talkie one prepared for technically in advance by the wily Hitchcock), "The Lodger" demonstrates a beautiful sense of subtext—of the gap between what people say and what is on their minds—which is rather an astonishing achievement in a silent picture. The later movies that were made in America, after the great English talkies ("The Man Who Knew Too Much," "The 39 Steps," "The Secret Agent," "Sabotage," "Young and Innocent," "The Lady Vanishes," and "Jamaica Inn"), were sometimes dogged by sentimentality and by an unattractive cynicism. But in these early films, which show the spirit and velocity of one of the very few English-speaking directors—Orson Welles is another—who could probably still survive and express themselves if they were deprived of sound, Hitchcock is dedicated to clarity.

His cynicism appears to be the cover for a pessimistic and vulnerable temperament. He has always been the calligrapher of off-center worry, showing us people quarrelling and interrupted by a charwoman, or a man in emergency with hiccups, or a crisis spun out because a dentist is taking his time; in the English films, where he was working in a social context that he must have had deep feelings about, the characteristic seems not a device but a true and stirring piece of observation. There is a wonderful scene in "Blackmail" with a working-class woman in her Sunday best being interviewed by a policeman. "Sir," she calls him. It was a different age, but reported with more truth, feeling, and affront than the push-button protest films that we punch out now about the pigs. "Is this your handwriting?" says the police sergeant. There is an agonizing wait while she looks for her spectacles to check up on herself, on her own scrap of paper, written on in the handwriting learned at a school that she probably left at twelve. Late Hitchcock would have manipulated the pause to imply drama and worry the audience; this Hitchcock is reflecting a character.

SEPTEMBER 11, 1971

In "Frenzy," Hitchcock is back in London after a long time—it's sixteen years since the remake of "The Man Who Knew Too Much"—working with his old fanged humor. The picture begins with a track up the Thames. A tugboat goes under Tower Bridge and pours out a feather boa of filthy smoke. The movie travels silently under the bridge, in one of Hitchcock's nonchalantly amazing shots. Then we are listening to a knighted buffer spouting propaganda to the press on the terrace of County Hall about how "your government" and "your local authority" have beaten pollution. "'Bliss was it in that dawn to be alive,' as Wordsworth has it," he says. And then the crush of reporters, courteously bored, suddenly has its attention caught by the sight of the naked corpse of a woman in the Thames, and rushes away from the knight. "It's a woman!" "It's a tie, all right." "Another necktie murder." After a quick change of scene to a suspicious-looking man (Jon Finch), who soon does up his tie with disagreeable pedantry, you mutter to yourself, "I thought as much," and then discover you were on the wrong suspect. From the very beginning of the film, therefore, you know the misapprehension that is to go on existing in the minds of the police. Hitchcock has always believed that suspense and surprise have nothing to do with one another. So much for the canard that people wreck everything by giving away the plot. Synopses seldom spoil the shocks in Hitchcock—except, perhaps, the ending of "Psycho." They do no great harm to "Frenzy"—which is Hitch back in an old form of *Punch*-Cockney thriller—because the weak-faced good-looker of a Covent Garden fruit merchant who is played by Barry Foster is very quickly shown to be guilty of the rapes and murders-by-necktie that are put down by the police to the sterling and rather bovine recalcitrant barman played by Jon Finch.

The man stalking the murderer is a detective from New Scotland Yard, played by Alec McCowen. An acerbic chap with Hitchcock's own twist of knowing humor, he is saddled with a loving wife of cloying cuteness, played by the brilliant Vivien Merchant. She is taking a course in Continental gourmet cooking, and he has to suffer for it regularly at the end of a long day. While she is seeing to the quails with grapes, dear, which starve him to death, he tips the conger eels and unspeakable bits of frog back into her dainty silver soup tureen and dreams of bacon and eggs and sausages, which we see him eating when he is at liberty at the office, tucking into a trayful on his desk. Late in the film, he explains patiently to his wife that a pull-in—crucially involved in one of the murder cases—means a place where lorry drivers can go for "humble food like sausages and mashed potatoes."

For a long time he is misled on the trail, maybe through hunger.

He thinks that the obvious suspect is guilty. Everything leads to the man. The barman, just sacked from his job for apparent thieving and blatant cheek, was once married to one of the later victims (Barbara Leigh-Hunt, playing a genteel woman who runs a marriage bureau). Another victim is played by Anna Massey, a skinny, poignant redhead, here doing a perfect London working-class bird's accent and giving a beautifully brainy, energetic performance. The plot depends on Sherlock Holmes detective business with an analysis of potato dust and on a rhythm of coincidences that move as fast as the shuffling of a cardsharper. The violence shown amounts to relatively little. It is transferred to the mind of the audience and turned into an emotion more like anticipation of the seemingly inevitable. The most upsetting murder isn't even seen. The camera simply tracks very slowly away from a closed door, down a stairway, through a front door, and then up to look in the window of the house on Henrietta Street—running at right angles to Covent Garden market—that holds the fruit merchant's flat, over an old publishing firm called Duckworth, which has a brass plate like a dentist's.

As in "The Trouble with Harry," the story has a sense of humor that seems very English. It may have been both consoling and astringent for Hitchcock to work in England again. He is mordantly good at conveying a certain rabbity working life. He does it here, for the first time in ages, with the parts played by Alec McCowen and Barry Foster. There is also a sort of sabre-toothed gentility that he greatly relishes, and no one else in the commercial cinema uses savage silence so well. In one three-minute sequence done without dialogue you can almost hear him enjoying himself. He is as fascinated by the twinges of domestic psychology as he is by plot, and he revels in air pockets of dead hush. Like Simenon, he cuts corners, and he has the cold control and insight of Simenon. He also has an instantly recognizable way of handling exchanges of looks and silences between people. The eternal imbalance of power in private relations obsesses him. He is the dramatist of edginess, and the reporter-poet of impossible small calamities, such as a flash in "Frenzy" when a man nearly gives himself away by sneezing. It is like the moment in "The 39 Steps" when events are held up by a traffic jam caused by a flock of sheep, and like the use of a facial affliction in "Young and Innocent." He thought of putting Cary Grant into Lincoln's nostril on Mount Rushmore in "North by Northwest" and sending this character, too, into a sneezing fit.

In "Frenzy," we are in Hitchcock's old world of using *Evening Standard* and *Daily Express* headlines to grab us into a chain of events. He instructs us always in the belief that catastrophe surrounds us and, like the blandly pretty flying kingdom in "The Birds," is likely to take over. In this film, as so often before—in "Rear Window," for instance—he manipulates one's frustration about a frantic honest man's possibly not being recognized in time as someone telling the truth. People in Hitchcock are always compelled to act out their natures, and so the world he creates is determinist. Mr. Memory, in "The 39 Steps," is destined by his talent to answer questions about the spy ring, and he gets shot for it. We, in our turn, are destined by curiosity to cliff-hang as Hitchcock pleases, and there seems no escape. He can make determinists of us all. It is this, more than anything else, that may really be sticking in our throats when we call him a gloater, or a showman who is a glutton for our punishment. He lives in a very fast-moving land, sharp with erotic and ironic detail, where the camera is often used subjectively as a character in the story. One would never find Hitchcock putting the camera in one of those impossible positions behind the steering wheel of a car or below the waste catch of a washbasin. He is interested by the mannerisms of hysteria, and there is an extraordinary vivacity about his social eye. The streets and clothes and expressions of a London that he sees rather as the old-style city are reported in "Frenzy" with the most fine-grained detail. One is taken into a territory of spirited visual gossip, conducted by a guide of lazy humor and command.

Hitchcock's Englishness has always had a powerful grip on him. With "Frenzy," we are nearly back in the days of his great English films—"The Man Who Knew Too Much," "The 39 Steps," "Secret Agent," "Sabotage," "Young and Innocent," "The Lady Vanishes"—which is astonishing for a man of his age and after the poorness of "Torn Curtain." This sense of nationality always gave his English work a pungency and a warm swiftness. He is lucky to have been able to draw on Anthony Shaffer to do "Frenzy's" sly screenplay, not to speak of a cast of first-rate, well-equated actors pretty much unknown outside England, so that audiences have no preconceptions about who are the stars and therefore unkillable. Maybe going back to England revived something about his technical energy and sharpened the famous cutting edge of his sense of family combat, though there is no abatement of the fact that he sometimes treats his audiences abominably. For instance, we are asked to believe that a hero now in his early thirties got the D.F.C. as a squadron leader, which would put the Blitz somewhere around 1960; and there is outrageous macabre use, clever though it is, of the "MacGuffin" that he says every thriller of his needs—in "Frenzy," a diamond-initialled pin. By "MacGuffin" he means something of crucial importance to the character that is of no weight at all to anyone else. Not to his public, because not to Hitchcock.

JUNE 24, 1972

The great Hitchcock, genius of stories about misappropriated guilt and frozen-looking blondes with red-hot souls, is being given a gala evening by the Film Society of Lincoln Center on April 29th. His long career has had steady themes. Counter-snobbery, for one. Displacement of an almost religious sense of sin, for another. Even in "Young and Innocent" (1937), he spiked courtly passages with marvelously funny surreal intrusions involving Mary Clare at a children's tea party; Derrick de Marney played the hero, accused of murder but palpably innocent. The tenor of the film is unusually sunlit, detectably embodying some parody of stage and screen comedies of the time. It is only at the end that Hitchcock's complicity with the audience asserts itself, when the villain is disguised as a dance-band musician wearing blackface but given away by his already established facial twitch, inducing in us the director's own relish of punitive last-minute recognition.

The theme of the pursuer, himself often pursued, who begins to incarnate the guilt of someone for whom he is mistaken or who was once his trusted friend recurs and recurs: in "Strangers on a Train" (1951), when a nice young tennis player in collusion with a lunatic is landed with the lunatic's motive; in the brilliant "Shadow of a Doubt" (1943)—screenplay by Thornton Wilder, in collaboration with Alma Reville and Sally Benson—when Teresa Wright as a niece called Charlie begins to sense, and even to take on, some of the dark side of her loved, murderously suave Uncle Charlie's character; in "Vertigo" (1958), when James Stewart as an ex-detective with acrophobia is assigned by an old college friend to follow a suicidal wife (limply played by Kim Novak) who believes in reincarnation, and finds himself, after racing to stop her vertiginous death and being pursued by his own block about heights, chasing a girl like her and persuading her to reincarnate the dead girl; and in "To Catch a Thief" (1955), when Cary Grant as an ex-cat-burglar is hunted by the police and himself hunts down an impostor.

The languidly humorous "Rear Window" (1954)—it is hard to get hold of prints now—epitomizes Hitchcock's gift for inspired visual gossip, including views of a pet-loving couple who let down their dog to the yard on a pulley, and of a dancer who limbers up while she has her teeth into a club sandwich. James Stewart, muttering about blood leaking from a trunk while he is idly nibbling Grace Kelly's mouth, gives the liveliest performance in a plaster cast that there can ever have been.

Certain motifs teem in Hitchcock. His favorite false clues intentionally irritate, like pebbles in a shoe. The name of the famous "North by Northwest" (1959), for one; there is no such compass point. The title is a worry, a piece of dust in the eye which can't be blinked away. So is Hitchcock's own brilliantly maddening slogan " 'The Birds' Is Coming." His films abound in red-herring scenes of unsettled memories which produce disquiet and lead nowhere, like the encounter in "Marnie" (1964) between the heroine and a man who remembers her in another guise. In "To Catch a Thief" there

53

are at least three false-trail villains. In one of his few comedies, "The Trouble with Harry" (1955), with Harry already dead at the start of the picture, the corpse, which is first seen buried in the beautiful bronze leaves of a Vermont autumn, becomes a red herring on an unprecedented scale. The body is found, disposed of, re-found, re-interred. A retired sea captain thinks he has shot Harry. A middle-aged spinster thinks she is responsible for the death because she hit Harry when he tried to assault her. His separated wife appropriates the guilt because she crashed a milk bottle onto his head. Harry's gaudy socks or bare feet commandeer every scene they are in. People trip over him, make arrangements over him, sketch him. The murder is everyone's own anise trail of self-recrimination, and the corpse is very funnily dealt with, as only a believing Catholic can be seriously funny about sin. One of the great lines of intentional bathos in all cinema comes at the moment when Mildred Natwick, meeting a panting Edmund Gwenn dragging the corpse, says, "What seems to be the trouble, Captain?"

At moments like that, one can't forget that Hitchcock once wrote titles for silent films. In a crowded elevator, a friend of mine heard him perking up the pall of abashed elevator-silence by saying with sudden crypticness, "Who would have believed that one shot could have made such a mess? Blood everywhere." His titles must have been very terse. It is typical of this generally kindly, winking man that the effect of his films should so often be described as scary but never as frightening. Real fear is something he undoubtedly feels, but I don't believe he would think it belonged in entertainment. It belongs with hellfire.

There are hints of his real fears, though, in his theme of the nearly fatal halt. In "Shadow of a Doubt" and in "Sabotage" (1936) people in unknown extremity are stopped by traffic policemen. Hitchcock has always been terrified of the police. In "Saboteur" (1942) an escaping hero has to hide handcuffs on his wrists. "The Wrong Man" (1956) takes an innocent hero through a grinding ritual of fingerprinting, form-filling, handcuffing, and inquisition by policemen repeating a Christian name that the character never uses. The director, born of poor parents in 1899 in a London suburb, has memories that die hard. His father was a greengrocer and a poulterer; perhaps the second profession explains Hitchcock's lifelong disgust about eggs. It is as great as his love of the trains and buses of his childhood, and his aesthetic distaste for newfangled planes. (Think of the terrifying crop-duster chase scene on a flat prairie in "North by Northwest.")

One suspects Hitchcock of a suppressed loathing of romantic music, because of his dislike of sentimentality; he now holds in low esteem his own "Champagne" (1928) and "Watzes from Vienna" (1933). "Secret Agent" (1936) has a scene in which a single organ note blares because a body has slumped onto a keyboard. You begin to feel that it is the histrionics of the Albert Hall cantata that are morally as well as literally the license for the attempted assassination in "The Man Who Knew Too Much" (1934, remade by Hitchcock in 1956). Just as music is not ethically neutral in Hitchcock's films, pet animals are not really pets but devices of criminality. They are trick canary songsters, as in "Sabotage," or signals at the start of perilous events, as in the pet-shop meeting in "The Birds" (1963) between the young lawyer (Rod Taylor) and Hitchcock's characteristic airless blonde (Tippi Hedren). Or animals may be represented as stupid surrogates for people, like the horse that Miss Hedren prefers to her husband (Sean Connery) in "Marnie." Anthony Perkins in "Psycho" (1960) stuffs birds as a hobby. Hitchcock is keen on taxidermy: there is an unbeatably sinister scene at a taxidermist's in his remake of "The Man Who Knew Too Much."

Hitchcock has always been agog about the behavior of people under pressure. He once—in a magazine called *Movie*—referred to the blitz in a way that made it sound like one of his own devices to find people's Achilles' heels of alarm about the unforeseeable. He understands plots about civilians under attack, so to speak: about people thrust into overwhelming danger while they are on holiday or absorbed in a test match, or playing an ornate practical joke, which is the starting point of "The Birds." He loves making the lofty heroine of "The Birds" squirm, and getting her cool nerves to crack, and putting her into high heels before making her walk through sand. Hitchcock's kind of revenge is on an irreligious otherworldliness. It isn't the mischievous sadism it is often taken to

55

be. In "The Birds" the characters who play out the revenge are the birds themselves, those creatures who for millennia have been used for food and quill pens and ladies' hats; they terrorize the heroine in a glass telephone booth where she is caged like a canary, and swoop down a chimney as if they were the Eumenides.

The juxtaposition of the pampered against the new or rabid or vulgar has always struck Hitchcock as something more than merely amusing. In "To Catch a Thief" the aristocratic heroine, played by Grace Kelly, is pitched against an ill-bred mother (Jessie Royce Landis) with such moral pungency that the moment when the mother stubs out a cigarette in a fried egg amounts to something more than a shot of food wastage. We see that this girl who looks like a jewelled chiming doll clock sprang from a fishwife parent, and she is not ironclad but simply new to the snobs' game. If there is one theme running all the way through Hitchcock's films, from the social gaffes or the unpracticed criminals to Robert Donat's speaking gibberish when he is suddenly plunged into a political meeting in "The 39 Steps," it is that everyone is a novice.

APRIL 29, 1974

With a kick on a cemetery headstone that has no body below ("Fake! Fake!" shouts the kicker), and a gentle, lethal plopping of brake fluid, the sound track of Alfred Hitchcock's "Family Plot" firmly plants us in a world in which the hallowed is a hoax and the mechanically sophisticated is dangerous to treat as a plaything. Hitchcock has never made a strategically wittier film, or a fonder; and this in his seventy-seventh year.

The beginning reminds us that the Master has always wanted to direct, of all things, J. M. Barrie's "Mary Rose;" and, though he once cheerfully informed me that he has it in his studio agreement that he is not allowed to film the play, the wily old jackdaw has managed to smuggle a whit of Barrie's fantasy into his new comedy-mystery. Mary Rose hears voices calling her from another world; at the beginning of "Family Plot," when Barbara Harris, as a ravishingly pretty and constantly famished con-woman spiritualist named Blanche, is conducting a séance with a loaded old biddy named Miss Rainbird (Cathleen Nesbitt), Blanche speaks in the voices of a woman and a man from the Great Beyond. The voices confirm Miss Rainbird's guilt about having long ago covered up the illegitimate birth of an heir to the Rainbird fortune. Then Blanche, exhausted by her bogus insights, returns from the Other Side and gratefully accepts a drink. "A double shot of anything."

Blanche works hard to make her wide-eyed living out of the dead. The offer of a reward of ten thousand dollars if she can find the missing heir is an amazing windfall. She generally manages frugally. Her boyfriend (Bruce Dern) drives a taxi. They exist on hamburger-munching and sex, both of which are perpetually being interrupted by twists in the Rainbird-heir mystery and by shift-work for the taxi company. The Bruce Dern character, called Lumley, puts up with deprivation better than his girl, whose temperament endearingly refutes generalities about women being too finely bred to have appetites. Blanche is a girl of simple longings whom fate keeps calorically and erotically ravenous.

Hitchcock has always thrived on making stories about couples. In "Family Plot"—written by Ernest Lehman, from an English novel by Victor Canning which has been transplanted to California—we see how his attitude toward casting has changed. Barbara Harris and Bruce Dern occupy the places that would once have been held by Grace Kelly and Cary Grant, or Kim Novak and James Stewart. The part of the glossy blonde (Karen Black) is now villainous, and the glossy blondness is a matter of a wig. Called Fran, she is in murderous collusion with a smooth diamond thief named Adamson (William Devane). Another couple. The two pairs are piercingly different. Blanche and Lumley adore each other, though they often seem about to throw lamps at each other; Fran and Adamson are partners in crime who cherish little love for each other and talk to each other with a formality that is eerily violent. There being no chivalry among thieves, Adamson unblinkingly sends Fran on dangerous missions by herself, for which she wears six-inch heels, black clothes, and the blond wig: at one's first glimpse of her in this disguise she looks as if she might well be a man in drag. The music-hall sight is funnily linked to the way Blanche's voice suddenly hits an air pocket and comes out as a baritone's at the opening séance.

One of the thieves' ploys involves a red-robed bishop whom Fran knocks out, in church, by plunging a loaded hypodermic through his vestments. No worshipper moves a muscle to stop her. People in church are in an inhibited and insensate state, says this film, which is droll about the religious as only a believer like the Catholic Hitchcock can be. Fran and Adamson tell the kidnapped bishop over an intercom that they are going to have to put him to sleep again; he complains that he hasn't finished his chicken. Blanche and Lumley, waiting over endless glasses of beer in a seedy roadside cafe for a cryptic and dangerous-sounding appointment, watch a parson drinking Coke with four Sunday-school children; the door opens, a dulled-looking girl comes in, and we laugh from bathos, because nothing happens except that the parson turns out to have imported the kids as a cover for a date.

And then, in a hair-raising but somehow majestically comic scene, Lumley and Blanche give up waiting for the man they were summoned to see, and find that they have at least met his work, for their car brakes won't function. Lumley is driving: downhill. Blanche adds to the terror by panicking. Hitchcock elects not to show us details of the dashboard. He simply cuts between views of the road and shots of Blanche nearly throttling Lumley, clasping him round the neck and providing the desperate man with the unhelpful information that her hamburger is making her feel sick. Hitchcock is good on feminine hysteria. One remembers Jessica Tandy crouched in a corner of her living room in "The Birds" (1963). He often has a wryly amused view of women's scares. I remember that he was once showing me his kitchen in Bel Air. Everything was spick-and-span. Not a cornflake visible. A desert for cockroaches. He opened a door, and icy air steamed out. The freezer locker: a whole room. I saw hams and sides of beef hanging from hooks like rich women's fur coats in summer storage. Hitchcock courteously bowed me in first. I hesitated and looked back, imagining the door clanging shut behind me. He knew what I was thinking, and I knew that he knew. A Hitchcock scene was in our imaginations, and an equally Hitchcock flash of irrational fear had come to pass.

Each of his films has been full of moments of red-herring disquiet, but he has never laid such a bland set of ambushes as in "Family Plot." The Master makes unsettling use of an oaken-looking woman in a jeweller's shop, whom Blanche cheerfully asks if her sign is Leo; of a brick wall that comes open and then closes hermetically, causing steep claustrophobia; of a fragment of bishop's red robe shut in the bottom of a car door in a garage, making one think of the gaudy socks of the unlosable corpse in "The Trouble with Harry" (1955); of an overhead shot of a weeping woman hurrying through a maze of paths in a cemetery, pursued by Bruce Dern; of a woman physician, a disgruntled old man in shirtsleeves, and identical-twin mechanics, who are successive false trails in Blanche's chase; of a genteel chiming doorbell on the front door of the thieves' house. Hitchcock's ominous mechanical devices and his dark clues leading nowhere build up in us a farcical discomfiture. We are like oversensitive princesses troubled by peas under mattresses.

But "Family Plot" does not rest on the fostering of anxiety. Hitchcock allows himself a camaraderie with the audience which makes this film one of the saltiest and most endearing he has ever directed. It is typical of the picture that he should have the sagacity and technique to bring the terrifying car incident to such an untroubling close. Only a very practiced poet of suspense could slacken the fear without seeming to cheat, and end the sequence without using calamity. With this picture, he shows us that he understands the secret of the arrow that leaves no wound and of the joke that leaves no scar. Sometimes in his career, Hitchcock has seemed to manipulate the audience; in this, his fifty-third film, he is our accomplice, turning his sense of play to our benefit. There is something particularly true-pitched in his use of the talent of Barbara Harris. She has never before seemed so fully used. The film finishes on her, as it begins. She goes mistily upstairs in pursuit of the enormous diamond that the villains have stolen. Lumley watches her. She seems to be in a trance. Maybe she has got supernatural powers, after all. She brings off a clairvoyant's coup, though we know more than her lover does. He is purely delighted by her. A Hitchcock film has seldom had a more pacific ending.

APRIL 19, 1976

OF SATYAJIT RAY

He is very tall. Well over six foot. Most Indians are rather short. He makes films that are nearly always in the forbidden black-and-white, and films that run the usual length, breaking with the Indian custom of dance/drama/Hindu mythology films mixed with cosmetic commercialism (heavily made-up starlets, men with glistening black moustachios). These films last five hours or more, and their market is mostly in the villages that house over ninety percent of the population: they are screened in cinemas that are generally open to the baking Indian air, with breaks in the programme for customers to buy sweet fruit drinks and betel nuts that stain the inside of the mouth with red. None of this is for Ray. He has broken all the rules.

E. M. Forster wrote, with irony, in A Passage to India, *of the tourist anxiety to find "the real India"; there is, of course, no real India, because it is a sub-continent. Its essence lies in a spiritual sense of flux, which Westerners call muddle. The five-hour-long films, hardly or never exported, tell us something true enough; Ray's films tell us something other, but equally true. Like the five-hour films, his pictures don't flinch from showing us the apparent*

61

confusion of India, but they are conceived with the exactness that may be the core of style. Of course India seems "muddled." How else, given its size, the wrench of independence from the British Raj, and the rupture of Partition, could it be anything else? But Ray is rare: in his elegant and literary conciseness, he is really a novelist working on film, who has created within his own terms a chronicle of what it is to be Indian and as scholarly as so many Indians are. The persistent sight of students in the poorest villages sitting in the dying light reading library books by the flare of petrol in tin cans is one of the memories I most retain of India.

"Charulata," Satyajit Ray's most nearly flawless film apart from his great Apu trilogy, is a flowing, opulent tale that seems to be lit from the inside like a velvet-lined carriage with a lantern in it rocked by a hot monsoon wind. The film carries an exquisite period flavor of the eighteen-seventies in Bengal. We are in a sunny garden with a swing on long ropes and statues of fat little cupids; a house with a birdcage shaken frantically by a sudden storm, and curlicue bannisters, and embroidered rugs; a Chekhovian atmosphere in which men lie on cushions eating sweetmeats and talking of Bentham and Mill. The inwardly fretful women play cards, embroider handkerchiefs and slippers for their husbands, use the swing while they hum pretty plaints that have an atmosphere of rounds, take down the birdcage during the storm, and accept that changing the world is not for them. Working at something private, like writing, is considered feminine and permissible, but publication is a masculine preserve, which Charulata barges into head on.

Charulata is the heroine of the film, which was made from a Rabindranath Tagore story. Though it was shown at the New York Film Festival in 1965, it didn't have a public run in New York until the one that has just started at the First Avenue Screening Room after the picture was dug out of a vault in Chicago. The character is played by a docile beauty called Madhabi Mukherjee. Her husband, Bhupati (played by Sailen Mukherjee; Mukherjee is a common name in Bengal, where Ray makes his films), is a bearded intellectual who runs an anti-British radical newspaper called the *Sentinel*. (Again, shades of the upper-class radicals of czarist Russia, this time of the seventies and of Dostoevski.) To keep his bored wife amused, he sends for his young cousin Amal (Soumitra Chatterjee), who encourages her to write. Amal is suspected by Bhupati of spiritual and social laziness in his easy acceptance of things as they are and of British rule as it seems it will always be. He wears a mustache. To an intellectual like Bhupati, he has the complacency of a sugar-fed artist as he sits around in his striped dhoti orating about aesthetics in a plangent voice, as if he were addressing a dying sun. Amal's interest in the arts enraptures Charulata. A powerful sexual bond grows between them, though it is never acknowledged openly, except in a freeze frame of their hands reaching out to one another at the end of the film. The story holds a peculiarly Hindu mixture of sensibility and harshness. Indeed, everything in it contains its own contradiction, like the god Siva, who stands for both destruction and regeneration. Charulata, who seems all shy acquiescence, actually has a backbone of steel that enables her to decline to emulate the apparent sweet yieldingness of the young Queen Victoria, of whom cameo daguerreotypes hang on the walls of the house as if they were icons of womanhood. Like Victoria, she turns out to have a startling will, although she belittles herself and says that she is incapable of originality because she doesn't know a lot. Ray shows Charulata symbolically obeying her age's code of femininity by looking at the street through binoculars. From afar, through the lens of the onlooker, she sees a poor man sheltered by a black umbrella in the style borrowed from the clerkly fashion of the Raj, as it is even today, when men in dhotis and bare feet carry the same kind of umbrella. In "Charulata," poverty is seen at a distance from this house of brocade wallpaper and lushness and a piano out of tune because of the damp heat.

The domestic scenes in the film are lit with life and affection, but Charulata's calm pleasure in her gift for writing is suddenly darkened when she is told, quite casually, that Amal was sent for to teach her: to bring her out, to release her in a way that would be publicly unseen, to quieten her pinings, to quell her loneliness while her husband edited papers about liberty and probably about feminism, though the Lord help us from letting it get into the home. Cockroaches, yes; damp, yes; conversations about rebellion, yes; yelling at a servant to bring tea, yes; giving care to a wife whose fidelity is taken for granted, yes; encouraging women's talents in the home—letting them embroider, scribble, read expensive books curling with the damp—yes; but equality for servants and masters, no; expressiveness for women, no.

What has been lyric becomes an unspoken tragedy when Amal is pressed to accept an offer of marriage to the youngest daughter of a lawyer. The marriage bears with it the chance of a trip to England. To the land of Shakespeare! Of Gladstone! The theoretically loathsome ruler is a country that actually commands the respect and yearning of the educated upper classes. Breeding and convention win Amal over. To love a married woman like Charulata would be impossible. She and Amal never show their passion for each other. It stays underground forever. The rules don't permit anything else. England calls. Ambition. Duty. Goodness to his busy liberal cousin, who may know everything or nothing. A tenderness for Charulata representing one of the many testing buried objects in Indian thought and behavior: maybe a mine, or maybe only a harmless hillock of grass burned by the sun. Passion is enclosed in "Charulata," as it always is in Ray's films—in "Devi," of 1960, for instance, in which a seventeen-year-old girl, idolized by her devout and sweetly dotty father-in-law, one day finds that he has secretly come to think that she is a reincarnation of the goddess Kali. He throws himself at her feet, and her toes suddenly curl up in fear like a bird's claws. Sadly inclining to his will, she tries to convince herself she can heal the sick, and once brings it off, with her adored nephew; but then he dies in spite of her, and she goes mad. Charulata has more genuine restraint, perhaps because she was born a century earlier. The film leaves one with a sense of great things unfulfilled but never of mania. Like Ray's "The Music Room," which has tones of "The Cherry Orchard," it has a style that is songlike, beautiful, sometimes turning into an abrupt and comic rudeness that again seems very Russian. Grape-lipped men lapse into English as Chekhovians dreaming of revolution lapse into French.

"Charulata" is gentle to loneliness in the well-off, it is beautifully written, and sometimes it is very funny. The music was written by Ray himself. Along with everything else, the picture is a fascinating fable about the bequest of Empire in India. Ray once spent a long time with Jean Renoir while Renoir was working on "The River." Against the gaudy background of the Indian film industry, there may well appear to be something Europeanized about Ray's humor and his low tones. To Europeans or Americans, though, his Forsterish irony seems deeply embedded in his style, and he obviously works from within in his sight of the Indian character. The film is triumphant in its comprehension of a period.

JULY 8, 1974

Trains: the hypnotic trains of India. "Nayak the Hero" was directed and written by Satyajit Ray, and most of it happens on a train from Calcutta. A film star called Arindam (played by an enormously popular real Indian film star called Uttam Kumar) is going to Delhi to get a prize. He begins at home, restlessly: making fun of a serious man who talks about horoscopes and says that it's a good day for contracts; sending a telegram; talking to a girl on the telephone. Arindam has a horror of signing contracts, of being tied down, of being recognized. He unconsciously puts on dark glasses when he is making excuses to the girl on the telephone.

On the way to Delhi, we are in the beguiling world of long-distance trains. People move in and out of compartments. The rich dine in the wagon-restaurant. Lying asleep in his clothes to the thrum of the engine, the actor has a dream about drowning in money. Later, a distinguished old passenger, epicene with near-senility and wearing a shawl over his head, asks the actor with the abrupt rudeness of age if he drinks. He can't bear the smell of alcohol, he says, brooking no protests. The actor is asked for autographs, and he is admired for being a champion at everything. A young girl comes shyly into the restaurant car to interview him.

65

Thin faces at a station press against the window. The girl shrinks back. The actor, who seems more lordly than he really is, tells her to behave as if they were on location and she were his heroine. His life is a blur of techniques. In the vertiginous hours between sleeping and waking, his nerves jump. His interview with the girl takes us into flashbacks of the burning at a ghat of someone he loved. Tears run down his cheeks from the heat of the flames. There is the vexing idea of reincarnation: true or not true? "If I am reborn, how will I know I am me?" The question is the actor's dilemma.

Arindam washes his face to wake up, and looks at himself in a cracked mirror. At whom? At a man with a fractured and fear-riddled temperament, he thinks. He speaks twice of something's being too risky. Once, the risk is contained in a crowd of autograph hunters who have been waiting twenty-four hours for a glimpse of him. The actor won't even get out of his car. This is Ray's ironic hero: a man of straw endowed with mistaken kingship, prone to bad dreams and to steps of caution.

The picture was made in 1966. It is the achievement of a great film director working outside his usual style, fumbling sometimes with surrealism, using flashbacks that flaw the usual concord of his sense of storytelling, but sometimes illumining it by lines that suddenly show character in movement, like the glare of a torch catching a figure on a staircase.

JULY 29, 1974

Satyajit Ray's "The Chess Players"—the first film that this Bengali has made in Urdu (with some English), which is much more widely understood in India than his native tongue—is about two sorts of rout. The setting is Lucknow in 1856. The British are about to take over the final part of the Muslim princely state of Oudh which remains to fall to the conqueror. The film sees it as the last cherry that Lord Dalhousie, Queen Victoria's Governor

General, wants to snap up in his lean jaws, which look in old likenesses as though the lines of rigor and discipline around the lower part of the face had been developed by locking colonial-jail handles with his teeth. The second rout, never to be acknowledged as concluded, is an endless game of chess between two plump highborn husbands known as Mr. Mirza and Mr. Meer. Mirza, played by Sanjeev Kumar, has a wife who is exhausted by the game and pleads for attention. Meer (Saeed Jaffrey) has a wife who thanks her stars for chess, because it lets her carry on an affair with her nephew, a scared young man who hides under the bed at a moment's warning.

There is a very good nasty performance by Richard Attenborough, using a Scots accent, as the British Resident, General Outram. His opponent in his larger game of political chess is the Nawab of Oudh, Wajid Ali Shah (Amzad Khan). The Nawab is a splendid musician and poet but no great ruler. For all that, he has felt it a monstrous indignity to have been deprived of his crown so that it could be sent to London for the Great Exhibition in 1851. Meer and Mirza, trying to forget the power of the East India Company, click-click at their game and pretend to themselves that their worst fear is that they will not be allowed to go on. After all, the Indians did invent chess, and spread it to Persia and England. And, after all, it was the English who sped up this intrinsically slow and thoughtful game by taking over the rules, just as the East India Company has taken over practically everything else. In the British game, the minister is called the queen. And the pawn can move two squares in its first move. And when a pawn reaches the eighth rank it can be exchanged for a queen. You must say the British are clever. There is a whole parable here of the way the British have managed to inculcate in the Indian mind the idea that Indians are slothful and unpunctual. The reigning Anglo-Saxon contempt for lax clock-watching still leads to such overanxiety on the part of Indians that an Englishman is apt to be wakened with breakfast at three in the morning when he has asked for it at five. Meer and Mirza discuss the occupiers' mania for speed. Steam engines are coming. The telegraph is already here, which means in their view only that bad news travels faster, there not being very much good news, or, indeed, much good around, apart from sanctuary in chess. Better to contain national wars in fights about the rules of the game, in squabbles about who touched a knight and then moved a pawn. These differences are healable. The battle between India and Britain for Indian independence will take a century. In the meantime, the East India Company, by telling the Nawab of Oudh that he is ruling badly, can make use of his wealth to fight in Nepal, in the Punjab, in Afghanistan. The Nawab, not by any means a malign man, takes refuge in poetry and music, and grips the jewelled knobs of his throne while Lord Dalhousie moves in with a plan to fleece the Nawab of his remaining lands. Meer and Mirza conduct their endless game in an unwitting cross-rhythm with the political warfare. They move from place to place. Wifely complaints nag. When you spend the night with a whore, women put up with it without a murmur, but when you stay at home and play a clean game, they pester. Sometimes, the players' irritable and indispensable intimacy with each other makes what they say sound like talk in Beckett. They find each other insufferable but remain indivisible. Like husband and wife, they are so close that they can't always tell who has been talking; like husband and wife, they are conjoined in trouble. Somebody steals their chess set. On a Friday. And the shops are closed on Friday. To think that such a beautiful new strategy should have been dreamed up only to go to waste! While the Nawab, to prevent an actual seizure of his throne, announces that anyone spreading rumors about an East India Company takeover will have his tongue pulled out, Meer and Mirza can talk only of its being such a beautiful day and nothing to do. However: invention. Hookahs shall be brought, as usual. A tomato shall be bishop, a lime shall be knight, a chili shall be rook. The Nawab, in his palace, is beyond such comfort. In a sad scene, he says that he is a poor ruler, and speaks with joy of the pretty sights of his reign: pretty girls in pretty uniforms on pretty horses. He remembers a song that he composed: one that he sang while a petitioner's request was being read out. The clerk's voice seemed to fade away. Queen Victoria has never composed a song, has she? The Nawab is no more belligerent than the chess players. He is merely sad that, with the British here, his benighted people should be pressed into service by the East India Company's rule, without pay, to be turned into the Company's best soldiers and take away the remaining half of his kingdom. The chess players flee from their beautiful Muslim houses to go on with their game. One of them remembers a broken-down old mosque in the country. They take a mat and a couple of hookahs. They can buy their lunch from a shop: kabobs and chapatties. Life can be lived on very short commons.

Back in the palace, the Nawab's mother holds out hope of mercy from Queen Victoria. The idea withers, in suffering and dignity. In the same mode, the broken-down mosque turns out to be a childhood memory of Meer's. The chess players contemplate playing in a field of mustard. A child offers them his house: an empty house, because everyone else has run away. He wanted to stay, because he wanted to see the red coats of the British. The last twenty minutes of this magnificent film are piercing about the end of things, about managing on less and less. Ray wrote the picture himself, basing it on a story by Prem Chand. The Nawab's decision in Oudh lies between giving up his throne and fighting the British, toward whom he and his family have felt friendly for more than a century. The decision is taken as the bloodless combat of the chess game begins again.

MAY 22, 1978

II

CINÉMATHÈQUE
AND ON

OF HENRI LANGLOIS

Perhaps much of film achievement lies in the history of the great Paris Cinémathèque. Henri Langlois, its onlie begetter, now dead, was a great friend. He gives the lie to the truism that no one is indispensable. He is. Powerful men in France tried to kick him out of his position as head of the Cinémathèque—a position that certainly wasn't moneygrubbing, for he couldn't afford even a telephone and instead left a string of restaurant numbers with the friends he trusted—but filmmakers from all over the world rallied to reinstate him. He was the meeting-point of Abel Gance, Jeanne Moreau, Jean-Luc Godard, strange fellows; apparently at work across a couple of generations. We all owe him a great deal. He fought endlessly, but only with the archivists whom he felt to be preserving film by the wrong methods. His friends were films, filmmakers, film fanatics of eleven or twelve whom he would let into his screenings for nothing because he suspected them of being a new Truffaut or a new Godard. He supported innovation and threw away nothing: not even a picture that he himself thought negligible, or some single can of film that he had rooted out in a flea-market. To the short history of cinema he has given nobility, and everyone who makes or writes films is by him ennobled.

The Decoy Fanatic: Henri Langlois

"If the history of film is fifty thousand films, then Chartres is fifty thousand stones," said Henri Langlois, onlie begetter of the great Cinémathèque Française, eating ginger marmalade with a teaspoon in Paris and afterward signing for an ordinary lunch for five other people, resting the bill on the jutting waist of his brown polo-neck sweater. The history of film at his Cinémathèque, in Paris, is much more, and also many more, than fifty thousand films. In any event, Henri Langlois, master celebrant of movie archivism, the Cerberus, saint, and spy of world cinema, is never quite sure how many prints he has. His passion for the preservation of film and his passion for particular kinds of marmalade eaten with a spoon both require a vagrant special knowledge. He would agree that the marmalade expertise has the less importance, but he takes it with equal seriousness.

It is his dedication to cinema that has built the Cinémathèque Française. The edifice is without heirs, since there is no one at all like him. Through the Cinémathèque, Langlois is the father of the middle generation of directors all over the world, and the grandfather of New Wave filmmakers like Truffaut, Godard, and Chabrol. The famous historian and collector, without whom the cinema might hardly know that it has a past, is completely devoted to film. He will raid the flea markets of Paris for a can holding part of a lost Buster Keaton two-reeler, he keeps the hours of a true eccentric, and he stores everything he can find. Films that other archivists had despaired of he used to restore by cleaning them frame by frame and drying them on a clothesline. The current headquarters of the Cinémathèque, which is in part privately supported and in part subsidized by the government, is the Palais de Chaillot. The Cinémathèque consists of three cinemas—two cinemas in the Palais and one on the Left Bank—and a museum, in the Palais. The films would take years to show end to end, and the attention that Langlois gives to each one is infinite; of himself he is careless to a degree that makes one think he may be cultivating the behavior of a fanatic bohemian to draw attention away from his craze for film, which has made him a center of government controversy. In February of 1968, French bureaucrats unwisely, and unsuccessfully, tried to unseat this hero of *cinéastes* all over the world—his fierce allies included Renoir, Kurosawa, Visconti, and Chaplin—for some less troublesome leader; they brought down upon themselves riots and protest marches that many of the political-minded believe to have been an unconscious training period for the events of May, 1968.

Langlois never forgets a film, but he often forgets to pay his own telephone bill. The phone is forever being cut off. When that happens, there are six or seven other possible numbers for finding him. Two of them are the numbers of restaurants. The rest are for phones in various nooks of the Palais de Chaillot. At one or the other of his cinemas there, he will often sit at a desk serving as an ad-hoc ticket booth and take admission fees himself, his gentle, film-soaked brown eyes benevolently watching out for some boy sitting round program after program for the price of one, as Truffaut did when he was a boy. "There is the new François, perhaps. Or there," Langlois will say, missing nothing, his huge bulk overflowing his little wooden chair. One thinks of him as a natural sitter; his body looks permanently bent into chair angles because of his having seen so many films. He has the daintiness of many heavy men. When he moves, he seems to have bulk without weight. It is as if he were filled with hydrogen, and he leaves companions racing far behind in his museum until he stops to pant against a table, gazing at a still of Marilyn Monroe or an early camera shot of Méliès—panting more out of some revived excitement than out of fatigue, which is probably the one human response he doesn't understand. His trousers seem innocent of ironing, and his polo-neck sweaters look as if they had been dug out of a schoolboy's trunk crammed with toffees and old magazines and football boots. His shape is roughly an oval, poised on a tip and slanting forward. He walks like a dolphin balanced on its tail, often raising its head to send out messages. His character leaps to lack of order. He is too busy for system—too busy saving film. He spends as few hours of the day as possible on himself. It seems entirely typical of him that

75

he once confused sleeping pills and vitamins, taking a sleeping pill after every meal and a vitamin pill at bedtime. No consequence, observers report. Marmalade and films kept him awake. "I could have been a marvelous madman," he whispered to me confidingly in Paris. "I could have contained my madness."

"Contained": apt. Though the fanaticism is certainly not a hoax, and though it sustains him as much as his friends do—as much as the company of anyone who loves film does—you have the feeling that the colossal, ostensibly obstreperous mad archivist is a decoy set up to draw the fire. The real man exists elsewhere: a fine-tuned poet drawn to serious conversation and to practical jokes that give no pain, and infinitely respectful whenever he detects creation. The point of setting up the decoy would be, perhaps, to grant himself time. His total absorption shakes off ninnies and allows him repose for looking and for the company of film, his friend.

He has enormous charm, of the kind that he responds to in movies. "By charm in the cinema, I mean the mythological charm of the fates, not the charm of a pretty woman," he said to me in Paris over an exquisite Chinese dinner at four in the morning, which is his usual hour for dining. He was born in Smyrna in 1914, to a half-American, half-French mother and a French diplomat father. Also from his mother, he has Irish blood. He often spoke demotic Greek as a child. He has a brother who is a lawyer, but Henri himself never passed his *baccalauréat*, because he saw six films a day. He was always the family black sheep. "My uncle thought I was a Communist, because I didn't play bridge," he said. Pause. "I still don't." Whenever he is in a sociable situation, he seems to become the center of a peculiarly convivial graveness, which can turn in a second into a humor that includes everybody. At the Academy Awards in 1974, when he flew to Hollywood to receive a special Oscar for his services to the cinema, he gave his thanks in French, which was translated; was responded to in French, also translated; spoke cheerfully, again in French, of the craze of the New Wave—and of Renoir and Abel Gance before them—for American movies, his words being again translated; and then made a rapid exit with a sentence in English, thus pulling the rug from under everyone. He likes a certain amount of sorcery and trick-playing. All this is taken by him with perfect seriousness. There is a beautiful American woman connected with the endeavor to found an American Cinémathèque—which is to be directed artistically by Langlois and run by Tom Johnston and Gene Stavis, two longtime colleagues of his in the enterprise—on a magnificent site under the huge pillars of New York's Queensboro Bridge. Langlois told me quietly that he thinks she is the heroine of an American detective thriller, so putting his finger on something arcane about her appeal, something unsaid and wizardly.

Over a lifetime, Langlois has helped to raise the cinema from the ghetto of art, but he minimizes what he did for the people of the New Wave through his passion for then unrecognized geniuses like Bergman, Ozu, and Kurosawa. (Langlois was the first to show Kurosawa outside Japan.) In spite of his scholarly love of silent films, Langlois says of Ozu, "What talk! What nuance of feeling!" Scarcely anyone else in the Western world perceived it in the fifties. But this man, living in epic disarray and apparently wedded to films, has a curious capacity for sensing the truth of feeling and the movement of mood in other countries, politically as well as aesthetically, and in the past as well as in the present. His instincts for shifts in the popular spirit work like antennae; they never seem to derive from anything he has read. He apparently knows things from the air. His intuition can in fact be traced to his born habit of paying heed to everything that passes by. No man can ever have given greater attention to events while looking abstracted. It is another aspect of his decoy apparatus.

We spoke at some late supper in Paris of the fallen idol of the car industry in America, and of the economic situation across the Channel. "You see, people in England have always had their faces bang up against the wall, and soon it will have happened all over Europe," he said. "As usual, it happened in England first." We were in a satin-lined restaurant with a perky waitress. She made him resentful for the first time since I had known him. "The restaurant is like a cheap drawing room. No, like a bordello," he said. "This waitress with a red satin blouse, she is not for women's liberation. I don't like her pensées." It was midnight—early for him—but we left for the fresh air and a tiny car with his old friend

Mary Meerson, widow of Lazare Meerson, who was a Russian-French movie designer famous between the wars, particularly for his work with René Clair. She speaks French, English, Russian, Yiddish, Turkish, Finnish, and Lord knows how many other languages. Courted all over Europe as a girl, she now has gaps in her teeth and the same bulk as Langlois, but she retains great funds of charm, loyalty, humor, and expansiveness. It is easy still to see her as a beauty, even though she walks with difficulty and takes no care of herself: or, indeed, of anything but film, Langlois, and all other friends to the imaginative.

A church clock struck twelve as we came out. "We must work," said Langlois, striding toward Mme. Meerson's little car. "Can you drive?" he asked me. "Unlike us, you would put a distance between yourself and the steering wheel, which juts into Mary or me. Though I should prefer that the gentleman do the driving. When you go to England, will you also be going to Ireland? They make there a special kind of marmalade with whiskey."

"Henri likes it very much," said Mary Meerson.

They have plenty of time for such talk. On the other hand, one can see that neither can ever have had much for hypochondria or snobbery. When Langlois was a young man, he was told that he had to go to the mountains for the sake of his chest. He went instead to the top of the Eiffel Tower every day and breathed the air there. He hoards time like a miser and then spends it on film, as if he were a boy throwing gold coins out of a train window in the dark to see them catch the light of the electric sparks. He spoke to me once of three days of officialdom that he thought of as wasted: "In those three days, I could have saved perhaps three films."

Out in a park, two young moviemakers named Eila Hershon and Roberto Guerra were with him when he saw some black swans. "Like a black-and-white film," he said. The swans had red beaks. "Like the heart of film," he said. He doesn't like gray marks on old movies and will do anything to be rid of them. Gray belongs on his clothes, he told me. An accident to anything but a film is something to be put up with unheatedly. And even when an uncatalogued film that is due to be shown in a program eludes him

78

temporarily, he makes something better of the loss. He believes in the creative force of the accidental, as Renoir does. "Vandalism lies in forgetting, in making do with little when much needs to be saved, in sleeping when you know films are being destroyed," he said. The apartment where he and Mary Meerson live has been gradually stripped of fine paintings to allow him to buy films. "If you don't save, you have not got. The important thing is to save. When you don't buy a Picasso, another museum buys it. But when you don't buy a film it is lost." A cheap table in the drawing room has a drawer that Langlois used for a long time to hold the takings from the cinemas and the museum in the Palais de Chaillot. He spends nearly all his own money on laying his hands on films, and on entertaining friends late at night: certainly not on clothes, though he is delighted by an African man's robe that a young friend bought for Mary Meerson. Mme. Meerson once made an effort to get him to Pierre Cardin for a suit. He wouldn't go. "Cardin must measure me sitting down, and come here," Langlois said. "I don't wear a suit standing up, after all. I wear it sitting down. Anyway, I like unidentified suits." Mme. Meerson buys him one-hundred-percent cashmere socks, but he habitually loses them after a single wearing. She doesn't mind, even though neither of them has a sou. Like Langlois, Mme. Meerson has a peculiar style buried somewhere, for all the surface muddle. They seem wonderfully happy together.

Around them the couple have collected many devoted friends. Actors, directors, old allies, young members of the New Wave:

Simone Signoret remembers him in the Occupation. Langlois would bravely indulge his passion for secrecy by passing furtive word to her around some café, where she would be sitting under the Nazis' noses, that he was going to show an outlawed classic that night in his mother's drawing room: "Half past eight tonight, 'Potemkin.'" The dangerous screenings were made possible by his having scattered reels of forbidden film among trusted friends. The spectators could all have gone to jail. "Simone could have been badly punished for coming," says Langlois about this stoic figurehead of resistance to authoritarianism. "Not only for political reasons to do with the Russians but because she knew and loved film."

A director young at the time of the war says, "Mary is so paranoid that the Germans were nothing. She and Henri were quite used to having no telephone and no electricity anyway, because they always forgot to pay their bills. Even now, Henri will sometimes say, 'The telephone's going badly,' as if being cut off by the telephone company for not paying one's bill had something to do with the service."

Renoir says, "He made a church for the cinema. He refuses to choose; if he doesn't like a film, he says, somone in the future may. It is very solemn, very gay."

Truffaut says, "Langlois is the man to whom we owe everything. He showed us all we know. He says that he just laid the table and we ate, but no one else laid the table."

Catherine Deneuve says, "He has made a bank for safekeeping, but he doesn't like vaults, because vaults give you a false sense of security. He says that in other countries films are kept in vaults and are never seen, and yet all the time the films are being destroyed. The Cinémathèque is the most reassuring thing in Paris."

Lillian Gish says, "Henri works for the nation, not for the state. Modern film is too strong for me, but he also keeps all the films I like. You see, a writer can go back to the words he has written, but films and actresses have only a very short life. To the cinema, Langlois is like a god. Nothing happens in the world of cinema that he doesn't know about. Have you thought about how much he has in common with Truffaut? They both remember only what they want to remember. Langlois says Truffaut has to travel with two tickets, because he is always losing one. I went to Paris first in the Great War, and then in the twenties and thirties. I saw Paris first when there wasn't a light anywhere. Only a full moon. Mr. D. W. Griffith and my sister and I could hear the bursts of gunfire. Paris was out of bounds unless you were there, like us, on special business. I had been learning French secretly. Youngsters have no fear." Miss Gish herself still looks very young: delicate, flower-faced. "That's why soldiers have to be seventeen or eighteen. I was in Europe in 1938. In Germany, I did all my shopping in the Jewish shops. We lived in the governmental district, which meant that we had heat. Sometimes I think of the cinema and how no other invention has so moved the hearts and minds of men, except perhaps for jazz, and, of course, printing. I remember in Yugoslavia seeing a man kiss the screen when one of Mr. Griffith's films was showing. M. Langlois would understand that, though I don't mean that he is sentimental."

Jean-Pierre Léaud, famous at fifteen with "The 400 Blows," arrives for a bistro breakfast at seven-thirty, looking sleepy, and says, when I thank him, "*Ah, pour Langlois . . .*" We eat croissants. He hasn't any money. He has walked from home. "Langlois has given us a window on films. He is our *grandpère*. Without him, the New Wave would not exist, as Truffaut says."

Abel Gance says, "He is the Shylock of films, thank God." The legendary Gance is a thin man, now over eighty, living among books written in many languages, in an incongruously shoddy modern apartment of which he seems oblivious. His real life is elsewhere: mostly in two new scripts he has written. One is about Christopher Columbus, one about Christ. Gance reads Sophocles and Shakespeare and Goethe. He sits alone with me after giving the most precise and gentle directions about how to find his apartment. He opened the door himself. Bent shoulders, handsome face, a body smaller than his clothes. We talk at his desk. He is flickering with interest in new ideas. "Columbus had a very concentrated vision." Hands round his eyes as if he were looking again through a viewfinder, as he did when he made his famous "Napoléon." He is wearing a suède jacket. There are neat folders everywhere. An old portable typewriter. He finds documents and lines from books to show me. "Words are on the wind. Images rest," he says.

Gene Stavis, a man who is Langlois's confrere in knowledge, and even in looks, says, "The great thing is that he doesn't treat anything as a problem if it isn't immediate, and for him the only pressing thing is to preserve films. We have to do it here in America, too. Japan also has a terrible record for preserving films. Langlois knows that filmmakers are a very rare species. There are not many men with the genius and stamina of, say, Renoir or Bergman." Stavis is a big man with a fine laugh, and an eccentric speed of movement rivalling Langlois's own. "The cassette revolution . . . Our immediate intention at the American Cinémath-

81

èque is to show videotape as well as movies, a history of TV as well as film. It's a scandal that so many bad film buffs and bad filmmakers are being turned out here. The point is to be able to show people that the things they admire have a past. I realize that seeing famous works of the past on cassettes or videotape is a little bit like showing Renaissance paintings through a microscope. All the same, though it may be a fad, it may lead somewhere."

Willard Van Dyke, ex-director of the film department of the Museum of Modern Art in New York, says, "Langlois is a genius, even if he is criticized for his method of cataloguing. If he creates chaos sometimes, he is the most creative man about chaos I have ever known. Archivists are bound to have disagreements, because archivists are bookkeepers; all artists hate bookkeepers above anyone, and I think there is a good deal of the artist in Langlois. He crosses the line all the time." A generous view to take, if you have ever listened to the run-of-the-mill quarrels of archivists about ways of preserving films. Langlois's belief is that some of his most physically fortunate films were the ones buried in chateaux during the war in cellars that had long been used for the storing of salt.

"Hamlet was often played in the early days by a fat man, when great stars were fat," said Langlois stalwartly to me as I followed him round his museum, he speeding ahead and puffing. His friends of old remember a time when he was very skinny, and bleary-eyed with looking at films. They say he could have been an architect. One can see it in the way he has laid out the museum, which originally had the unpromising shape of a train. Now it seems like an Aladdin tunnel, full of entrances at odd angles. There are a D. W. Griffith contract, an 1892 Eastman camera, one of the earliest Lumière Cinématographe contraptions (1896) with a contemporary playbill, posters and photographs, a reproduction of Méliès's studio, a tiny dress and jacket that belonged to Bessie Love ("It's beautiful, no?"), a set structure for "The Cabinet of Dr. Caligari," Garbo's first costume, an Eisenstein design for "Macbeth," an audiovisual film strip of a Diaghilev production, Buster Keaton's hat, Chevalier's boater, a Mae West hat burdened with trimmings, an Esther Williams bathing suit, stills from "Citizen Kane," a dress from "Gigi," a Sophia Loren dress that Langlois stops beside in exasperation at the way passersby have messed up the folds. He arranges everything himself, with a natural feeling for the very elegance that he would despise in some social celebrity who might be asked to run the American Cinémathèque. "If they looked for someone elegant, it would be ridiculous," says the colossus figure of world cinema, arranging film stars' clothes with more style and fondness than any window dresser. "I did all this on very little money. People gave things. Scripts, designs, clothes, whole sets. As to raising money, I am a specialist in making gaffes. For instance, I ask a millionaire for some money for the Cinémathèque, and I find myself saying, 'We won't have any of that horrible plastic.' But, you see, the gentleman made his fortune out of plastic bottles. All the same, in others I prefer *bêtise* to *politesse*. That is why I liked de Gaulle. He made many gaffes, because I think he never felt quite secure. Not like most politicians. Security makes laziness, and it requires energy to commit a gaffe. It is unforgettable that at the start of the Nazi Occupation de Gaulle committed the, shall we say, gaffe of offending the Germans. This must be very interesting, the national characteristics shown during the war. The French prepare the Resistance, for instance. The Americans prepare the conscience." He paused, and thought of something. "The English fought," he said gently, going on to speak of the Blitz.

Sitting exhausted in a back room of the museum devoted to silent-film mementos, drinking it all in like a hippopotamus at a pool, and looking at von Stroheim's gleaming white greatcoat, he said, "When I was a boy, I saw German films, French films, Italian films, but I missed the entire American silent cinema. It was the same with Japanese cinema. Now Ozu is acknowledged as a master, but a while ago every time a great Ozu film was shown there were only ten or twenty people in the audience." Kurosawa designed the layout of kimonos hanging on the walls of Langlois's Petite Salle, a little cinema that, like a Japanese restaurant, has comfortable cushions for seats, with no backs: Kurosawa pinned the clothes into the positions of dancers making stylized gestures and put them behind sheets of mesh. "As I have said, Ozu has a quality of nuance that is unusual in the talkies. Often one learns a great deal by showing him without subtitles. If it is true, as I think, that the Cinémathèque Française played a role in the New Wave, it was because we didn't have enough money to subtitle prints." I later watched him showing Orson Welles' "Macbeth" to a class that he was teaching. For quite a time, he turned off the sound. "You see?" he said to the audience. "It is made like a silent film." But his admiration is not for the antique in any recondite way. It is simply for the lucid. His great love is for Jean Vigo, the master who made "L'Atalante" and, above all, "Zéro de Conduite." Langlois said in his car as we were going somewhere from the Chaillot, "Vigo avoided the horrible disease of naturalism. Sound and sight merged for him. A silent film, it has to be said, is often flat. Sound creates an ambience. False, yes. As the great Picassos and the Eiffel Tower are false to realism. No, to naturalism. The Eiffel Tower is not remotely antique. It's a pun. It's false. That's the interesting thing. That's the paradox."

In his adherence to the simplicity of silent film and also to the complication of any talkie that has been imagined with cinematic purity, Langlois seems to be contradicting himself. It is one of the singular things about him, his friends believe, that he can say opposing things and make you reconcile them. "Films with subtitles on them are for the ladies of the Sixteenth Arrondissement," he will say, at the same time struggling to find exactly the right subtitle from the workings of his own mind in preparation for a class. He writes not only subtitles but poetry. Seeing him one day, I told him that I had had a dream at four that morning in which he had rung me up at four in the dreamed morning and read me a poem he had just written in Greek. He looked skeptical and convinced at the same time. "How is that possible?" he said. I repeated what I had said, and he said, "Last night, you see, at what must have been four in the morning I finished a poem in village Greek—that is, in French translated into Greek with the help of a friend, because I can hardly remember Greek now, in spite of speaking it when I was a child."

Typically, the Dionysian antiquarian has an Apollonian and modern taste in poetry and films. "He has a fantastic intellect, but it is not logical," a famous old friend says. "Henri believes that logic is a way of saying no." So it goes. Langlois lives by the calm of the art he most admires, but he also flourishes through erraticism. "In the ancient Greek idea, it is disorder that produces order. Disorder is energy," he said, casually defending a lifetime that looks squall-ridden to outsiders and to squabbling rival archivists but that artists recognize as a signal of quiet water in which to drop anchor and work.

"When we first started the Cinémathèque, it was called the Cercle du Cinéma," he told me. "It got going in 1935. Then my friend Lotte Eisner, among others, helped in the war to hide our prints from the Nazis. She did it at great danger to herself. We had prints everywhere. We hid them in the Château du Lot, most of them. We called it the Château de Lotte." Lotte Eisner, a courtly, arthritic cinéaste, is a gallant and scholarly German friend of many years. Langlois and Mme. Meerson will suddenly send her a delicate cake and she will make it the centerpiece of a tea party in the packed little library of her apartment in Paris, where she works on books about masters of the silent days. (A book of hers about Fritz Lang is to be published in America later this year.) She is one of many Jews in France whom Langlois went on seeing staunchly all through the Occupation. Mm. Eisner, who has taken French citizenship, spoke to me at one of her tea parties of his coming often now to tea, this whale of a man. "I say to him, 'Henri, you've gone through all the chairs. Please don't sit on the Louis Treize.' So he says, 'I'll sit on the floor.' You know that neither he nor Mary has a watch? He often rings up in the middle of the night, if he has paid his telephone bill and the machine is working, and I say to myself, 'Henri, do you know what time it is?' "

I said, "I expect he does know. He's never late, by some miracle. I've often noticed him looking at his wrist, even though there isn't a watch on it."

Lotte Eisner nodded, and poured more of her fragrant tea at a splendiferously laid table, hemmed in by fiction in many languages and by shelf upon shelf of reference books about German and Japanese cinema. "I say to him sometimes, 'Henri, you must have had a watch in another life.' He believes in reincarnation, you see."

It may be this belief that gives Langlois the paradoxical attribute of at once seeming to have all the time in the world and making decisions in an instant. The decisions are often veiled in unnecessary secrecy, as though his life were bugged and had to be led furtively. Perhaps that is because of his instinct for the usefulness of decoys. Towards his duties as an archivist his attitude is peculiarly his own. He would love to save every foot of every film that has ever been made. He refuses to pay attention to this age's idea of what is trash and what is crucial, let alone to use his own standards of the historically durable. He prefers storing films in wood to scaling them in steel, and he prefers showing them to storing them: "A film has to breathe." About the point of keeping movies whether he likes them or not, he says, "Even bad films—bad as we see them now—deserve to be saved." I don't think I have ever heard him say of any film that it is worthless, though he is famous for his occasional tempests directed at audiences whom he regards as ignoramuses—at an audience that doesn't recognize Ozu, for instance, to whom he will retort silently by turning off the film and showing a Mickey Mouse.

Not that he disdains Mickey Mouse. He recently had a Disney season, and he has a passion for American cinema. "This is why the American Cinémathèque could be so important," he says. (The designs for the theatres and the museum that are to be housed under the Queensboro Bridge, once the money is in, have already been done by the architect I. M. Pei. They are spectacular. They react to the site.) "America has the real Picasso of cinema in D. W. Griffith. Yet he is often left to molder. . . . I found a film of Griffith's that had an illness that was spreading like cancer. The thing to do was to cut fifty feet out of it. In Griffith's own country, they wanted to destroy the whole thing." He went on to speak of the time of decline in American filmmaking, when film producers ran studios as if they were matters of real-estate administration or showing off. "As these men had automobiles, as they had mistresses, so they had studios. However, things are changing, no?"

Lillian Gish had said to me in New York, "It's terrible that it has been left to French and English cinema archivists and film lovers to interest Americans in their own movie history. In their own social history, even." Talking American social history in a Greek restaurant on a recent visit to New York, Langlois told me about a film record of Watergate that someone has put together to donate to the Cinémathèque Française. "Watergate!" he said, pouring Greek red wine. "In France, we are used to all that, O.K. But Americans forget that they came to America to be rid of it. Well, this has been a bad time. Before, Harding put his trust in some criminals. More lately, the criminals have had such power that the people themselves have had to put their trust in them. Now, as to the American Cinémathèque project, it would be logical for Americans, who in this case have antiques as old as anyone in the world, to have a place in which to watch. These antiques are of immense value. The destruction process must be stopped. There are many things to which time gives life. Making a judgment against something is gambling against the future. We shall have the old trouble with archivists, of course. They tell us always that the original parts of old films explode. But you see me, and I have been a projectionist for many years." He was clearly undented. "One always says that one's competitors' products explode. In the case of the English professionals, they are inclined to say that old prints are noxious." He ate stuffed vine leaves, and then some moussaka as one of several main courses, looking remarkably unpoisoned and rather serious. "These fights are ridiculous. In the old days, there was only one real difference between the other archivists and me. This difference was that the government institutions in other countries had money. I was never bureaucratic-minded, but all the same I had my work to do."

Langlois treats a lost film like a quarry to be coaxed, lured, hunted down, and nourished back to health by hand. He is a great teacher, his pupils say. One of them remarked after a lecture, "He ties things up in a knot. Very complicated. And then the knot slips, like a rope trick, and everything becomes simple." Everyone thinks he is devoted only to silent cinema, but he was one of the first authorities to recognize Kenneth Anger. He brought Persian films to the West. The success of Satyajit Ray is partly owed to him. He sees a lot being done in the future with a new public. He said, another day, when we were walking in Paris, "At the Cinémathèque, we have tried to learn to have no prejudice against any film, including commercial films. Before we began our efforts, people would have said, 'These films are senseless.' I don't try to make a chart of importance, and certainly I am not for the old against the new. Cinema has to be seen not from a historical viewpoint but from an aesthetic viewpoint. On the other hand, one has to remember that there are often aesthetic importances not visible to us at the moment." He will stop on the street and stand there for hours to talk abut film. "We must have slapstick, for instance," he said, halting now. "We know these days that it was aesthetically important, but when Keaton was working he was not taken seriously." We went into a restaurant, and he turned away from a suggestion of escalope Viennoise to go on talking. "Keaton suffered because of the bourgeoisie, and perhaps that is why I don't like Vienna very much. It is a place of the bourgeoisie. The Viennese men of the bourgeoisie don't read. They only know how to make love. Love in a bad way. Also, you see, escalope is nothing to do with my origin. It's not natural to me." He grinned.

Like many heavy people, Langlois is finely calibrated, with ideas that have a mysterious and visionary effect on people around him. He is impatient with the frivolous, and he thinks that a lot of archivists and thinkers stint on work, but he is also tenaciously patient about waiting for change to come. In the films that most interest him, he finds half-hidden signals of things on the brink. He often seems to be talking about other possibilities that lie buried in great cinema. He sees Shakespearean things here, you think: the prophet of a new order coming in at the end of a familiar reign, like Fortinbras, and the same emotions that are expressed in Goneril's line "An interlude!" in Shakespeare's amazing moment of quick, sad scorn for the immediate which should be spoken without weight and surrounded by no great pauses. It seemed typical of Langlois when he suddenly said in a crowded street, grasping my arm and not even stopping in his hurry, "True cinema is the world of beyond." He turned toward me. No haste then; only interest. "Yes, is that true, do you think?"

MARCH 24, 1975

88

Old Master: Abel Gance

Abel Gance, who has been to cinema what Picasso was to painting, was born in Paris in 1889. He is a thin, frail man, housed in a frugal modern Paris flat crowded with books and neatly stacked folders. His study is full of incongruous modern furniture and poor reproductions of antique occasional tables. In these ersatz surroundings, he plans films that have as expansive a vision of the world as his great chronicle of Bonaparte, which he has made in four versions; the latest was made in 1971.

You might suppose that Gance could at this point give himself a respite. On the contrary, he has written detailed scripts for an epic about Christopher Columbus. The man who discovered America—yet whose name was not given to either of the continents he had led the way to—should be celebrated, Gance strongly feels. He has no doubt that he has the time to do it. "One lives as long as one has things to do that are necessary," the old man said to me a few years ago, he at his piled desk, planning. "It is when one has finished that one dies." His vision of the films he wants to make is a vision of cathedrals. "Cinema will reinforce men's energies, and suppress their twilights," he said. He thinks poorly of modern movies' progress. "Unlike Racine, who says that what one hears is better than what one sees, I believe for myself that the opposite is true. Or can be true. But cinema now is underselling itself. There is woodworm in the timbers. Commercialism. Thin theorizing. The hulk will go down. Film is forgetting the finest words in its vocabulary. One should restore them."

Gance speaks of Columbus as of a friend. "He died poor. I said to myself, 'That's an injustice to be repaid,' considering the struggles he had in Spain in setting out on the endeavor, which, after all, had no visible end. He didn't know that he was going to discover a new world. Or that he would have the misfortune to bring back gold. He endured the political dramas and the travail of navigation. His enterprise embodied an internal ethical drama of total gravity, like

89

Hamlet's. Do you know about his death? A Shakespearean tragedy. And in his own lifetime no one even knew where he was born."

It took young men from the *Cahiers du Cinéma* group—especially François Truffaut and Jacques Rivette—to recognize this prophet who is still with us. The present glorious version—"Bonaparte and the Revolution"—is described in a Gance subtitle as a *"fresque dramatique en deux époques."* It provokes thoughts of Griffith and Eisenstein, von Stroheim, Lubitsch, and of the great Romantic painters, and often even of Godard. There is an impression of rush: swift cutting, images crammed with the churning races of the Revolution. Alternating with them, and so given a tonic poise, there are closeups, stills, and engravinglike images of grand rooms. No one who has entered filmmaking since Gance has so fully and fluently used the grammar of cinema. "Enthusiasm is the great condition of life," the old man said to me in his apartment, looking with vivacity at the piles of work planned.

This splendid feat of intellect, education, and imagery includes, in its 1971 version, which runs four hours and a quarter, some of the best parts of the nearly five-hour 1927 silent version and some of the 1934 sound version (which Gance was able to post-synch without trouble, because he had originally written lines of actual dramatic dialogue for the same actors to mouth in the silent original). There is a third version—a hundred and thirty-five minutes—made in 1955 and called "Napoleon-Bonaparte," which includes one of his four famous 1927 triptychs, anticipating Cinerama by decades. Together with a sequence that was an augury of 3-D, and an insertion in color, three of these triptychs have been lost. But according to Robert A. Harris, an eager American film authority who is working in Rye on what he hopes will be a definitive reconstruction of the 1927 original, one of the great French fanatics among film archivists thinks that he has located two of the missing triptychs. Gance, ahead of his time, used hand-held cameras and, sometimes, cameras strapped to the back of a horse or to a pendulum.

* * *

"Bonaparte and the Revolution" begins with Beethoven on the sound track. Gance is interviewed. He speaks of Bonaparte and Talleyrand. There is some mixed footage in sepia, and the famous Gros portrait of Napoleon. Gance has retained the film score by Arthur Honegger. Alexandre Benois was the art director. Albert Dieudonné plays Bonaparte. Antonin Artaud plays Marat. Gance himself plays Saint-Just. We see France in confusion. Foreign invaders, formless republicanism. Bonaparte in a Paris garrett, almost twenty, rejected as a military student, demoted because of a silly matter of boots; already alert to the people's misery, made visible on his wall by the shadows of citizens passing in the street—warriors carrying weapons that are a mixture of real arms and farm implements. And then the King, in a panelled room at Versailles. The King hears the populace roaring outside. "Is that the wind?" the blinkered monarch asks a Minister. "No, Sire, it is the Revolution."

Danton, with a violent mass of black hair. Robespierre, the most silky, the most dangerous. Saint-Just, noble-nosed, his hair dressed so that he looks like a High Romantic garden statue. The differences between the men's physical types are striking. They are images of the differences between the men's concepts of the effect that violence will have on the Revolution's course. But, for all the wrangling, there is a hairdresser at work, making curls while the republican potentates make plots. Danton emerges from a conference chamber to go into a meeting hall filled with a bottled-up mob. Wild applause. There is the first performance of Rouget de Lisle's "Marseillaise." Danton seems to sense a rival. His meeting with Rouget de Lisle has the lighting of a painting by one of the French Caravaggesques: it looks like a Georges de La Tour. The King's cannons are fired on the citizens. "The sound of a crown falling," says Camille Desmoulins. We have seen Marie Antoinette sitting in the Assembly; she is still enough of a despot to hide fear, but her eyes move uneasily from side to side, like water in the jugs of a ship in storm.

The people are taking over. But under whom? We see the King looking back at his possessions as he flees. The populace sacks Versailles, uncomprehendingly destroying what is now its own.

Bonaparte is repelled by the lack of order, and probably Gance would agree with him. Brutality has dominion. We see the cut-off ear of a Swiss Guard. The people are made witless and lustful by the lack of a ruling ethic. The seductiveness of rebellion and looting beckons oppressed people into many bordellos of opinion.

Bonaparte returns to his native Corsica, ordering law without bloodshed. The equivalent of 1792 in France, with its decline of revolution into barbarity, is not to come to his homeland. He will make a new revolution. But the Corsicans treat him as a traitor, feeling themselves to be at least half for England, which is Corsica's proposed ally. "Am I French or English?" says a peasant soldier desperately. "Tear off my uniform and my skin comes off with it." Shouting that "France is the mother of us all," Bonaparte makes a cowboy's leap out of an inn window and takes down the town flag. Its billows dwarf him. The composition is straight out of the French classical baroque. He races for the sea and a boat, and catches the wind with his captured tricolor, which acts as the sail. On the same day, in Paris, Charlotte Corday stabs Marat in his hip bath.

Bonaparte becomes a general. Chaos still reigns. Royalists and revolutionaries are still arguing for their separate causes. Gance's Bonaparte is on neither side: he makes it clear that he doesn't like the men who have made him a general, but that he feels obliged to take on the role, because France is menaced. In a line here, Gance hits on the key error of the Revolution: the people's mistaken impulse to "name a soldier or a dictator to rid us of these scoundrels." Name a scoundrel-ridder and you are likely to be saddled with a tyrant. The first part of the film ends with a shot of Bonaparte asleep in the sun, covered by flags draped over him by his mesmerized soldiers. Such is the despot's skill: he has made an adoringly patriotic army out of a lot of tired cynics, and he has done it because he posesses a despot's energy.

Second epoch. The Assembly. Saint-Just defending the Terror. Closeups of the other, private sort of terror passing over his own face. We see a quill pen writing the death sentence for enemies of the prevailing faction of Revolutionists; Gance makes much use in this film of beautiful writing, often shown upside down, always elegantly illegible, so that calligraphy becomes something as abstract as costume. Bonaparte is imprisoned, is rapidly freed, and even more rapidly falls in love with his Josephine, from Martinique. The sequences about his marriage are a consummation of Gance's humor. Bonaparte is given acting lessons in how to propose to a woman. Then political conferences take precedence. But Josephine arrives, so Bonaparte clears out the men; bungling gallantry, and amused by himself, he kneels on a cushion and speaks his rehearsed lines. Acceptance. Another victory. But he can spare only two days for his honeymoon before he has to win Italy. For the marriage ceremony, his beloved Josephine has not had time to get her birth certificate from Martinique. So she uses her sister's— thereby taking four years off her age, says a narrator. In Bonaparte's case, he borrows his brother's birth certificate and ages by eighteen months. No matter. Get on with it. The two idyllic days seem pictorially to embody everything most glorious in French Impressionism. The couple's love theme on the sound track is "Voi che sapete." When Bonaparte has left, she sings it to herself.

Time moves. A change in the temper of the period. The dandies and dolls of the post-Revolutionary era, with their fun about a game they call Guillotine, are not suited to the austerity of Bonaparte. Their waste of spirit does not invite him. He needs adversity. Once again, he creates a victorious army out of bedraggled and outnumbered troops. He wins Piedmont. Before the battle, Gance shows us a lost alley cat peering out of a cannon. Why anything is happening no one in the army knows, but the soldiers are ready to die for this great man who barely notices them. The people of France have found an emblem in Bonaparte, just as Bonaparte has found an emblem in the eagle, which appears in some of the multilayered images that are one of Gance's great cinematic innovations. While the undersized military philosopher thinks of the globe that he means to make his republic, exhausted soldiers are having to fight in the most hectic, muddy battle scene in any film I know of, apart from the one in Orson Welles' "Falstaff." The young general, sleepless with amibition, has stalked the camp the night before the battle. But, in the military review before that, a little drummer boy without such drive has fallen into his drum with fatigue and fright.

"Our enthusiasm and the 'Marseillaise' make up the difference," Bonaparte has said to his outnumbered troops. Gance's point about Bonaparte is that once he has decided to act, he feels no need to convince the people that he is right: he believes that results vindicate. Bonaparte is "Heroic" because of his tenacity and the world breadth of his revolutionary vision. Gance has a subtle sense of the shifts in shame and guilt as the Revolution goes its way. Robespierre is spiritually doomed as soon as he signs his name to Danton's condemnation. When he tries to absolve himself of the sin by making his signature on the death document a miniature of his usual one, he is only compounding the wrong. Gance represents Bonaparte as a genius who achieves his vision without the imbalance of Saint-Just. "Even Marx and Engels spoke of Napoleon with an admiration that might surprise you," Gance said to me. "They seized his republican ideas. The trouble was that events forced him to create European kingdoms so as to get rid of European feudalities. Which was to replace one disaster with another."

There is a famous piece of crosscutting in the film, beautifully described in "The Parade's Gone By," by Kevin Brownlow, who has himself worked for years to find lost cans of Gance footage in the Paris flea markets. The crosscutting is between the struggle in the Assembly and Bonaparte's struggle in a storm at sea on his way back from Corsica. Gance devised it in 1927, for the silent version of the film. "I had to find a way to show that he could stay afloat through all the tempests," he told me. "France, too, was in the middle of a whirlwind, nearly submerged." Whenever Bonaparte is onscreen in this sequence, the frame seems to boil with superimpositions. Bonaparte is racing to give matters his stamp. He is possessed for the moment by the idea that "we governed by the guillotine those who had the right to be governed by justice." Earlier in the film, we have seen him alone in the Paris Assembly, haunted by the utterances not only of recently executed politicians but also of long-dead men of literature and ideas, who clearly represent to Gance his own colleagues in a life of reading. The phantom of Robespierre says, "If the Revolution does not grow beyond our frontiers, it will die where it is." As Gance puts it in the film, speaking as much for himself as for any past revolutionist, "Happiness is a new idea. Barriers still stand between religions, between ideologies. We should mingle in the rebellion." The juxtaposed combat in the Assembly and storm at sea was suggested by a line of Victor Hugo's: "To be a member of the Assembly was to be like a wave on the ocean." Gance lives with his thinking forebears.

Perhaps a shot that moves one as much as anything is the prophetic technical courage of a rapid image that uses advertising typography just as Godard does. For all that Gance has already bequeathed to his descendants, his influence has a noble life ahead. His films, technically wondrous, are unique in the cinema in the ideas they excite. They make it obvious to any child that problems of barriers are not fundamental but only didactic. There is some vital lesson in Gance's own performance as Saint-Just: in this version we see Gance, whose life has exceeded film's, in an added silhouette shot taken when he was eighty-one, representing a figure of history who was guillotined at the age of twenty-seven.

In Gance's great earlier film "La Roue" (1922), about a young man and woman falsely brought up as brother and sister, the young man is in love with the girl, who he knows is not his sister, and desperate about her indifference. "She can't see my suffering under the layer of soot," Gance wrote for the character. One thinks of this splendid old man sitting in his small study, showing no sign of the toll taken by the mishandling of his works but conceiving noble new commissions.

SEPTEMBER 6, 1976

A Sense of Dream: Jeanne Moreau

After Jeanne Moreau was in Louis Malle's "The Lovers" (1959),
film fans in France began calling her Jeanne d'Arc du Boudoir.
People in the profession who knew her better countered with
Jeanne la Sage. We were recently in the country in France, together in the beautiful place she has made of a century-old farmhouse
above Saint-Tropez. We went for a walk and saw a child watching
some piglets. "I like children. I also like the children of pigs," she
said solemnly. "Pigs are innocent and honorable." Of this woman,
François Truffaut, who directed her in "Jules and Jim" (1962) and
"The Bride Wore Black" (1968), said to me, "She has all the attributes of a woman, together with all the qualities one expects in a
man, with none of the inconveniences of either." Peter Brook, who
directed her in "Moderato Cantabile" (1964), said, "She is one of
the most remarkable actresses I have ever worked with. She has a
somnambulistic quality." Orson Welles, who directed her in "The
Trial" (1963), "Falstaff" (1967), and "The Immortal Story" (1968),
said, "She has the sense of drama and the sense of dream." Tony
Richardson, who directed her in "Mademoiselle" (1966) and "The
Sailor from Gibraltar" (1967), said, "She is more informed, committed, and passionate than any other actress I know."

Yet Jeanne Moreau herself says, "Being another character is an
absurd ambition. I hated acting the novelist's wife in Antonioni's
'La Notte,' in 1960. There are people like that poor woman, of
course, but not for me. That is not what love is like." There is
despair in the beautiful downturned mouth but also ready blithe-
ness. "I hate people who say, 'You're a real pro,'" she says. Her
word for what they are trying to get at is "précise." "Acting isn't a
profession, it's a way of living, and it's one that I may—I don't
know—leave behind. I would like to be a good director. I would
like to die a good writer." In New York, she had laughed and also
said, "I would love to be an architect. How many of these buildings
are scaled to the human size? And how many were built by a
woman?" In the South of France, where she seems most at home,
she spoke less harshly of herself as an actress: "When you work

with a new director, you open the door. *C'est le début, l'initiation.* I think that's why I'm related so deeply to the countryside. Everything begins here. There's nothing in it to disturb the consciousness." She traced the indented date—1860—on a stone fountain outside her house. "In a city, I would never be able to create a place like this. In the country, you watch a river. In the country, a house is built for the flow of the family. The fireplace is not a sign of the power of the head of the household. It's connected to family organization. In a plane, I have the impression that I'm going to be intimate with whatever city we're all travelling to in this great ship that used to express aspiration, but it doesn't happen. I like small harbors for the same reason. Everything there is connected to the convenience of the people who live around them."

We went inside, out of the light, and up to her bedroom, where there is a Picasso drawing of a woman and a little boy. "In fact, why are we connected to artists?" she said, with her legs tucked under her on the bed. "The Picassos I love most are the early ones. But his passion to paint, that's the thing. In Avignon, he was like a man losing his blood. He painted and painted, and sometimes you are linked to. He understood that art is not autobiographical. I suspect autobiographical art. Perhaps having such a relationship with the facts and the self is dangerous." She went out of the bedroom into a gallery that overhangs the drawing room, and put on a record of Billie Holiday. We listened for a while, and then she began to talk vigorously of Truffaut, who is her great friend. "People have accused him of being 'too sweet.' What is too sweet about affection? About kindness? The thing that is too sweet is what is vulgar and simply fishy—a fish going bad."

She has planted a lot of the trees around the house, which is shady against a brilliantly sunlit landscape of chestnuts. On a clear day, you can see the Alps. There are many fountains in the garden as well as the one outside the front door, where one day she carefully arranged some roses so that they could be seen through the mild plashing of water. She has a whistle like a schoolboy's, done through her teeth, and she suddenly started whistling for birds, which knew her call and came to perch on the stone edge of the fountain bowl—not to be fed but to watch. A certain ugly bird she particularly likes. "There was one morning when the other people in the house and I were having coffee here and the bird came and sat next door to the butter and stared at us as if we were more interesting than the crumbs. Which, of course, we weren't." she has two wolfhounds and a spaniel, which she makes no great fuss over. Characteristically.

The drawing room is double height, with a beam two-thirds of the way up that shows where hay used to be stored. There are wicker chairs—one or two with parasols over them for the summer, when they are moved outside. A low corner, with a little built-in daybed, has walls covered with pictures of Orson Welles and Jeanne Moreau in Seville. "In one scene of Orson's 'Immortal Story,' which was shot in Seville, he filmed with no lighting apart from candles with four wicks each," she said. "Everyone said it couldn't be done. He is a sculptor in clay. If he has to transform a Spanish village into a Chinese fair, he can. He has ingenuity. It goes with his skill as a magician." She talked for a time about the puny parts he has had to play to stay solvent. "Orson is an uncommon man when it comes to money," she said. "He never has any, and then when he is in the middle of shooting a film it is as if he were on an island away from worries, and he orders a dozen pairs of silk underclothes, and meals from Fortnum & Mason."

She lit a huge log fire, showing a bandage on her left knee. "I fell when I was in theatre rehearsals of Frank Wedekind's 'Lulu,' in Paris," she said. Then, pretending to be serious: "I am an Aquarius and so I have very weak ankles. This hurt knee is the *other* one, not the 'Lulu' one. When I was a little girl, I was built like a tomboy. I was always running, climbing trees, and falling off bikes, and always had big scabs on both knees. You must be careful on the stairs here. The step at the top is higher than the rest. I like to wonder what mistake the man made—or perhaps he did it half on purpose. Some of the best directors I have ever watched value chance, know how to use it. I don't believe it's a good thing to be extremely clever. A director like Jean-Pierre Melville wants so badly to be brilliant, to startle with clever cutting. It seems cold. Sometimes I think how few men there are who love the camera now. They are not astonished to have it in their hands, like Lumiere or Keaton, or like women directors, who I believe will keep that innocence. Clever men often use the camera to prod you into excitement, not to find out what is in the script and the actors. But Orson, now, with 'Citizen Kane,' he was so young he was in love with the camera. He didn't manipulate it; he was saying, 'Let's see what we can make together.' Of course, with women's films there *will* be dross. There will be a poor commercial cinema of women's films, but one hopes not too much."

She made rabbit stew. The kitchen is a typical South of France country one, with an old oak door carried on big iron hinges, a dark oak chest of drawers, a table that was once used for preparing game. Over the oak chest she has put up a print by Picasso of a girl's head. There is a beautiful old pair of kitchen scales near the stove. A married couple who work for her had the stew with us. "My godmother is going to give me two geese with bouclé frills around their necks like nightdresses," said Moreau. "We have a very old turkey here, because I am given one every year, and once we were all away at Christmas, so there was no reason to kill it."

"Do you do the killing?" I asked Louis, the gardener and man of all work, who comes from the Ardennes.

"Yes," said Moreau.

"Do you like it? Some countrymen don't mind," I said to Louis.

"No, he hates it. After doing it, he can't eat," said Moreau.

At the end of the meal, she reached behind her into a drawer of the chest, pulled out a box of buttons and a needle and thread, and made a rose out of silver paper for my daughter, sticking her tongue out as she did it, and sewing a red button carefully into the middle of the pleated foil. She collects knickknacks—buttons, gloves, shoes, little cardboard boxes that may come in handy—and keeps them together very neatly in places that she knows blindfolded. The buttons are all old ones, multicolored, like little jewels or children's toffees.

Later on, up in the gallery, which is filled with her books and with processions of small objects given to her over the years, I noticed a file of tiny ivory Chinese horses. "I like arranging them," she said. "They are the soldiers of fortune." One of them, near the back of the line, was on his front knees with fatigue. The head one was looking back. "Each one is quite different. Very Chinese. I want to go to China. With Mao, I felt anything was possible. Not like the Russian Revolution, which made a prison. The politics of the left in Russia has killed art, not to speak of so many people. It is not like England, where the left-wing young men of the mid-fifties tore aside the veils of the intellectual lackeys; or the French Events of May, which produced so much. The truth is that there is a certain poetry that politicians cannot trap, and sometimes it emerges even in Russia and Czechoslovakia. In art, we sorely miss the spirit of the six million Jews whom Hitler slaughtered. They understood that truth. I am thinking about a story told to me by a Russian Jewish doctor friend of mine who survived concentration camp. We were talking about what is indestructible. He had a friend in the camp who outlived fear and torture by playing chess games in his head. Sometimes he would go through old games that he had already played. When things got extremely bad, he would invent new problems for himself, all played in the head. It was, of course, the mind that saved him, but not without suffering. When people are alive, they have many deaths: not only cowards die a million deaths. What is incredible about existence is its toughness in extremity. The Russian doctor made me think of Louis here. I think the reason the doctor survived is that he knew that each human being is one of many. Louis is small but very strong. I saw the part of the Ardennes that he came from. It was ravaged by the end of the war. I was surprised you ate the rabbit stew, because I know how much the English had to eat rabbit for years, even after the war."

"The whale meat was the worst," I said.

"The English in trouble are like the Italians. They have a vivacity that is not aggressive."

Jeanne Moreau has a strong moral sense that works like the instinct of a countrywoman for detecting, say, thievery on a farm or a fox among the chickens. She spoke of a figure of an African goddess that she was once given. "It looked two ways, good and bad," she said. "It had two faces. I threw it into a basket of apples, but that didn't remove the stink I could smell. Then I had it in the car and I was passing a waterfall. I stopped and threw it into the river. I knew that it had to go into violent water."

We went toward our bedrooms. She is, after all, and among many other things, an actress. She said, making an actress's slip, "I hope I sleep well."

Playing a recording of Prokofiev's "Classical Symphony" in the gallery, she spoke about England. Her mother is English. "Now that everyone is poor in England, that's liberty. That's why you say it is such an invigorating country to be in just at the moment, though its friends are sorrowing for it. The thing is, outsiders see only the loss of empire and the economic crisis. That will pass. In the Industrial Revolution, England was forty years ahead of everyone else. The present money trouble has come about because the English are inventors, not businessmen." Moreau has a sense of national differences. Her books tell one something about the spread and exactitude of her tastes. She has many art books, D. H. Lawrence, Balzac, Jack London, Giraudoux, Malraux, Proust, a volume on Joan Crawford. She loves books of reference, and her questions are as eager for information as her talk is to provide it. Her country house is a place for thinking. It is full of corners where her friends can be alone and read. She must be one of the best-mannered actresses in the profession.

"When I'm acting, I feel I have no family—only the director," she said. "It's a dialogue, not a monologue. Luis Buñuel is one of the men I have most loved working with. It's not for any applause. That's wanting response, not reward—it's dying of lack of company, not of thirst. I have made a lot of box office duds." She has always been profoundly dedicated to directors, and has a private and lasting affinity with the ones she admires. "Some actors are creative without wanting to take over the film. A director can give you a good part, but you can give him back just as much as you're rich enough to suggest to him the thousands of doors to open. One discovers the character during shooting. It's an encounter." She has acute stagefright. "But what is good about stagefright is that it's transformed into concentration as soon as you're working."

Louis Malle, who directed her not only in "The Lovers" but in

101

"The Fire Within" (1964) and "Viva Maria!" (1965), says that she is one of the actresses who must build up into a scene. "She is not at her best in the early takes. She has to construct a contact."

"Making a film is like life aboard ship, except that every day is an emergency," she said in the South of France. "And then there is the aloneness afterward. Of course, there is loneliness and being alone. Being alone is an opportunity, yes? Except, perhaps, the tragic aloneness when you are physically ill. Emotional loneliness has a cure."

On another day, she said, "Actors shouldn't ask questions, they should do things. That's what Peter Brook thinks. I was impressed by the way he worked. When we'd made 'Moderato Cantabile,' he was asked how I did it. He said it was sometimes an actor's desperation to be able to give anything that is needed. To me, the Method preparation for concentration is some actors' way of doing what I try to do in a different way. I can't use thought and intelligence while I'm shooting. If you think too much about the character— Well, intellect has nothing to do with acting. Thought can go on before. Then you just have to be here, present. Suppose the director says that pages twenty-two and twenty-three are cut, and he says that instead of showing you standing in front of Claridge's and buying Dunhills we'll show you down at the swimming pool. Well, you just do it, because you are the character. You have to live up to the character. I think that this passion for nakedness in films about love is often beside the point and won't last. It's an exaggeration of the time. When you want to do something, you overemphasize. Mystery is a taste that we have lost, but it will come back. Maybe the longing to see the naked body is a longing to know everything about someone. But you find then that the body itself is a cover. That's the reason the way one is dressed has meaning." Moreau is one of the best-dressed women in the theatre, with natural style and a nearly bygone feeling for prettiness. Not for her the overall and Earth shoes and stamped T-shirts of film stars just as beautiful.

"A director's instinct and an actor's instinct will coincide if they're attached to the idea of making the character distinct, and not debasing it," she said. "There are never ten ways to do something. Only one. That is a question of morality. You have to be true to yourself and to others. The plot—that is, the character narrative—takes you with it. Virginia Woolf once said that the plot is like a river: it carries you along and it shows you the countryside around the people." She changed a record, and then said, "For some reason, I was thinking of Buñuel's 1972 film 'The Discreet Charm of the Bourgeoisie.' About that film I felt like a child. With Buñuel, one feels that anything can happen. For instance, a dog can speak. I always had that dream in childhood."

Moments of her own performances came to mind: the unforgettable half smile of triumph at the success of a dark compact just before she kills herself, near the end of "Jules and Jim;" her self-mocking suggestion of conquest in love in Roger Vadim's "Les Liaisons Dangereuses" (1961); the moment in Buñuel's "Diary of a Chambermaid" (1965) in which she bends herself to her master's fetishes, looks resigned, but shows her heart to be scornful and chilled. She is a woman of invention beyond the scope of most actresses. In Jean-Louis Richard's "Mata Hari" (1965), besides acting magnificently, she pulled most of the dialogue together, with the help of Truffaut. "You don't have to do anything in front of a camera," she said. "You just have to be concerned." About an actor trained in the Method, when he was wondering what his motivation was for picking up an ashtray, she said, "You want to say to him, 'Just pick up the ashtray and shut up.'" She has a capacity for transmitting extraordinary intensity of understanding between her and other characters, which is one of the reasons she enjoyed making "Viva Maria!" with Brigitte Bardot. "Films tend to say that women can never be in rapport with each other": a thought that obviously prompted much of her own film, "Lumière" (1976), written and directed by her, and with her playing a part in which she is intimately concerned with several other women. One has the feeling that, unlike many actresses in the English-speaking commercial cinema, she could never fall into reposing a character on being hagridden or having a fishwife's emotional range. There is something about her, clear to all the great directors she has worked with but hard to pin down, that always transmits a concept of eternity and of a better world elsewhere.

In Paris, last year, when I was seeing her before she married the American director William Friedkin, we spent time in her beautiful apartment in the Rue du Cirque. It had a main room with pale-orange muslin curtains and an orange carpet. Jeanne Moreau talked, over lunch, about other people's films. "The best period in the American cinema was the thirties and forties, when actors and actresses were under contract, and not maneuvering on slippery ground from one film to the next. People were craftsmen then. They didn't think of themselves as being artists. A film took ninety minutes, no more, and each frame had to be full. What strikes me now when I look at those older films is that they are so packed with energy. It grows in one's mind: the music, the editing—everything. If one wants to learn what to do, one not only watches Fellini, one also watches Howard Hawks." When she was casting "Lumière," she chose Keith Carradine because she found herself dreaming over an early photograph of Gary Cooper. "I wanted a man who had those purely American qualities—the simplicity and integrity and innocence."

She keeps small notebooks with her for writing down details of characters in a new film she is working on: their roots, their originality. The story is set in France between Bastille Day of 1939 and September 1, 1939, the day the Second World War began. One character used to live in Poland: Jewish, a doctor. She has read endless newspapers of the day. "I want to make a film that says something about the older men, their relationship with the land. Their anguish over the 1914-18 war—that they had fought in it and won it and then lost all the same. Now there was this new war, which was to produce Vichy: another defeat, and this one full of remorse. After Munich, men in the French countryside lived their lives in a spasm of false shame. They thought, This happened twenty years ago—how can it happen again? They felt that it was their fault. Their feeling for the land is important, and the memory of their past, when the men were called on to fight again and then to have their country occupied. The connection between God and farming and the Church was still the same as ever; it created a powerful feeling about Good and Bad. These men felt that everything had become Bad, and couldn't believe that it could be so. Even if people are well informed, they have very little of what one can truly call information. People who work the land say 'That can't be' about a drought. 'There hasn't been one for twenty years.' Young men who lived in the country had heard of America as the land of gold, India as the land of jewels. They had heard their fathers talk of the Great War. They couldn't imagine their own Europe and themselves involved in its private bloodshed again. It was a legend. In 1940, the women were already talking very independently about this men's war. The women's-lib movement started after the war, when some of the men came back. I'm so deep in this film already that I hardly notice Paris. In making a film, one is making a complete world, but it relates to . . ." She traced a shape with her finger on the table meaning "nowhere." "There is total intimacy among the people working on the film, and no resentment about the loss of it afterward."

Another time in Paris, when Jeanne Moreau had had to put thoughts of her film aside, because she was working on "Lulu," we met at a bistro and she again drew with her finger on a table. "I have been thinking about the Berlin Wall. The situation would be this. Two figures, a man and a woman, start off walking quite normally. They break into a run. They reach here. The woman trips. Maybe they don't know each other. They are killed." She ate for a minute and then said, "When 'Lulu' is finished, I shall go back to the country. Though sometimes I have a sense of nonsense in the country. Not a thought but a feeling. It is because the country is so strong. There is this feeling of nonsense even in Paris about such a situation as we have in the German capital. As I began to say, the French countrywomen after the last war understood what was happening much better than the men who survived. The deeper you go into life, the more you have to forget everything."

Jeanne Moreau was born in 1928. Her father, who died three years ago, was Anatole-Désiré Moreau, the owner of a Montmartre restaurant called La Cloche d'Or. Her mother is an English former dancer, Kathleen Buckley, who danced with the Tiller Girls at the Folies-Bergère. The Moreau family is descended from farmers. Born in Paris, Jeanne, as a child, used to spend her holidays at Mazirat, a village of about thirty houses in the Allier Département, between the Loire and the Cher. Her best friend, who lived in Vichy, where Jeanne and she were both at school, died of croup when Jeanne and she were eight. After the outbreak of war, Jeanne and her mother and sister were obliged to stay in Paris, because her mother was an alien. (Her father was cut off from them in the South of France, in Vichy. He was a soldier there. They struggled to join him, and finally succeeded, but it took fourteen months.) "I read many books far too soon. They make me sick even now, some of them, with terror and fascination. I read Zola when I was thirteen. My father often sent me to carry a bowl of soup to the film ticket-seller, and the man would say, 'Wouldn't you like to go in?' Once—I must have been sixteen—my father took me to see 'La Bête Humaine.' He fell asleep, but I was carried away. I was a good student until I was sixteen. Then I went to see Anouilh's 'Antigone.' I heard my mother say to a neighbor who would be sympathetic to my longings, 'I have a daughter who wants to be an actress.' I went to the Conservatoire National d'Art Dramatique. My parents were separated when I was at the Conservatoire. Then I joined the Comédie Française. Some things about it were disgusting. The big stars would take parts just to stop others from having them. After that, there was the Théâtre National Populaire."

She has a natural feeling for the theatrical. She said to me in New York about "A Chorus Line," "It's real because it's fake. When mirrors on the stage are turned onto the audience, that is extraordinary. People in the audience are forced to look at themselves in a mirror. It is a great moment. The reflection of those pale faces of the audience, as if they were the ones who were auditioning! When I was young, I couldn't dream of that sort of poetic device. Soon after the Théâtre National Populaire, I was in a Paris 'Pygmalion' for two years. One of the wittiest plays, whichever language it's performed in. I was often sad then. I was shy, totally diffident, at the end of the war. I felt as if I had started talking only a short while earlier. Before that, it was an epoch of silence. Perhaps my silence made me feel unusually close to my sister, Michelle Cavanaugh, whom I could always talk to. I was married to the director Jean-Louis Richard when I was twenty-one. Our marriage was dissolved shortly afterward, but he is still a great friend. We had one child. A son."

When I was in London last year, the telephone rang and Jeanne Moreau asked me from Paris if I would go to see her sister in a hospital in Fulham, because she was concerned about her and couldn't leave Paris herself. Jeanne has powerful family feelings. She telephones her son, who is now nearing thirty years old and lives elsewhere in France, practically every day. His name is Jerome. Jeanne is nine years older than Michelle. She seems to have been a very motherly sister.

Michelle Cavanaugh is much like Jeanne in the legs—she sits like her, with fine calves tucked under her—but quite unlike her facially. She was reading Bertrand Russell when I went to see her. Jeanne had asked me to take her a particular scent, and a nightdress, as a relief from hospital clothes. The requests were very precise. The nightdress should be white cotton and simple, with no sleeves. Michelle laughed about her love for Jeanne and said, "We have an overdeveloped independence, both of us, like an overdeveloped muscle. I live mostly in Ibiza. My therapist thinks I shouldn't, but he's never set foot there. He thinks that because he's very possessive. Not like Jeanne." Michelle Cavanaugh apologized for having a therapist. "Once, Jeanne said if she hadn't been an actress she was afraid she might have been a neurotic. Later, she told me that her real reason for being an actress was to fight self-deception, to find the truth in the characters' predicaments. She has been through much more than I have."

Jeanne Moreau said to me in Paris one day, talking about her family and the planning of her next film, "My mother's father— English, of course—was responsible at the outbreak of war for the protection of the people of Littlehampton. My mother and my sister and I were in England, and with the first of September, 1939, my mother wanted to go back immediately to France. We took the boat from Newhaven just after New Year's Eve and arrived back in Paris at the end of February. Mazirat, where we had spent so much of our lives, was the root of many things I want to think about that have to do with the war. The institutions were always run by the left. But people were still related to the Church and sent their children to the Church school. It was an accommodation. And it was very healthy for the balance of life in the village. There were internal fights, it's true, but it's also true that fights—not wars—are good."

This was when she was rehearsing "Lulu" in Paris. As with many French rehearsals, work started after lunch and went on until the small hours. She was wearing a short fox coat that looked fake because it was dyed pale-blue: appealing, on this beautifully dressed actress, who is an old friend of Pierre Cardin. She would concentrate totally on what the director was saying, repeat the same movement or fragment of a scene again and again—one of the movements being a climb up a ladder, which resulted in the fall that injured her knee—and in a break she would come downstage to kiss an inexperienced young actor, run over to a box in the darkened auditorium to ask if I was interested. "Lulu" is a difficult piece, and she did it superbly. She has always been remarkable for choosing worthwhile, hard things to do, and rejecting the common-place. "People don't seek power, I think," she said to me once. "They seek the possibilities for doing things."

Another day in Paris, she said, in English, "Men can scream, women can whimp"—meaning "whimper." It was one of her few mistakes in the language. About women's liberation, she said, "I am not a feminist, but I can understand that people who are discontented cannot hide it. That the rich are powerful is a fable. It is not the rich who are powerful, it is the people who feel themselves free. The women's movement is about the fact that men have imposed on women emotionally. I myself think it's more that they have deterred us intellectually, robbed us of the faculty of invention. But one is not given such things—one has to take. It's easier to live by blaming convention, but nobody insists on its rule, apart from oneself. I've noticed that the women who are most resentful about conventions are often the ones who most want them. That year called the International Women's Year—it sounded fine but it wasn't very serious. Every year is the year of men and women."

When she went to Washington to introduce "Lumière" there, she made this speech, in English: "Thank you for coming to my first film. There's no time for long speeches. Thank you. Goodbye." This first film is imperfect, but it is full of interest: it has common sense, and is not a whit autobiographical—which it has sometimes been taken to be, simply because it is about an actress played by Jeanne Moreau. The director was involved to the fullest when she was making it, in her usual, unique way of seeming to be a little underwater while she is working. The film is about a woman who, though she has a genius for friendship, commits follies of egomania and thoughtlessness, especially toward a dying doctor, wonderfully played by François Simon. The director edited some of the film by cable from Hollywood to her editor in Paris, and told me that she hadn't realized until she saw the final cut that the last words in the film were "Forgive me."

March 13, 1978

The Urgent Whisper:
Jean-Luc Godard

Jean-Luc Godard gave me a red plastic chair to sit on, facing him across a clean white Formica desk. I looked to the left at an agreeably dilapidated olive-green-corduroy armchair.

"You feel you are being interviewed," he said, from an identical red plastic chair on the other side of the desk, trying combat but failing to be fierce.

"Only as if I were being tested by an oculist."

Godard took off his glasses. They are clear ones now; once upon a time, he wore dark ones perpetually. In self-protection? As a weapon? I think because the colors of the world looked to him unbearably bright. His films since then suggest that he takes it for granted that many things about the world, though all but blinding, need search and speculation. So he wears untinted glasses.

"Tell me the words you read behind me," said the oculist, sucking his pipe and watching.

A purple poster on the white wall behind him said "LA TRISTESSE." A clipped page of cartoons beside it was headed "LA FOLIE." A small distance away, a meticulously scrubbed blackboard had the words "DENTISTE, VENDREDI, 10 A.M." chalked up and ringed round.

Godard's world, of course: so, Godard's codification of a Godard vocabulary. The words were surrounded by air, like ideas. We were in a Godard film, which habitually makes of print something close to an image of a human feature, just as a Godard shot of a hand is used like a word.

"I had forgotten that you would see 'DENTISTE.' Your eye swings round beyond a hundred and eighty degrees," he said. There was a considerable silence, and no need to break it. I remembered that when he was making his first feature film, "Breathless" (1959), he is said to have asked what the convention was about the maximum camera swing acceptable to the eye in a single shot. He was told that it was a hundred and eighty degrees. He immediately asked his cameraman, Raoul Coutard, to use a great deal more.

With a dead-straight face, he moved up the comfortable old chair for me. He was wearing an azure-blue polo-neck sweater and gray trousers. He has a cleft chin, good hands, and a wary look of being about to spring away from dangerous situations. His expression is less implacable than he probably imagines, this peculiarly convivial and questing hermit. His friends ("I have very few friends," he asserts firmly, in a typical style of testing intimacy by keeping it at bay) tend to say of him fondly that he is impossible. His medium is not violence, and they know it. So do we, who watch his films and recognize him to be one of the great poets working today in cinema. He is a rare man, as innovative as Braque, and a being who is at the same time hesitant, melancholy, and blithe. He seems to despair of himself daily. He presents himself as being severe. But he will make dead-eyed concessions to funny truths, as his friends and allies find. He tries very hard not to laugh, but he has a sense of the ludicrous which equals his capacity for being bored. He also owns up to the pressure of feeling which is so strong a characteristic of his piercing company. "The left appears to me to be sentimental, but the right has ideas that have turned to stone. I am a sentimentalist, so I am on the left, for this among other reasons," he says, arguing out the point with himself.

He has lately fled from Paris to Grenoble, where we were seeing each other. He has a house at the end of a small street, near the River Isère. His living room has two front doors, at right angles to one another. I think he likes escape routes.

"You tapped at the wrong door. Tomorrow, come in at this door, will you?" he said.

"And out?"

"It is a door you can come in at and go out of. A very functional door."

His living room has a blood-red Maoist poster, lettered in Chinese script; a red Formica dining-room table with four red Formica chairs; bristly mats patterned in bright yellows and blues, like doormats drawn on by kindergarten children; a huge window at one end covered by a straw-slatted blind; an open-rise staircase with olive-carpeted treads, separated by the air that Godard finds so full of motion. On a big brown cupboard door there is a very small newspaper clipping glued at a minutely particular place. A room celebrating space, primary color, simplicity, graphic design, words.

The Chinese script of his poster is beautiful. "I want to go to China when it is out of the mode," he said.

We talked about words and films. He has a very quiet voice. "A studio like the one I have here is both a library and a printing firm, where you have to both print the book you want to read and read the book you want to print."

A friend of his of thirty years told me that Godard's ferocious early longing was to write like Stendhal. Now he makes films like no one else in the world, this polemicist who can never prevent himself from expressing himself poetically. When Godard began to make movies, aesthetics grew twenty years older and audiences twenty years younger. In his presence, one is struck by his exactness. As he talked, he moved his ashtray to a precise place on his desk. Another day, as he was following me in through the front door—one of the front doors—I noticed an instruction on the door saying *"Bien essuyez les pieds, s'il vous plaît."* So I wiped my feet well. So he looked back, and nodded with a drollness that his immobile face did not mask. "Good." There was a Godard silence. If one stays untalkative with him, he generally goes on to say something more. "We do the cleaning ourselves." We? He and his girl, perhaps? He is in love, with a vehemence matching the vehemence of his films. Or he and his devoted technical crew? Or he and cinema? Cinema is his ally, his kin.

"Could I see your studios?" I asked.

"Yes." Godard started to put out his cigarette.

"Coat?"

"No need."

He let me out of the inadmissible front door and sped along the street. I had been expecting the journey to involve a bus ride, at least. But he opened a door twenty yards away, and there were the studios: in a converted garage, chopped up into a sound room, a mixing room, an editing room. Each one was full of glittering technical equipment. We might have been in a space-research center, except that one of the rooms also held a Ping-Pong table.

"You play with Grenoble friends?"

"I am mostly alone in Grenoble," he said, but he grinned.

Godard's films have a way of communicating the sanctity of isolation.

"The artist and the scientist are similar. I mix images and sounds like a scientist, I hope. The mystery of the scientific is the same as the mystery of the artistic. So is the misery." One could see the letters merging, changing, plundering each other, as they do in the iconography of his films: "MISÈRE," "MYSTÈRE." "Though in the West there is the difference in what is expected. The artist in the West—unlike the artist in China—is considered a figure of amusement." In Godard's "Made in U.S.A." (1966), the characters whom the film finds interesting are the very ones who hold themselves in contempt and "whom I call the *gauche élégante.*" He finds that the curiosity of scientists, like the proper inquisitiveness of filmmakers, can be falsely mollified by the use of words. "Scientists are always looking for answers and then putting them into grammatical form when they should sometimes be put into image form. In their research papers, their words often hide what they see. I think that's why the problem of cancer will not be solved: because the solution is hidden by the writing. Sometimes what a scientist says is muddy because what he writes is hidden by what other people have written twenty years ago." Literature beside the bed. His upstairs room is piled with books, old and new. This film scientist reads.

I asked him whether there was any fiction he had read lately and liked. He walked about, and said, "I read mostly historical texts." He added that he has always found the documentary the more attractive road. "It's a road leading to fiction, but it's still not a road, it's bushes and trees. I haven't read fiction in twenty years," he said, pretending casualness. He cultivates indifference, this passionate man, just as he defies fondness and at the same time dispenses it. He asked me, in urgent league, to translate some English directions about an editing machine.

We talked later, between silences, about conversation, and about its likeness to scientific research: about both of them being deeds of motion along an unlit corridor in which a participant will bang first against one wall and then against the other. Looking for something and finding something else. Research being an activity without company. Godard both defends and possibly regrets his isolation, but he would fight to the death for the right to solitude, which is something different. "Solitude is a strong position. The position to refuse." He contests by silence, just as his silence also expresses the courtesy of declining to waste someone else's time.

So we began to talk about noise. Not sound but noise. His films have more and more often provoked thought about the intrusion of noise. "I am very interested in noise," he said. "Even when a small blade of grass is growing, there is a noise between the grass and the earth. Ah, I can ask you about something." He left the desk where he was sitting, and went to get a brochure, which he found in a second. "What is souffle in English?" I suggested a translation that was electronically wrong, and he got a technical dictionary. "It's 'hum.' " His English is good. He learned it mostly in America. The pamphlet was about a piece of recording equipment. "I'm very interested in talk," he said after a pause in which he had been propped against his doorjamb reading his pamphlet in dead silence. "Ah. A *souffle*, which is a low-volume noise—which can, of course, be talk about, shall we say, a cup of coffee—is diagnosed here as 'a leakage between two channels.' There was an article in *Scientific American* by an expert on modern communications. He practically invented computers. A signal between the transmitter and the receiver goes through a channel and noise is added, he wrote. A matter of signals. Conversation between intimates: a leakage between two channels."

Like the films he makes. Semaphore signs, emblems sighted from far away, seepages of talk.

"A film is an image on an image on an image. The images will say 'I love you,' then 'I don't love you,' then 'I love you' again, but in a different way. This can be done without universities, without expensive equipment. Universities are depressing. Equipment leads to control by the rich owners of the equipment. A film should build images in a way that is quite different from TV. Television is a looking machine. The killings of people on TV don't have the effect the assassins want." Godard has been working for TV, not surprisingly alienating bureaucratic dullards. French TV refused to show a commissioned film of his in 1968; London Weekend Television refused to show one in 1969; Italian television refused yet another, also in 1969. All the same, he prefers TV to theatre, and at last the preference is beginning to prosper, with French TV now showing work done in the brilliant little Grenoble lab. "I hate the theatre. Perhaps because actors are shouting. Or because they are serfs. I prefer sport, which is a more free kind of theatre. I prefer the Olympic Games."

We played Ping-Pong, fairly well. He plays chess extremely well.

"To learn to put questions differently. A good film is a matter of questions properly put." Again and again, this has been the guideline of Godard's thinking. He believes in novelty not as an aesthetic good but as an armament. "When you are hit, one of two things can happen. Either you think better afterward or you become more concussed than you were before."

114

* * *

Godard was born on December 3, 1930, in Paris, of Protestant parents. His father was a doctor. Jean-Luc went to secondary schools in Switzerland and Paris, and then to the Sorbonne, where he took his Certificat d'Ethnologie. He was a member of the Ciné Club du Quartier Latin, and in 1950 he founded the short-lived *Gazette du Cinéma* in the company of the directors Jacques Rivette and Eric Rohmer. In January, 1952, he began writing for *Cahiers du Cinéma*. About then, he travelled a great deal in North and South America. His mother was killed in a motor-scooter accident in Lausanne in 1954. That year, he was working on a dam-construction site in Switzerland, where he made his first film—a short, called "Opération Béton" ("Operation Concrete"). Before that, he had been a delivery boy, and then a cameraman for Zurich TV; after that, and after a short named "Une Femme Coquette (1955), written (after Maupassant), filmed, and edited by him in Geneva, he again ran into the dog days, apart from occasional critical writing for *Cahiers du Cinéma* and *Arts*, and had odd jobs, including Claude Chabrol's old post as press officer for Artistes Associés. His first French film was called "Tous les Garçons S'Appellent Patrick" (1957). The script was by Eric Rohmer. There is a shot of a man reading *Arts*, with concentration on the headline "The French Cinema is Dying Under the Weight of False Legends." Godard has begun.

His famous "Breathless" makes many early statements that he has gone on to support in succeeding stages of his career. Technically, there is already the fondness for master shots or closeups and little between. In content, there is the fascination with the Marx and Coca-Cola generation, and the feeling for the character played by Belmondo, a character who has consigned himself to an outward imitation of Bogart which lends him Bogart's facial gestures and mannerisms but not his inner life. The Jean Seberg figure already represents Godard's lasting feeling about his women characters: that they are mysteriously the mainspring of action, where men are passive. The film is filmically amazing, and to the point for a whole generation: energetic, brave, desperate. At this beginning, with "Breathless," one feels that Godard himself is at his last gasp. The

115

rest of his career so far touchingly seems an effort to regain his breath.

In "Le Petit Soldat" (1960)—with Anna Karina, whom he married in 1961—there are the lines "The time for action has passed. . . . The time for reflection has come." The film is typical of Godard in striking the least insistent note the hardest, and in launching contemplation. The hero, Bruno, is betrayed in the simple idea he holds of Veronica, an idolatry he has shown in comparing her to great paintings. As in "A Woman Is a Woman" (1961) and "Vivre Sa Vie" (1962), the place of women in society's mind is the central metaphor. In "A Woman Is a Woman," Godard joyously apes Lubitsch. We are in an imagined Gene Kelly musical, with imagined Michael Kidd choreography. It is Godard's first color film and his first in wide-screen: an *hommage* to pretty women, to fun, to Hollywood when it is vivacious. He abhors the piece now as bourgeois, but a great man's works stand: this one for, above all, its activity and its communication of love.

"Vivre Sa Vie," in twelve elegantly ordered parts, holds one of Godard's earliest open admissions of the struggle between voice and image. Over the stately, beautiful alternation of closeups and long or medium shots, there is the sound of a narrator's remote voice reading statistics. "The fight between images and sound," said Godard in Grenoble, about "Vivre Sa Vie," and then about the path he laid for himself with it. "It's not combat, but it's also not just an adding together. Whereas film traditionally makes either the dialogue or the images no more than a supplement to meaning, as one puts a stamp on a parcel." The theme of "Vivre Sa Vie" is prostitution. The idea, expanded, recurs in a lot of his other films: the concern for throttled voices without a vote that would be recognizable to the conventionally clever. About his thematic use of prostitution he said, "It's not the cant about women as objects. I have felt all my life that women are much more *actively* intelligent than men." But this activity, the source of women's brio and gaiety, can also hound them from meditative life and be as much a source of torment to them as the passive role that Godard accords to most of his male characters.

"We have to ask ourselves questions," he said, walking about

116

and then swinging on the back of the comfortable olive-green chair. We had a conversation both facing in the same direction, because I was sitting in the chair. "Does one say one is not content because one is not free? Or is it that one is not free because one is not content?"

In "Contempt" (1964), based on Alberto Moravia's novel "A Ghost at Noon," Senecan serenity is pitted against the edginess of modern man, and Godard uses a documentary style that allows him the freedom to emphasize things that would pass one by in a movie with a traditional narrative. "'Contempt' is a simple film about complicated ideas," Godard said. It contains a quote in which Lumière, the great early man of film, calls cinema "an invention without a future." Godard has given it a future. He has done it by always attempting to return to zero, to make films as though none had ever been made before. He has never asked an easy question. We call the Second World War "the good war": are we right? ("Les Carabiniers," of 1963.) How can a man free a woman? ("Vivre Sa Vie.") How can a Westerner aid an Asian? ("Far from Vietnam," which he contributed a pensive segment to in 1967.) He knows we are indeed far from Vietnam, but there is a Vietnam at home where we are all combatants. What about the potency of the near-at-hand? ("A Married Woman," of 1965, augured by "Vivre Sa Vie.") What are we building? He shows us an answer in "Alphaville" (1965), a vision of the future which was actually shot in contemporary Paris. We are in an underworld so dark that characters have to use torches in the daytime. Lemmy Caution (a pun on cochon), played by Eddie Constantine, is like Mozart's and Schikaneder's Tamino leading Pamina through the dark of mistrust and eternal tests into the light above. They almost need to run. Many of Godard's films have endings about flight.

In 1968, Godard linked up with Jean-Pierre Gorin to form a production group called Dziga-Vertov, christened after the director who, in the Soviet Russia of 1918, founded the famous newsreel group called Kino-Glaz (Film Eye) and with it created a film method that is close kin to Godard's in its oddly lyric technical energy and in its passion to pursue the differences between the truth told by the camera's vision and the truth told by the eye. In the Godard-Gorin "Une Film Comme les Autres" (1968), one sees people in meadows discussing politics. There are snatches of speech, of people reading from newspapers. Always, this Godard implication that the fragments of life would make the most splendid whole if only they could be put together with faithful patience. I imagine that this intellectual underpinning is among the reasons his friends cling to him—friends like Truffaut, an old, old confrère—even when he is being most difficult. He is now a loner, no longer in partnership with Gorin, backed into a corner, working, thinking. Brecht said, "Thinking comes after defeat and before action."

Anna Karina says to Jean-Paul Belmondo in "Pierrot le Fou" (1965), which is another of Godard's many films about people and missions betrayed, that she doesn't know who he is. Then she turns to the audience and says, "I don't know who you are, either." Doubt stands. Godard is an artist, not a tub thumper. He trusts that he has thought of something, he imparts it with gifts that defy the desolation of his findings, and then he thinks he may be wrong, and goes on to make a film to contradict himself. He has tried to understand, among other alien things, England and English factory life, in "British Sounds," of 1969 (also called "See You at Mao"), with its famous ten-minute tracking shot down an assembly line under the voice of a little girl reciting her Marxist catechism.

"To liberate sound from the tyranny of sight," said Godard in Grenoble, experimenting idly with a tape recorder that produced furry bouncing sounds, like new tennis balls hitting the skin of a drum. He clicked off the machine, because there was no speech on the immediate tape. He hates the inane, we know from his films, just as we know that he hates the seducing apparent zest of criminality. Both opinions are strongly there in "Masculine Feminine" (1965), the picture that best of all captures what it was like to be an undergraduate in the sixties. It is a story of the receding brain, like many of his most eloquent nightmares. Five deaths recorded; total apathy expressed by the characters. Paul, the interviewer-hero, steps backward from a jerry-built apartment building at the end and falls to his death. A girl who wasn't even a witness tells the cops, "He wanted . . . I think he wanted to take a moment for some pictures." Longing for distance kills, says Godard. And in the

Dziga-Vertov film of 1971 called "Vladimir and Rosa," about the Chicago Seven, with its intentionally only half-intelligible conversation between Godard and Gorin pacing up and down on either side of a tennis net, Godard seems to be posing a notion still more perplexing to him than anything in Descartes. "I think, therefore I am": O.K. But what about feeling? Is it true that "I think, therefore I feel"? How can people feel when they intellectually *think* that they feel?

All the same, to think is the thing. Action in Godard's films comes too late and unprofitably. In "Weekend" (1968), the ground of the past has been razed. The vestiges of a culture try to scrounge a noisy existence in the countryside. "Weekend" powerfully reminds one of Godard's feeling for history, as when Paul Gégauff plays Mozart on a piano among the poultry in a farmyard. Something triumphant in the absurdity of music's existence in this mud remains our coinage, says Godard. If only we can hang on to it. Reassemble things. You think of "One Plus One" (1968), his Rolling Stones movie. It is perhaps his most reticent work. It intercuts the sights and sounds of revolution outside with repeated fragments of the Stones working in separation from one another in a recording studio, listening to themselves on earphones. We are dependent on technical equipment—yes, of course, says Godard, the technical fanatic. But we are relied upon to make something coherent of these recorded pieces of distorted human behavior which take us into the dark of our souls, which show us the back of the moon.

Chaos and banality, with Godard's poetic overlay of idealism and involvement. In "Le Gai Savoir" (1968), a character called Émile Rousseau, who advertises himself as the great-great-grandson of Jean-Jacques, is stumbling around a disused TV studio with a character called Patricia Lumumba, symbolic daughter of the Third World. They embark on a series of late-night dialogues. Begin again. Decompose. Recompose. Start from zero, as before. There is an examination of language. Patricia and Émile are alone in a black vacuum. A voice incessantly comments on the action: we are hearing Godard, an heir of Rousseau the humanist romantic, of Picasso, of Mozart, of Hegel, of Renoir, of Joyce, of Bogart, of

Dostoevski. Godard's source is in aesthetics, and he sees aesthetics as ethics. "Simplicity is virtuous, candor is elegant. And in film you could say that imperialism is a sect of people who want to make people make movies their way." His men, like Keats, dream about a death without substance: "To cease upon the midnight with no pain." It is not the legacy of Hollywood's unwounding killer movies which gives Godard's heroes their implacability in the face of death; it is his own observation of our time's lack of any feeling of responsibility for death. The needle goes into the frog's leg, the nerve jumps, but no judgment is made. "Without a political basis, collective creation is really no more than collective eating in a restaurant," he said to me. In "La Chinoise" (1967), about a cell of five disorganized young French leftists—a student, an actor, a peasant, an economics logician, an artist named Kirilov, after Dostoevski's character in "The Possessed"—radical efforts scatter like grapeshot for lack of communal purpose. "The trouble in the West is that we are overfed aesthetically," said Godard. "The Third World's problem is that it is starving. We consume things that are unnecessary artistically. Half of our films, three-quarters, are unnecessary, but we do not realize it."

I asked him about the films of two of his erstwhile friends, and he said, in the expressionless manner I had begun to recognize as a signal that he was saying something close to his heart, "They have been making bourgeois garbage and I have been making revolutionary garbage."

"That's cant," I said.

"Yes," he said.

We decided to go for a walk. "Now, 'Pravda,'" he said of the film about radicalism that he made in 1969. "I would put a label on it and say that this is a garbage Marxist-Leninist movie. People like Jerry Lewis or Laurel and Hardy—if they had been working in 1917, they would have made genuine Marxist movies. One sees it in China now, I believe and hope. Think of Laurel and Hardy in revolutionary China! Just think of Laurel as a political commissar and Hardy as a peasant! Well, at least I know now what not to do anymore. I've visited a house that I'll never go into anymore. We mustn't make what the Chinese call sugar bullets."

I don't know how anyone could call this man's films disdainful, which is at the moment such a widespread response. He is Orpheus stumbling through the underside of our world, stubbing his toe in the dark, but not looking back.

"It's very hard not to be conditioned by the films one has made. Not to make in the same way the journey one made first. One has to work differently if one wants to have different ideas. Thanks to the help of others, I have started a little association in Grenoble where I can work like an artisan. Up to 1973, I was working traditionally. But I wanted to be more independent. We're shooting in 16 mm. and 8 mm. and blowing up the image. I like using video." An old crew member of his says, "He liked playing the dope about production, but he was really very smart." "With video, you see it at once and then there is time to think," Godard said. "With conventional shooting, the time is taken up with waiting for rushes. And one watches performances too much. Actors are only the annex of a film." When Marina Vlady asked Godard how she should prepare for her role in "Two or Three Things I Know About Her" (1967), he said that she should just walk to the location each day rather than take a taxi. Not prankishness: simply a characteristic way of aiding an actor unconsciously to absorb a film's topic, without diagrams.

Jack Palance, the annex of "Contempt," had been told by Godard that he was to play an Italian producer. Then he found out he had to play an American producer. "Jean-Luc was feeling a little— er, talkative," says Suzanne Schiffman, who knows a good deal about Godard's silences, having been his continuity girl on twelve of his films (and also Truffaut's co-scriptwriter on, among other pictures, "Small Change"). "Well, Jack Palance went into a corner, and three of us started laughing, and Jean-Luc laughed, because he knew he was being impossible. Working with him was like playing a game of cat and mouse. Actors never knew if they were getting things right or wrong. He could be violent and rude, and all the crew loved him. We were like a family. No family is easy."

"Why did you split with Gorin?" I asked Godard.

Godard said, "It was like a marriage. Perhaps no marriage should last too long."

Silence.

"I may be wrong," he said.

Mme. Schiffman says of Godard's notorious intransigence, "He's not democratic, but he is probably revolutionary. Also, he is no autocrat. If he screams at an actor, he doesn't mean it to count, because he believes that the actor shouldn't get hurt. Once, he yelled at Raoul Coutard, and Coutard ran out into the street, and Jean-Luc ran out after him, and it was like a love affair gone wrong suddenly."

On a Godard picture, an American actor used to Stanislavskian methods asked what he was supposed to be *feeling* when the script told him to shout: whether he was furious or pleading. After ten minutes with one of Godard's crew, Godard having refused to talk about motivation, the actor bawled and was both furious and plaintive, which was what Godard wanted. In "Vivre Sa Vie," a bit-part actor doing a scene with Anna Karina also made the mistake of asking him what he was supposed to be feeling. Godard answered him with stage directions: to stop here (at a chalk mark), to untie his shoes, to walk over to the window, to look left. The scene came out handsomely. Godard's famous hermeticism and taciturnity are easily admired as part of his temperament, as long as both are left untampered with and are also unfeared. His motives are never, by anyone's account, brutal. (Fritz Lang said to a young man who had been working on his pictures and wanted to go on to directing but feared the authoritarianism, "Don't worry. I was a long time getting nice on a film.") Godard is always most mannerly toward his topic. "He dreams of a film's being technically easy," said one of his former crew members. "He would like to swallow a film by mouth and have it digested in one day. He isn't a methodical man. He hasn't a political head: what you see is a man protecting himself from being a poet."

Godard, another day, refilled his pipe and there was a pause. Then we spoke about books, and afterward he said, "A script or a TV program is only a printing of the result of letting loose a story at a certain time. At the moment, I like to make, say, two films of one hour each, like TV programs, linked for cinema. If you work in the style of an amateur, they leave you alone. Our problem is to work like an amateur but in a professional way."

* * *

A young technician in a mackintosh came into the room and talked rapidly about a minor problem, which Godard and he solved in a moment or two.

"We are in no way a group," said Godard solemnly, denying the obvious camaraderie that had passed between them. "I never worked really with a group. When I worked with Gorin, it was not a group."

A brown-wrapped cigarette. He said, "I dream of doing manual work. Coal-shovelling. In movies, it's difficult to find manual work. What comes first is the editing of what I see—editing in my head—and then the script materializes out of the footage."

Barbet Schroeder, who acted in "Les Carabiniers," said later in Paris, "Jean-Luc used to improvise the dialogue from pieces of paper in his pockets. He would always tell the actors what to say. He never allowed them to improvise. Even when he was directing without sound, he used to tell them what gestures to use."

Suzanne Schiffman said, "He usually had a script to submit to the backer, but he didn't care about it, because he wasn't going to follow the script. When I was working on 'Contempt,' I understood that it was a film to explain why he couldn't make a film. It was Anna Karina's film, of course." (Now his ex-wife.) "The only real way he can communicate with people is through cinema, so even his love for Anna was best communicated through film."

"How old is your daughter?"

"Ten," said Godard.

"Is she solemn?"

"Yes," he said, indifferently. But Godard's indifference hardly foxes.

"Pretty?"

"Yes." Again, the enactment of indifference. Then, very fast, after a pause, a Godard confession of intensity: "Talking about amateurishness, of course, if one wants to make a movie about one's daughter, no CBS or NBC is going to let you, but in Grenoble—we came here because we like mountains—in Grenoble you do what you want." Slowing down, he said, "No, what you *can*

123

want. This is the more difficult thing, isn't it? We want to make films that the average mother in a cinema finds that she wanted to see but hadn't known she did. This is very enjoyable. This is play." Pause. A paradox or a parallelism often follows one of these pauses. "There should be love in work; there should be work in love. Not every artist seems to love work. To love it is a privilege. After all, bosses love to work, and they are some sort of artist, because everybody is." He inspected this remark as though he were holding a piece of film up to the light, and grimaced slightly and said, "Well, Nixon loved to work."

He sighed, and admitted to a faint longing to be a mogul. "I should like to be the boss of a small Paramount, as you see. In order to make money. In order to make more movies. To make a film," he went on, with determination, and in spite of knowing what he does about the difficulties, "you need only some photographs and a cassette."

He seems very much aware of the danger of didacticism in art, though he would not call the danger aesthetic. "When you use the camera as a weapon, you become an informer," he said.

From working in what he now thinks of as some factory of film, engaged only in repetition, he has moved into the field of maneuvering to achieve the original with each film. It is his nature never to be sated by what he himself has just invented. Of his "British Sounds," still thought on many sides to be raw cinematically and politically, when it is simply new, he says, "It is not good that we are still obliged to use Marx quotations instead of the words of the worker."

More than most visually gifted people, he has the verbal man's interest in distinctions. "There are films on politics and there are political films," he said. "Yes? The films on politics record activity, but they are not part of that activity." We talked, between gaps, about the notion. And about the opposite also being true: that there are certain films that are political because they seem the product of inactivity. Antonioni's "The Eclipse" not only portrays inertia but also characterizes it. A "film on politics" is a film in which the fiction and its ideas aren't put into question by the political element. A "political film" raises doubts.

"We might talk about the ideas of criminality," I said. His films, though they were often veiled in his early days as American gangster stories, are about many sorts of crimes: they are about crimes of the kind of apathy that he himself pretends to but belies by his flame of intent.

"There are criminal informers," he said. "I mean, criminal non-informers. In an actual criminal case, the criminal is the journalist who reports the case without naming the real disease, like a doctor who talks to a patient without giving a name to cancer."

He puffed on his pipe, and we spoke of many things. "Film is revolutionary art," he said unexpectedly, "because it is the sensation of movement, and such a sensation doesn't exist with a Grecian urn."

I say "unexpectedly" because Godard's talk lies largely in earnest-eyed fooling. He is much interested by the world's buffoons ("Les Carabiniers") and by the idea of wisdom in idiots. He is also greatly concerned about the resources of fakery open even to a human being whom he knows as well as he knows himself. "With 'Breathless,' they said I was respecting the public, and I said I was fooling it. The truth is I was fooling myself, because I was pretending not to know millions of the audience. It is a matter of the difference between what is entertaining and what is interesting. Which you could say is the same story at two different epochs. Two different lightings of the same room."

The little newspaper cutting on Godard's cupboard is about an imprisoned boss. The boss's head was shaved, and the workers rioted. "They wanted him back. They wanted to be ruled. This pining to be ruled. It is true of cinema. It props up the commercial system. People say they want to be independent, but what does it mean when they have a swimming pool to keep up? They have the swimming pool because they want to depend. Video is interesting because you are working in a way that *doesn't* rule you. It was possible for Mack Sennett not to be ruled, but not for us. If you write in a film script, 'The boat sails from Southampton,' you think you rule what you have written about, but the fact is that the line rules you. The front office will throw you out now, because you have written such an expensive line. But things are changing.

There was much more money invested in 'Gone with the Wind' than there is in films today. There are fewer long shots now. If you are making a film with Steve McQueen, you can't make long shots of a ball scene, because there is so much money in Steve McQueen. Most of the long shots now are in TV. With a crowd around the American President, you have two thousand extras for nothing."

Godard reminds me, above all, of Brecht. They have the same guttersnipe lyricism, the same inclination to paradox, the same capacity for an arid theorizing that is eloquently contradicted by the easy amplitude of their work. Godard has never been to Brecht's Berliner Ensemble, but this ghost-ridden, tacitly comic man, dedicated to the noble structure of accuracy, responded at once to a mention of Brecht's poems. He answered, "They are optimistic when I am sad. They are written from a standpoint of not being certain, and it's a very good way to convince. They say that the world is not sad, it is big."

OCTOBER 25, 1976

"Two or Three Things I Know About Her." It is one of Godard's most beautiful titles. Yes, you think, that's Godard—laconic, tentative, decorous. Not at all the savage tub-thumper he used to be taken for, until we sensed his style. This is a truly speculative man, a passionate witness to an epoch that strikes him as both barbarous and majestic, a poet with a temperament of rage and urgency held in check, a dogmatist laying down no law, a learner hard-driven by the idea that we are ignorant and don't even know that we are ignorant. His films are often full of quotes, but he is the opposite of a showoff. He sometimes sounds, in fact, as though he were truly terrified that he might turn out to have been one of the last bookish men on earth. He can seem to be passing on for the record what moved him long ago—an impulse that his youth and politics make poignant. The world he creates is scaringly modern, but he speaks of it in his films almost as if he were a vestige of some other time, noting casual slaughters that the assimilated inhabitants take for granted. Godard's films would not carry such a charge of love and anger if he did not feel himself mysteriously

126

supplanted. There is the same energy of the displaced in Shakespeare and in Swift. Some tribe has left the earth, say his films—*my* tribe—and taken away the dictionaries. But the memory of something lost goes with a furious connection with the present. If Godard characteristically seems nonchalant, I think it is only because the glare of the world he is attached to is too blinding for him to stare at it for long. And when he looks perfunctory about character, it is an act of courtesy, not of indifference: he wants to leave air around people. It is necessary to let them live their lives. He would not wish to scrutinize them out of existence. He allows infinite room for their stammering and their ambiguities. Some of them spout tenth-hand dogma, learned by rote from pulp fiction about sex or from rabble-rousing books, some of them scrawl cant phrases on walls, but all of them know for certain only one thing—that they are not yet dead.

"Two or Three Things I Know About Her" expresses, to begin with, the consciousness of a lower-middle-class young wife in the outskirts of Paris who lives in a modern egg box and goes on the streets, respectably parking her children, to earn enough loose change to buy the clothes and the smokes of a bourgeoise. The social irony is a simple circle, perfectly and swiftly made in Godard's particular way, and the girl's consciousness of it is both bombarded and blithe. She takes it to be a fact of her city. The "her" of the title probably refers as much to Paris as to the heroine, who is played by Marina Vlady. The picture begins with the sound of a whisper—Godard's mind—nearly drowned by traffic. The whisper goes through the movie, worrying away at scraps of thought about existence and language through the racket of cars and building sites. As in most of Godard's work, the split between the subjective and the objective in the film is not simple. It hacks the picture down the middle, in fact, leaving it spilling some of the director's blood, though the blood is made to seem tomato ketchup, because a light self-mockery is his manner. It is a system of apathy that conceals violent feeling. The subjectivity is all in the whispers, barely audible, intermittent, quoting words from Wittgenstein, from the process of this filmmaking, from Communist newspapers, whatever. The objectivity is about the enacted drama, the characters in the film, the visible. Godard is the most Brechtian of directors. Marina Vlady first appears as herself, named as herself, noted as being "of Russian extraction." She turns her head. Then she is introduced as the character. "Not of Russian extraction." She again turns her head, but now the other way, because the actress's point of view has switched to the audience's point of view. She speaks "as if she were quoting truths," which is the way Brecht always wanted actors to speak. In a wonderfully managed scene in a dress shop, she swivels from naturalistic behavior to direct talk to camera. Godard's contemplative moments are sometimes derided for literariness, as though they were doomed to pretension in any film, whereas they would do fine in a book. But this man, in the middle of meaning to kick away our sympathy, actually holds us in thrall by a technical mastery that razes to the ground most of the dumb received ideas about cinema. His technique serves exactly what he means. So when he says "The city of the future . . . will almost certainly lose part of its semantic wealth. Certainly . . . Probably . . ." it doesn't for a moment seem an assumed anxiety; it is his own, and a typical salute to dubiety. When he says, as the heroine has her pretty little red car washed, "Why do we take better care of objects than of people? Because they exist more than people do," it isn't one of our vapid cult-cynicisms, because we have already seen a good deal of the fugitive attention paid to this usual but particular girl. The gaps that have troubled linguistic philosophers trouble her without training. The reason for my tears is not described in the streaks on my cheeks," she says to the camera, quite fiercely. Godard forswears the forces of sympathy and audience participation, which are perhaps forms of fear, but this does not keep him from a furious pity and expressiveness. There is a sight of an old man telling a story to a child who isn't allowed out of a modern apartment block to play. Once, the heroine runs around Paris, intoxicated: "I was the world," says the commentary for her, speaking about the present in a typical past tense, "and the world was me." In a café, covering a held close-up of a cup of swirling *café filtre*, there is a long voice-over monologue about the subjectivity that suffocates and the objectivity that alienates; only Godard, maybe, could make this amazing pole vault over

128

the difficulties of getting us to pay heed in the cinema to pure talk, and only Godard would risk at the end of the monologue the beautiful acknowledgment of the epiphanic power of listening to the world as if it were a fellow-creature. In spite of systems that make us "greatly evil without realizing it," this is the way Godard sees Paris. Raucous, avid, in straits, interesting, "Mon semblable."

Another Godard film opened last week in New York—one made in London and called "Sympathy for the Devil." The Rolling Stones are rehearsing. There are Cokes, and paper cups, and recording earphones, and the usual fascination of watching people at work that holds good even for people mending a hole in the road, although these are no road menders. The Stones are hellbent, hard at work, and they have the world in their pocket. To someone English, their voices and their ease press a button about the social history of England that is as emotional as, say, mention of the Jarrow Marches combined with the great blue jokes of Max Miller in music hall. But it has to be said that—leaving aside the Stones' niceness to each other, and their amiable horsing around, and their easy acknowledgment of Godard offscreen ("Ca va?" says Jagger, thinking meanwhile about what the hell to do with his song)— there is something rather safe and short-cutting about the revolutionary song they are rehearsing ("I stuck around St. Petersburg, When I saw it was a time for change./I killed the Czar and his ministers . . ."). I'm not sure that Godard endorses it as expressing any sort of radicalism he admires. He simply gives an account of it. Over and over again we hear it, fragmented, in work. Between rehearsals in the recording studio there are shots in a bookshop of a man reading quotes from "Mein Kampf" that refer obliquely and rather alarmingly to totalitarianism's version of the star system ("The principle that all culture depends on men and not the reverse") and to divisive radicalism when it is running amok without a head or a soul ("Nothing great in this world has ever been achieved by coalitions"). The Rolling Stones' song has something about the Blitzkrieg. I wouldn't say that the link is either confirmed or denied by the film. Godard is too complicated, ferocious, and poetic a man to start bearing down on a Pop group for implying more than it means. This is a wryly sophisticated film. Woven into the sound track there are readings from a ridiculous pulp-fiction book that combines the clichés of pornography and James Bond slave-girl stuff with the star names of politics and public life. The parody is far out, accurate, puerile, and funny. " 'O.K.,' grumbled Pope Paul. . . . 'This is man's work.' " And then there is rhetoric from the Black Panthers getting through a badgering interview and reading in fugue from Cleaver for the benefit of a tape recorder in the middle of a car dump. Godard uses interviews like no one else. He can make them seem a genuine disputation, or the work of an obscurantist shoving dimes into a speak-your-future machine that intones doomy things the customer wants to hear, or the assault of some loud-mouth hammering on the brain of a gentler being who simply wants to shut up. There is a beautiful long sequence in which a girl called Eve Democracy (Anne Wiazemski, Godard's wife) is pursued in a field by a man with a battery of sewn-up questions: "The Occident is fighting Communism because the Occident is Faustian?" And "There is only one way to give up being an intellectual revolutionary, and that is to give up being an intellectual?" The girl representing democracy—beleaguered, milky democracy—wanders around in pasture so lush that it makes you want to moo. She goes silent at the triteness of the questions and then reluctantly says only "Yes."

As the Stones' song slowly comes together, with Jagger again and again going through the line "Let me introduce myself," and the beat changing, the world outside the recording studio begins to cohere in revolution. White girls in nightdresses, who look like models in ads, and who have been slavered over by blacks with exclamations in the style of Victorian pornography, lie dead and bleeding on a beach. Other girls with cannier minds have survived to chalk up some of Godard's sardonic schoolboy puns on the Thames Embankment and on garage doors. They wear trousers and cowboy hats, and they look a lot more themselves than the girls in nightdresses. They are the outriders in Europe of Women's Lib, perhaps—the film was made in 1968, after the Events of May in Paris—and Godard probably means to do them an honor by

130

having them not open their mouths, since the articulate in this film have as little understanding of what they're saying as a ticker-tape machine has of its tape. Godard's affection is extended toward the stuttering, the uncertain, the black manglers of borrowed white language, the English musicians deaf behind earphones and stumbling toward technical solutions.

Like all Godard's films, this one doesn't finish. It merely stops. The producers tied things up too neatly, against Godard's will. Godard wanted silence under the final shot, in which Eve Democracy's dead body is hoisted away on a camera crane labelled "Sam Mighty;" the producers laid in a track of the final version of the Stones' song, belying Godard's meaning that a revolution is never finished. In the same spirit, Godard's own title was dumped. He called his film "One Plus One;" the sum remained to be added up. "Symphony for the Devil" is the producers' title, and it strikes me as silly, reactionary, and having nothing whatever to do with Godard's tone, which is always meticulously subtle and meditative just at the moment when his shots have been toying dangerously with the calligraphy of advertising slogans and chalked-up war whoops. Godard's films live on these hostilities; finely calibrated thoughts, crass images; nonchalant behavior, desperate events; beautiful girls, ugly sexual profits; brand-new situations, stale language; a film style like a child's picture book but employed by a mind with the concentration of some aging, cornered man who has been working away at a café table for a long time. There is no one at all like Godard in the cinema. His films have moments of grace that suddenly flood the daily world with an amazing light from— what? A new sun that has nearly burst out? Again and again, watching his peculiarly simplified films, one has the feeling that he has just hit on something he has spent a long time thinking about and hoping for. He has an unsleeping eye for humbug and humiliation, for the things that modern people put up with, for affronts endured with dignity and fun, for political situations that seem too densely consolidated by talk to be budged, for the comfortlessness of a world full of expensive, ditchable commodities. When he paints a world of the dispensable, he certainly includes his own films. As he mentioned once—and it haunts him—people will say that they've seen an old Eisenstein film but never that they've read an old Balzac novel.

Two or three things one guesses about Godard. That he thinks the fine arts are dying. That he is nervous and deeply intelligent, and hidden behind dark glasses only because he finds the real world unbearably bright. That he is kept alive by creative vivacity in a world he finds lethal. That if he makes a mistake in a film and changes course halfway through to a style that puts him a mile ahead of himself—like Shakespeare in "Timon of Athens"—his answer is to finish the present piece and use the new impulse to go straight on to the next film. That he chooses to veil fear as energy, and always to address himself, not us. There is nothing demagogic here. If we were to describe his presence through his films, and our response, we might say that we are both trembling slightly.

MAY 20, 1970

A man whom we will call the hero of modern art is an agnostic. An agnostic is a man who doesn't know. But our hero knows that he doesn't know. Therefore he is not an agnostic. But he doesn't know that he isn't an agnostic. Therefore he is an agnostic. But an agnostic is a man who doesn't know, and our hero knows that he doesn't know. And so on.

Like buffaloes raising water from an Indian well by going on a seeming journey that actually takes them round and round, modern Western art plods this loop in logic. No type of mind in contemporary fiction could speak to us with more timeliness than the agnostic's, but most examples of it are products of the buffalo fallacy. By the very force of their cry that they don't know, they make us feel that they do; the coloration of their rhetoric denies what they are saying. Jean-Luc Godard is a man of another sort. Even though he has lately dubbed himself a didact, he continues to make the films of a poet who is one of the few pure issues of our epoch's doubt. With Beckett, he stands almost alone. "I do not know whether I may or may not know," says his work—in which it is altogether like "Waiting for Godot" and "Endgame."

132

Twenty-three of Godard's films are playing this summer at the Carnegie Hall Cinema. This week, we can see "Pierrot le Fou" (1965), one of the intellectually most beautiful of all the products of his skepticism, which should never be mistaken for the scathing kind. "I'm not sure that this is so," his films seem to remark. "I wish I could be certain. However, there is always the possibility . . ." For a lot of fiction-makers now, agnosticism is an affectation masking cynicism, which is of its nature unbudgeable. The true agnostic, on the other hand, wishes like hell that he did believe, and could weep that he can't. Thus Beckett's Hamm about God in "Endgame," in a cry that the English Lord Chamberlain, then ensconced as play censor, was idiotic enough to take as irreligious: "The bastard! He doesn't exist!" Godard is Beckett's true kin.

"After he had reached the age of fifty," says Jean-Paul Belmondo as Ferdinand, reading aloud about art to his very small daughter from his bath, "Velázquez no longer painted anything concrete and precise." Velázquez became less interested in figures than in spaces between figures: restated by the Belmondo character later on, the notion is the essence of the film itself. The story (very loosely based on a novel by Lionel White) is about the despair of a man trapped in a matter-of-fact marriage, and the lyricism of his subsequent escape from it with a girl named Marianne Renoir, played by Anna Karina. Ferdinand, christened in audacious honor of Céline, has just lost his job in TV. He and his wife go to an advertising party cluttered with topless women and buzzing with talk. Sometimes the people there will chat in advertising mottoes, with the unreal informality and eagerness of intimates in a commercial praising a brand-name food over a dull dinner, at which the colors of the movie will change to black and white under a wash of one violent tint. Marianne has come back into Ferdinand's life—after last encountering him five and a half years earlier—as a babysitter on the night of this party. When he goes on seeing her, the practicality and lightness of her spirit give him room to breathe.

Because the hero is a writer by nature, the film's typical Godard habit of using quotes—words and images both—seems more literally apt than usual, as well as being time-honored in the older visual arts. One thinks of Courbet quoting Baudelaire in "L' Atelier." Whole chapters of the astonishing film are made up as if they were collages of the borrowed and valuable. There is much narration and soliloquy in place of conversation. The characters do not often speak or act; it is more like them to report what they are saying, or to announce how they have acted or will act. The lovers, after much travail, much fun, much exploration of the space that so interestingly lies between them, blow up their car next to a wrecked car to cover their trail, and trek through France from north to south. We see them walking in a river that may be the Loire. Later on, when Ferdinand is beginning to write in her company, we see Marianne Renoir (there are many collage shots of Pierre Auguste Renoir's paintings, and the reference to Jean Renoir's "La Chienne" is plain) walking in water near the Mediterranean. We keep moving from the reality of the film—which is, as Godard always remembers, a created reality, as made up as any comic book or any pop movie—to scenes of parody and experiment revolving round comic books and pop movies. Belmondo Ferdinand, whom Karina Marianne calls Pierrot, will say something that he himself intensely means, but in a facial and vocal imitation of Michel Simon. Or there will be a scene of fooling between these actors who act the lovers, which will be quickly succeeded by a scene of the same sort of fooling at a still further remove, done as if in a Hollywood musical. Or an imaginary shooting will take the form of a shooting in a gangster movie, and then a "real" bloody incident in this piece of fiction will follow it, with people's voices more low-pitched and naturalistic than they are in the earlier and more obvious imitation. It is typical of Godard that what we see in both the gangster-movie parodies and the "real" acts of violence are scenes that seem to have been transmuted into modern paintings, which is one of the things that give the film its quality of the implacable and obdurate. Or, again, there will be a Chinese-box puzzle about the made-upness of names. "I'm *Ferdinand!*" yells the man at the girl who calls him Pierrot. But he is Belmondo, of course.

The repercussions between the imitation of actuality and the imitation of imitation are dazzling, quizzical, and more beguiling than the Brechtian Godard probably intends them to be. I don't suppose Godard can calculate how engrossing his unique methods of alienation often are. He means to put us at a distance when Ferdinand/Pierrot says into his driving mirror that he sees the face of a guy who's about to drive off a cliff at sixty miles an hour, but what happens is that we are stirred. Ferdinand/Pierrot/Godard is a touching man. He feels powerfully about words, for one thing. "Let's tell stories. The right words may move them," he says.

A political film by Godard—and his work has always been political—is not a film about politics but a political act that is just as direct, effective, and bare as the motion of casting a vote in a polling booth. In "Masculine Feminine," there are references to the assassination of Kennedy; in "Made in U.S.A." to the Ben Barka affair; in "Le Petit Soldat" to the Algerian war; in "Pierrot le Fou" to the Vietnam war and to Angola. The references are made schematically, in the form of revolvers, machine guns, cars, money. Godard's method of demonstrating something is always to take apart. A peculiar alertness to atrocity is given to an audience by the sense of logic which ensues from his technique. His films accord calm and pattern to disquiet and disarray. At the end of "Pierrot le Fou," the hero has an augured sense of loss which he ranks as pulp-magazine jealousy but which makes him kill Marianne. Then this very modern and doubting holy fool blows himself up. He wraps a strip of bright-yellow sticks round his head and then another of bright-red ones. The sticks, which are dynamite, look like kids' tubes of paint. Godard is saying that playthings kill, but he is also saying—perhaps with more sensibility than his fierce didactic self would want—that Ferdinand/Pierrot is a cruelly deluded humanist, too little in the world to know that his actions will have consequences. At the last second, with death irredeemably in motion, he decides he would rather not be dead. As a writer, maybe, says the film, he was doomed, because he lived overmuch in his imagination; he should have lived in the present, like Marianne, who kept being enthralled by it. The truth that Godard's characters "exist" is something that is apt to strike any one of them out of the blue, impelled by who knows what. It can happen during a pause in conversation. The knowledge that time is limited and invaluable will also hit Godard's people suddenly, and it will affect them in different ways. If a man had slipped off the Empire State Building and if he knew that he had ten seconds to live, what would his mind do? Run over the past? Scatter? Collect itself to a point? Count the seconds? Make a wish? Experience fall?

"I watch myself filming things and people can hear me thinking," said Jean-Luc Godard in an interview in *Le Nouvel Observateur* in 1966. No other director alive so wonderfully uses improvisation. For Godard, making a film is a foray like the progress of a regiment advancing through a strange country and living off the land. "Pierrot le Fou"—unscripted, and looking deceptively unplanned—actually falls into three carefully written and fluent chapters. The first part is animated by the lovers' frantic departure. The second part, full of soft, slow, fixed shots, is contemplative and halcyon. It is a chapter about two people living out of time and playing in Elysium. In the third part, Ferdinand/Pierrot is jerked from bliss into a universe in which life is again finite. But Godard, of course, is not definable as a pessimist. He is a most passionate agnostic and his don't-know vote is curiously reviving, because it is always exuberantly expectant about what is to come next. The end of a Godard film is not the end of a sentence; it is the silence following an unfinished phrase. It is a halt, unpunctuated, on a note of intense interest, which for someone of Godard's cast of thought is the same thing as hope.

"Pierrot le Fou" is an extraordinary film. The word "beautiful" describes it thinly. People are shown here in the midst of our Watts Towers existence, in an edifice of detritus—broken bottles, bits of colored glass, seashells. It is an existence of having adventures, of making do, of going on reconnaissances into the thought of writers and painters of the past, of surveying history, of listening to car radios. We are in Godard's familiar world of flashing city lights, rusty trucks, twisted steel, car accidents, murders. Red is insistently used. It is the color of blood, of traffic lights, of roses thrown away, of cheap clothes: the Godard paraphernalia. "How I hate blood!" says Ferdinand/Pierrot. When I came out of the film into New York, the reds of Manhattan stood out as if no other color existed: "Don't Walk" signs, neon, a red feather boa, fire engines, brake lights, a circling beacon on a police car. Godard is a master colorist. A red bicycle pump seen by him is like a guitar seen by Braque. "Pierrot le Fou" is one of the earliest films that were truly in color, along with Antonioni's "Red Desert" and Resnais's "Muriel." Godard uses color as a central character: beside "Pierrot le Fou" a black-and-white movie seems a duologue lacking the density of a subplot. "Pierrot le Fou" is an exhilarating and matter-of-fact film, with a questing turn of mind. One learns from it something new about didactics, about play, about thinking and recall, and about Velázquez's spaces between people, which in Godard's film have everything to do with the concept of extending politeness to a man's intellectual life.

Ferdinand/Pierrot is like one of the Velázquez characters he reads about to his daughter. As Godard's characters often do, he behaves as if he were a member of a race of "clownish freaks dressed up as princes." At the start, when we see him in his unholy, stately life, he is leading the existence that Velázquez so often painted: "caught in a mesh of etiquette, plots, and lies." On the evening of the mindless advertising party, his wife, dressing, says, "I'm wearing my new invisible pantygirdle, which you can't see." His retort, to wife and life, is to say, "After Athens, after the Renaissance, we are entering the civilization of the rump." He says later to the Marianne Renoir of Karina, whose beauty has never been more breathtaking or beloved, "There are days like this when you meet nothing but squares, and you look in the mirror and don't like yourself." She rescues him, for a time; he looks again, and, for a moment, feels more benignly toward the spectacle. The eyesight she endows him with is partly a matter of unconsciously sharing her own stores of curiosity and impulse. When they are driving at night somewhere together, there is a held shot of their two faces seen through the car windscreen, obscured monotonously by arcs of blinding spots of light that the highway lamps throw onto the glass like tracer bullets. The couple are alone together for a while in an unfindable place, as people are in Godard's marvellous accounts of breakable intimacy: they are a little in France, a little in role-playing, a little in an adventure in their imagined America ("The Statue of Liberty gave us a friendly wave," said Ferdinand/Pierrot as he drove out of Paris), and a great deal in one another's heads. Runaways? Only in a sense. Their pragmatism brings them straight up against the facts of the present and actual. Ferdinand/ Pierrot, looking at the moon, describes "a man crossing himself like mad and trying to run away." The Russians stuffed the man's head with Lenin, he says, and the Americans stuffed it with Coke: "The Americans and the Russians can shoot it out." The lovers seem to be hikers on hilly and unknown ground, but Ferdinand/Pierrot's knowledge of the past is a map. Their exigencies have all been gone through before. This is the point of all the collage quotes from Velázquez, Baudelaire, the Renoirs, Picasso's Pierrot, Céline, Lorca. Uncounted centuries have smoothed the rocks of the terrain, like so many tempests.

JULY 14, 1975

III

WOODY/DIANE

The opening description of Woody Allen was written in 1974. Since then he has made a lot of films that I hope you will have seen, including "Interiors," which is superficially in a quite different vein to his other work. It takes the risk of being serious, which of course Woody Allen has always been, but in this case the content is serious to the point of being racking. When I say "risk of being serious," I mean that audiences in general find it hard to forgive someone who has made them laugh for taking another turn. To Woody, who is a man with an uplifting gift for friendship, "Hurrah, bravo, welcome." And the same to Diane Keaton, his staunch and beautiful partner, whose scenes with him are always a miracle of private alliance transmuted for the public eye into something close to Beckett in its swiftness of communication—a communication much like the communication of a long marriage, in which neither partner is quite sure who is finishing whose sentence. Miss Keaton is miles beyond most of her contemporaries; because of her seriousness, fun, fidelity to self-formed notions, and sense of longevity of work, she has giant strides to go.

Guilty, with an Explanation:
Woody Allen

Woody Allen lay down in a commando position with a BB gun on one of his New York East Side terraces, outside a pair of French windows, and took potshots at some pigeons that fondly think he wants them there and that he emphatically does not. Feathery things seem to bother him: dowagers' fussy hats, bouffant hairdos, pigeons most of all. His penthouse duplex is a pigeon heaven, and nothing he tries seems to turn it into a purgatory for them. In his usual mood of seriousness about jokes, he once went to a Manhattan novelty shop and bought some coiled rubber snakes to frighten the pigeons off, but they treated the snakes as a welcome. Then he got some patent stuff to slather onto his terraces. It was supposed to rid one of pigeons. By "rid," he thought vaguely, the manufacturers meant that the pigeons would take umbrage at the smell. He went to bed. Next morning, he told me, he came down and the terraces were littered with pigeons stuck in the stuff. "I didn't know what to do," he said. "I was all alone. They were struggling. In the end, I had to *prize* them off, *one by one* with a *spatula*." His brown eyes looked larger and more appalled than ever behind his black spectacles, which are like the headlamps of a beautiful prewar car and give him an authority that he feels obliged, being an honest recorder, to undermine.

He wears saddle shoes, nice checked shirts with indescribable jeans, and, outdoors, a khaki fishing hat and a khaki battle jacket. "I have a tendency to wear clothes that don't match," he said mildly to me. The same day, when we had gone a long time without eating—the prospect of eating not being something that draws him much—his mind wandered to hospitality. "There's some chocolate pudding," he said, sitting on the floor in his drawing room, and then, lowering his voice like a spy, "I don't know how good it is." He paused, and whispered with restraint, "I hate the maid."

This maid, now gone, must be about the only person who has ever riled him. He said to me meticulously one day, speaking with his usual obvious truthfulness, "I don't get angry with people. Only with machines." His red hair is a false clue as far as any sign of flaring temper is concerned, as it often is in redheads. (Jean Renoir, for instance, who was a redhead before his hair turned white, is the mildest of men.) This self-despairing, hardworking stoic, who is one of the funniest men in the West—difficult to speak fairly for comedy in China, though there was recently a high-level International Conference on Humor held in South Korea—gets maniacal only with things like secretarial and kitchen gadgets. "I used to rent electric typewriters," he told me, "and then I demolished them somehow, and the people used to demand that I replace them. My ineptitude is the reason for my not being able to cook. I always wreck a kitchen. I smash things up." The mood to wreck doesn't sound at all like a temper fit: more like melancholy, as though mankind had deserted him, leaving him alone with a lot of cogs and things that whir. When he mentioned anger with people, he stood quite still. But when he talked about machines he shifted his feet all the time and moved his arms like the wings of one of his bogged-down pigeons.

Denigrating oneself is often taken to be a disguised way of denigrating other people. Woody Allen is one of the clear exceptions to this truism, which may arise from the reign of psychoanalysis in the Republic. Allen himself has been in analysis for fifteen years, with a woman. You feel that he regards the process as Sisyphean: a brave endeavor on her part to hold together a spirit impelled to scatter by centrifugal force. Analysis is one of his cluster of earnest undertakings. At the end of a day's shooting of "Sleeper" in California, he said, "I have an analyst's session by telephone, and then I have to practice my clarinet or else I'd lose my lip, and then I have French."

"Why French, on top of everything else?" I asked.

"I only had eight hours a day in pre-production," he said, "so I thought, Why don't I learn French? And now I feel guilty if I don't do it."

Daily life for this brilliant, courteous man seems to be a matter of endlessly fending off guilt, which settles on the balconies of his intellect like the pigeons on the terraces of his apartment. His films

143

reflect his suspicion that he is a fraud, and thus indubitably, hopelessly guilty. In "What's Up, Tiger Lily?," through the use of soberly inappropriate English dialogue, he dubs his own worries and crevices of self-doubt onto a Japanese melodrama. The film speaks for the lack of confidence that he knows so precisely how to use without begging for pity. "The last time I made love was on the Titanic. Unfortunately, we never finished," and "I can't break the door down because of my bursitis." (He washes his hands of himself physically. Having no idea how nice he looks, he jerks himself into spasms of self-repair: he plays tennis, for instance, though he says he is a hopeless athlete. "I'm fairly good at Ping-Pong," he once told me, trying to be accurate about himself, as usual.) His view of himself gives him an innate sympathy, in his writing and his films, for the rundown and the out-of-step, and especially for people who bring bravado to their straits. The hero of his "Take the Money and Run" holds up a bank with shy lack of technique ("Abt natural. I am pointing a gub at you," he writes to a teller), and then argues courageously with pedants in the bank who deride this inscriber of unreadable demand notes for being a rotten speller. In the middle of some perilous adventure on a ship in "What's Up, Tiger Lily?," Allen dubs a villainous Japanese toughie—who is actually giving grim directions to his nerveless gang—with queasy reminders of naval-training films warning pupils of how easy it is to sink.

Woody Allen sees even the human face as questionable. The nose strikes him as a particularly doubtful feature, hovering always on the edge of farce, and possibly more acceptable when flattened out by a steamroller into a large piece of leather, as it is in "Sleeper." Defiance sustains him, though it is always summoned up with difficulty, as if a waif were lifting dumbbells. In "Bananas," he calls himself Fielding Mellish: "Fielding, meaning strong, or with strength." In "Take the Money and Run," a commentator following the collapsible career of Virgil Starkwell (Woody Allen) shows him taking to crime at an early age and says, "He is an immediate failure." When he is trying to get into the Navy, he disappoints some psychiatric examiners by seeing an ink splotch in a Rorschach test as an elephant making love to a men's glee club.

Woody Allen's analyst must be fond of him—of his painstaking approach to her work, of his punctuality (which applies to everything), and of his devoted, apologetic way of delivering his obdurate bag of bones to her doorstep as faithfully as a dog bringing a sausage to lay beside your fevered head on the pillow when you are poorly. Fidelity in an analysand is little enough but as much as this one can offer, his manner says. Woody's temperament makes him admiring of all talent, haplessly determined in extremity, and technically fastidious (though he obviously sees himself as brash and all thumbs). One feels that this frail man suspects himself of weighing two hundred and forty pounds and of treading on everyone and every piece of outlying furniture. The suspicion has nothing to do with his real weight, which can't be more than a worried hundred and fifteen pounds or so. His long red hair, which hangs around his neck like a setter's ears, frames punctilious anxiety.

He is in awe of any comparably good comedian. Another eye, another universe. He said, registering relief, "It's a reward to be able to see the world through someone else now and again. W.C. Fields, for instance." He has an original and resolute mind that soars off into studious idiocy, but he characteristically seems to look on it as being in need of overhaul—of dry cleaning, and perhaps starching, with any possibly beneficial chemical additives. "I have a *slight* intellectual component," he said to me gravely, and went on to tell me that he wished he had eyes like Chaplin's ("deep sockets"). He worships Chaplin, and Groucho. Even Harpo is nearly up to Groucho for him. "Harpo's a lowdown comic with brainy instincts. It's a fine combination." Of himself he says, more than half seriously, "I have an intense desire to return to the womb. Anybody's." His life, which looks so gifted and rewarded from the outside, seems to strike him as misbegotten and beset.

We went to Trader Vic's in Los Angeles. Typically, the staff flattered him. But typically, also, they insisted that he wear a conventional jacket instead of his own (the khaki one, which looks as if he had just struggled to Camp II on Everest). "They always do that," he said to me quietly. "They don't *mean* to humiliate you." He thanked the donor and politely shrank inside the hideous lent jacket, which had shoulders reaching to his elbows and made him look like the flyweight youngest son of a poor family that handed down to him the clothes of five older heavyweights. Places other than his New York homeland and, especially, other than Hollywood—that forcing house of orthodoxy, with its tenets about the pursuit of virtue, godliness, slimness, and faultless digestive tracts which its fads pour out—would be friendlier to Woody Allen's singularity. On the other hand, no place but America would be so receptive to his fascinated and benign view of modern civilization's phenomenal oddities. It is no surprise that he responds eagerly to Jacques Tati, who has the same startled but benevolent acceptance of the sophisticated lunacies that have crept up unnoticed on most of the world. Woody Allen has a perfect command of the language of TV, of drugstore orders, of psychoanalytic banalities, of the enviable American comic genius for going too far, of the kind of bombastic and hopeful flirting with ironclad girls which dates back even farther than Groucho's with Margaret Dumont. He hates and fears mechanical jokery almost more than he hates and fears kitchen gadgets. He started to write gags when he was fifteen—in high school, where he unconvincingly describes himself as having varied from "below average to way below average." At Trader Vic's, as he seemed sometimes to be sinking unheard inside the horrible lent jacket, he had a rum punch without rum, because he doesn't drink (or smoke), and had zealous discussions about funniness and films. The seriousness probably has a lot to do with his funniness. It certainly has everything to do with his imperturbable tenacity, and his easy temper when he is directing the films he writes. I had just watched him acting all day on a sound stage, editing in his head as he went along. He had been encased in an armored headpiece that horribly augured uses for steel two hundred years hence. His whitened, slapstick face—"Sleeper" revives a great film tradition—was steaming under the makeup. His only relief had been a Hershey bar, but his equanimity remained unstirred and the atmosphere had spread. "Tati and Jack Benny want actors to be good," he said once. So does Woody Allen.

"'City Lights' and 'The Gold Rush' and 'The Navigator' and 'The General' are the four great comedies, aren't they?" he asked, as if anyone else would know better than he would. "They have a resonance. Because they're serious. Tati is serious." He had a think, looking eager but doleful. "Comedy is such hard work, isn't it? And maybe it isn't *that* important. Not enough to make a fuss about. Not like drama. Drama has romance."

"Hasn't comedy? Keaton?"

"Yes, but drama . . . I worship drama. Beckett . . . His rhythm, too."

"Keaton once told me that he and Chaplin missed the sound of the cameras cranking after they stopped making silent films. Because of the rhythm," I said.

We talked about that for a bit.

"Beckett is a beautiful comedian, of course," he said. "Never frenetic. The exact opposite of 'It's a Mad, Mad, Mad, Mad World.' 'Mad World' wasn't *about* anything. Well, though, as we were saying, comedy is such difficult work. You'll see people on a comedy with long faces, wondering where the laughs'll come, how to get them, how to get the rhythm right. It can make for a terrible atmosphere. When I was writing for the Sid Caesar shows, they were a mass of hostilities and jealousies. On the other hand, someone told me that on the set of a heavy Ingmar Bergman religious drama people are kidding all the time."

"That would be partly the repertory-company mood? Everyone knowing everyone else?"

"It's all very hard work." He sighed. "I like work. I'm going to be out of a job soon, when this film's finished, and I don't know what I'm going to do."

"Write your one-act play? The last of the three that go together? The ones you're going to direct?"

"Yes." He cheered up and had some egg rolls. "It's a question of technique, isn't it?"

"Someone first-rate once said that all artistic problems are really technical."

"I think that's right." He always looks as if he were taking a watch apart when he is thinking about an idea or dismembering the works of a joke, which he does devotedly, as if he had a magnifying glass screwed into his eye. "Fellini is perhaps the great tech-

147

nician. His camera movements." When Woody is talking about camera movements, he will swivel two fingers of his right hand like a pair of compasses in geometry. And when he is planning a cut in production on the set, he unconsciously moves his fingers apart as if they made a sling with a stone in it that a small boy is about to shoot off.

"Fellini, now," he said. He made a slow movement with the two divided fingers of both hands without noticing what he was doing. "People will go around and the camera will pan and the circle will be complete. But comedy's different. In comedy it's very difficult to do *anything* filmically. Everything has to be spare and quick and precise. The match has to be struck and the flare has to go up. None of the things that really good directors like. It's best in comedy to work directly on behavior, like Mike Nichols. Not on effects. You can't afford to have any of those Kazan travelling spots and shadows."

"Why do you think there are so few funny women?"

"I have to admit I don't adore comediennes. Is that because one has preconceived ideas of what women should be like?"

"Fragile? But Keaton was fragile, wasn't he? and M. Hulot?" I said.

"Yes, I'm wrong. I don't know. Elaine May I like very much, and Barbara Harris. I think it's because they don't seem at all technical. With Fellini, I'm afraid it's a little like listening to people playing a perfect scale. It's very beautiful, but it's only a scale . . . With Antonioni, now, though I suppose he might be called a bit precious, it's all in the rhythm, and that comes out of the material." He made his editing movement again with the fingers of both hands. "*He's* serious. And he moves around things. I hear he once did a play and he couldn't bear the way he couldn't get the audience's eyes to see from behind."

Eating Chinese spareribs and lifting the shoulders of his lent coat loftily, he said, "I used to look wonderful smoking." But smoking took time. One's impression is that he gives up anything that takes time from work. He has a Hammond organ in his New York apartment which is practically untouched. Like many good jazz musicians, he can't read music, but he can pick out any tune on his clarinet from a hum. Again, one has the feeling that he is happiest when he is doing something he can shape by hard work, although he cherishes the rawness of Dixieland jazz (which he plays), and the accidents or chance happenings in his films. He works in the cutting room for hours to preserve the accidents that came up during shooting. "If people only knew how little control you have over films. You're constantly dealing with catastrophes. I like them. Of course, the mishaps of editing add to them. Editing 'Play It Again, Sam,' I would suddenly get hysterical with laughter, and the other people in the place wouldn't know why. It would often be when I'd put half of a scene at the end and half at the beginning. That can sometimes work wonderfully. It's one of the good accidents in life. Most accidents are negative. But in entertainment and—er—*art* there's something about a serrated edge."

While he was sitting skulled in his mock-steel on the steps of his caravan, he had said, "I always think the next thing I do will be fun. Then when I do it I don't like it at all." He said much the same thing later, while he was in New York, editing and mixing "Sleeper" for hour after hour without a sign of impatience about the long business of splicing and putting together cuts, and with a perfect memory for the rhythm of a scene. "Eisenstein is my god," he said to me once, pulling down his fishing hat and obviously wondering whether he planned his pictures carefully enough. The only thing he does to while away the anxious time in the cutting room is to shuffle cards, without playing with them. They get agreeably dirtier day by day. He patiently showed me how to shuffle like a poker player. Shuffling one day, he told me that he had spent his poker winnings long ago on drawings, which he still has. One of them is a Kokoschka. Otherwise, apart from things like a beautiful big Edwardian hat that he bought for his beautiful chum and acting partner—an endearing and luscious comic with a mockingly beady eye for her lusciousness and an unusual leaning to slapstick, who was in "Play It Again, Sam" and "Sleeper"—he hasn't much feeling for possessions, though he has a lot of feeling for New York. "I hate Los Angeles," he said in Hollywood, in a Mata Hari whisper. In New York he looks different, though striding about in the same saddle shoes—busting through puddles and hailstorms, troubled maybe by thoughts of the pigeons collecting while he is out, but a free man. "I hate fussing with luggage. *Things*," he said. "Los Angeles isn't a place for intellectuals. Not for genuine intellectuals. Nichols and May are genuine intellectuals. So was Benchley." He has a great addiction to Robert Benchley and his straight-faced theorems about The Blind Explanation: "There is no such place as Budapest." Not that he is averse to sending up false highbrows in public. He has a likable disrespect for lofty religiosity and opaque innuendos in art. He once wrote a parody of Bergman's "The Seventh Seal": the heavy-laden spiritual game was not chess but gin rummy. "Great humor is intellectual without trying to be. You can teach people a little math or a few chess openings but not how to write jokes. It's a bizarre talent. Reduction to economical essentials. It has something to do with logic and something to do with literature." We discussed holding the name "Kierkegaard" up to a mirror to see whether it read as weightily backward: Kierkegaard intrigues him, and often comes up in his films and essays. "Something also to do with the mind of a chess master. That leap. I'm scared of dead patches."

Woody Allen works all the time. "I've got a workroom with a typewriter and all that stuff, but I only *copy* onto a typewriter," he said in his New York place. "I really write in the bedroom. I sometimes wonder if I'd be less depressed in a two-room apartment, like the one I lived in when I was married the first time" (his second marriage was to Louise Lasser, who was in "What's New Pussycat?," "Take the Money and Run," "Bananas," and "Everything You Always Wanted to Know About Sex but Were Afraid to Ask"), "or in a nine- or eleven-room apartment like this, whichever it is." He looked round it absently. "I come down from the bedroom for a snack or something, but mostly I like the bedroom." He cheered up and said, in a mock-confidential voice, "I think I can say, though this is not for publication, that I have the most beautiful apartment in New York." It is, he explains carefully, two apartments knocked into one. It has two kitchens. Only one is used. His apartment is hung with the beautiful drawings that he bought when he won at poker long ago. The drawings were an Incentive.

They definitely don't count as Possessions, or Clutter. Nor does a book someone gave him about Walt Disney, whom he adores. He was gravely interested in the fact that I liked Minnie Mouse's feet. "That's very rare," he said, and he pondered it for a while.

Allen was born Allen Stewart Konigsberg in 1935 in Flatbush, where his father did "a million little short-lived jobs" and his mother kept the account books in a flower shop. He says that he didn't make his parents laugh. "I don't make anyone laugh. Not offstage," he said, wondering solicitously whether he was being a disappointment. "Do you mind? I'm just not funny in private." He is, but he is also a beautiful audience. "I don't say this facetiously or modestly. I'm preoccupied with problems and work, and I'm certainly not the delight of any party. There seem to be a couple of different types of comedian. Some perform at the drop of a hat. I know I'm not always on. About Keaton and Chaplin: I think Chaplin is funnier but Keaton is more uncompromising. Keaton's films are Spartan. They're clean and clear and very American. Chaplin is more of a goof-off. The way 'City Lights' just pulls itself up short of sentimentality every time is something I idolize. It says a lot about love. Once I've done a script of my own I try not to read it again, because it becomes a little bit less funny. I don't rehearse a film. I never know where I'm going to put the camera. Funniness is organic, like sitting around with a lot of people when something loopy happens. What you write is not what you shoot at all. I've shot the middle of a movie again and again and eventually put it somewhere else. I love annihilating film when we're cutting it. Getting it down from a hundred and twenty-four minutes to eighty-nine. I think eighty-nine minutes may be the perfect length for something funny, don't you?"

If he sometimes sounds disorganized, which is probably a manner to encourage other people in a muddle, he actually knows exactly what he is doing. He even knows where the stamps are kept at home, which is more than can be said for most people as rich and busy as he is. (Not that he doesn't know that he's blessed with fortune at the moment, though he disbelieves in luck. For all his lack of superstition, he plays fortune-telling idly with his pack of cards in the editing room while a film cut is being spliced, and once turned up a significant-looking card for me. "That's the money card," he said, meaning to brace. "Unfortunately, there's nothing to it.") One Sunday in New York, as he was seeing me to the elevator, he gave the elevator man a stamped, handwritten letter to mail to the House of Representatives. It held a signed form protesting about Nixon. You could imagine him filling it in and signing it: "Woody Allen." Then "WOODY ALLEN," in case no one could make out the writing or no one had heard of him. He reads the *Times* carefully, though he had missed an item about policemen's wives' being worried about the influx of policewomen who spend eight hours a day with their husbands in patrol cars ("I can see that this is a matter for serious concern," he said), and he has a theory that the *New York Review of Books* has to be read at once, or else it piles up and becomes a matter of guilt." For him, guilt seems to come in the realm of failed chocolate pudding. He is delighted to find someone who doesn't feel guilty, and is buoyed up by anyone relatively free of depression. "That's wonderful," he said when I was laughing at something. "I'm sorry about having a cold today. I hate not being well." He shook himself like a pony shaking off flies in hot weather, and attended as closely to what he was saying as to filmmaking or writing. "I just happen to be able to write dialogue. Being a dramatist and being able to write sketches aren't the same thing at all." It comes down, perhaps, to the rhythm that he troubles about so much in speech and film editing and writing. When he collaborates, as he has often done in the cinema—especially with his friend Mickey Rose, and with Marshall Brickman on "Sleeper"—you have the sense that he works like a conductor. He is as organized and solemn about humor as he is, for instance, about keeping an appointment to have a health checkup for the sake of his accountant—which he takes seriously because it's the man's job. He has respect for jobs and loves efficiency. While the throwing-together of his two apartments made them rubble, he lived without grumbling at Delmonico's. Though no cook himself, and sore about rotten ones, he adores Julia Child. "I'd love to use her in a film one day. The beautiful way she chops onions. She's funny because she's engrossed in what she's doing. One understands, of course, that one's very lucky to be paid to do one's hobby. When I go on vacation, which is almost never, I always end up writing."

He made some coffee for us, and we talked about shiny dark coffee beans, the romantic big hat (three dollars) waiting upstairs for his girl friend, silly presents, drawings (he has an American primitive painting that looks a little like a Matisse), music, whistling ("I was a fine whistler long before I could play the clarinet"), hating holidays, liking work. He goes mute in the presence of joketers. "When I was very young, I wanted to go to Las Vegas and play the big hotels with the best jokes I could manage, not those terrible drunk jokes and wife jokes."

It is typical of his assiduity that he gets his clarinet overhauled every year. He has been playing it since he was sixteen. It stays in his car—even when he is in Hollywood—next to a copy of the *Times.* Though he is political-minded, he would probably think it a piece of showing off to reveal that. He tends to hide his instinct for political inquiry, as if it were a lot less important than, say, his instinct for tidiness. He once wrote "A Brief, Yet Helpful, Guide to Civil Disobedience" for the *Times:* "The Russian Revolution, which simmered for years . . . suddenly erupted when the serfs finally realized that the Czar and the Tsar were the same person." He has a parodist's perfect ear for literary styles. There was lately a piece of his in this magazine which exquisitely mixed the styles of Kafka's notebooks and of the diaries of an introverted Bloomsbury diarist: "Should I marry W.? Not if she won't tell me the other letters in her name." The first piece he remembers writing, also published in this magazine, was a chess contest conducted by testy correspondence.

Some of the factual things written about him sounded as if he must have produced them himself. A grave entry in "Current Biography" of 1966 explains that he is a standup comedian: "That is, a performer who confronts the audience in a standing position and tells jokes." He had already been playing the Blue Angel and the Bitter End in New York and the hungry i in California, among a lot of other famous places. But I don't think the memory of Flatbush, poverty, the two-room apartment, and his tumultuously unhappy first marriage has ever left him; or the feeling of being a schoolboy in the subway writing gags for attribution to people in gossip columns, as he once did. His time off with the clarinet—performing on Monday evenings at Michael's Pub, on East Fifty-fifth Street—is something that he seems to treat almost as if he were playing truant from Latin, though he takes his Mondays very earnestly. He likes using his band's Dixieland music in his films. At home, he practices to records. He enjoys it more than analysis, to which he is loyal but which he compares, after all these years, to vitamins: "It doesn't make any difference if I go or if I don't." When he is playing, he has the same sense of rhythm that he responds to so much in film, and the same instinct for improvisation. Plunge in. O.K., march tempo. B-flat. He always wants the band to be cruder. The serrated edge again.

He works like the devil on the later physical stages of a film, so as not to be overexplanatory. He has a technical passion, in writing as in film editing, for finding the startling cutout point. He often seems glum at work, like a lot of comics, but never lost. He is supremely educated in his sense of punctuation and other means of stopping short. It is an instinct that he morosely supposes to be peculiar to him; he is surprised when you laugh at something on the Moviola while he is sitting there looking expressionlessly at what he has done. When he caught me laughing at things on the Moviola, he said, "That's very *positive* of you. People *never* laugh in an editing room." And next he will pick up a ringing telephone—he always answers the thing himself—and cheer someone up or make a date, walking about, because the phone has a long cord. ("Pacing time.") Then he will hang up and come back to the Moviola. "Well, it's a matter of playing the blues and having a go."

"I always see myself as a Jewish uncle at some event. Not the hero, you understand. Militarily speaking, too, I am definitely 4-P," he said at his place one day.

"If I hadn't been a writer, I'd be very poor," I said.

"Would you, too? Ah. You *could* have been a meter maid or an actress, but, as I wouldn't want to be an actor in a play, I don't suppose you'd have wanted to be an actress. Writers aren't good actors. Speaking somebody else's words all the time. Embalmed if you're in a long run and out of work if you're in a short run. But rehearsing is terrific. You know something? The nuisance when you're alone is that you start thinking about the poor luck everybody has. Because the worst thing that could happen to anyone is getting older. It's like drawing the ace of spades. And everyone gets it. Though being very young isn't always great, either. It can be like living in a concentration camp. A bum's life or a comedian's life is liberty, on the other hand. Like being just the right age all the time. If I hadn't had this ridiculous capacity for being funny, I'd have been a bum. Or a messenger boy. Coming uptown with an envelope. Your day's your own. That's freedom."

FEBRUARY 4, 1974

"Love and Death"

Woody Allen's imperially funny new picture is named "Love and Death," a coupling of big concepts that says at once where the story is set. We are obviously going to be in the land of "War and Peace," of "Crime and Punishment," of "Fathers and Sons," though we turn out to be not really so much in Russia as in Russian literature. It is a literature seen through Woody Allen's unique prism of the grandiose but hesitant, as if it were being read by a student racked by anxieties about both the afterlife and the common cold. Mr. Allen, who wrote and directed the film, plays a nineteenth-century Russian named Boris. The weedy hero, swamped in progressively madder and longer-haired furs, which he begins to wear at breakfast, spends the picture surveying the course of his life in the best manner of his birthplace. His narration on the sound track is full of aperçus about agony and of manic confidences about his inmost yearnings; for nineteenth-century Russians, to publish a memoir was a sack of soul.

Boris's father is well heeled. This causes his sensitive son great hardship. The family, Boris tells us, has always had both a summer

155

and winter estate. The old boy, being a complete nut, also owns another piece of soil, which he carries around with him. It is a smallish sod, easily kept in a pocket. He reveals later in the film that he is planning to build a guesthouse on it. "With a little, little swimming pool, for fleas?" his radical son fills in, paying as much attention to the visions of rich dodderers as he can muster. Perhaps Boris has been sickened of the grand life by the fact that his father plainly needs a padded room of his own more sorely than a guesthouse. Anyway, though Boris is highborn enough to talk sonorously about having had his first experience of death from a serf, he nourishes furtive liberal leanings and tends in extremity to disguise himself as a waiter. The *luxe* of his beautiful floppy blouses is an embarrassment to him, you feel, like the matter of his breeding. He gives you the impression that in modern times he would cleave by nature to the anonymous clothes of a college kid plagued by bookish worries; his true class is not a nobleman's but the class of St. Petersburg 1798. We see his very Slavic preoccupations already troubling him when the film shows us the embodiment of him at the age of twelve, played by an earnest-looking, skinny child with the name Alfred Lutter III, which sounds as if it were made up by Woody Allen to give the boy a sense of security. The young Boris, looking charmingly like his brilliant, nervous aftermath, asks what happens when we die, and whether there are girls. The adult Boris, boasting in a throwaway voice of having grown to full manhood, but looking only slightly older and no less skinny than Alfred Lutter III, has the same unanswered questions on his mind. Living as he does in an extremely Russian setting of relatives and metaphysics, he reminisces on the sound track about Uncle Nikolai and his wonderful laugh (a shot of a bellowing man with a face like an adenoidal dolphin); confides that he lately had a strange dream (a shot of a number of upended coffins on a long lawn, with waiters rushing out of them in a kitchen temper before decorously dancing together); and conducts talkative scenes of passion with Sonja, his cousin twice removed. (She is played by the vividly alert Diane Keaton, one of the few witty women in public life so far who have managed also to be clowns without feeling unconsciously bound to mock themselves.) Sonja, says Boris, concealing his natural uncertainty beneath dash, is an incredibly complex woman. He treats his beloved as if she were a brainy sophomore with whom he dreams of being wonderfully unhappy on a run-down estate full of discontented serfs, pickled beets, and sexy duologues about the epistemological questions of the universe. The word "epistemological" is one that fascinates them both. Sonja, an idyllic beauty with her hair drawn back in an early activist bun, suggests with interest that the quickest analysis of her complexity would be to say that she's half saint, half whore. "Here's hoping I get the half that eats," says Boris, not caring which. The way the idea is built and wrecked is very much the method of the beautifully hilarious film: some piece of high-flying talk, veiling considerable tentativeness, will characteristically collapse into a piece of surreal common sense about looking out for No. 1.

Both love and death represent questions of glorious and appetizing pain to the High Romantic and bespectacled Boris, who approaches them with a surging soul and a rather testy intellect. In the case of love, his general approach is that it is by nature and privilege agonizing but that sex is underrated. Sonja tells him that sex without love is an empty experience. He feels that, as empty experiences go, it's not bad. Boris has a fine empty time with a posh and farcically beautiful countess (Olga Georges-Picot), except that he nearly missed it because she didn't express herself clearly enough for his lucid taste when she was making the assignation. "My room at midnight," she said. "Perfect," he said. Pause. "Will you be there, too?" The film often makes the point that, where lustful intent is concerned, clarity is all. A man impersonating Napoleon says to Sonja, "Shall we to bed?" Entirely confused, as Boris would be, she asks, "Shall we *what* to bed?" She was meant for Boris by Heaven. When the duality of Mind and Body comes up, Boris is a great respecter of Mind, which you can feel him confusing at defeated moments with the severely educated Sonja, but he is forced to notice that Body has all the fun, and he sometimes wishes that Sonja and he would stop their philosophy exchanges and have it, too.

Boris is deterred in love by a severe case of hypochondria ("an ulcer condition" and herpes). He is equivalently deterred in war by pacifism. To his loutishly brave family, who egg him on to fight Napoleon, he correctly describes himself as a militant coward. He vehemently does not care at all for killing people, and he is not in the slightest persuaded by current jingoistic talk about the dangers of the French invading Russia with all their rich sauces. He can't pull a trigger on a man he thinks is Napoleon; he can't take it in that a battle prospect strewn with corpses is a scene of anything worse than the results of Army cooking; and his only successful dealing with a weapon is as ammunition, in a stylishly shot combat sequence in which he plays a human cannonball. The Napoleonic battle scenes—wonderfully photographed by Ghislain Cloquet so that they look like Goyas (and rivalled in beauty only by a dinner-table scene in which the exquisite Sonja snores while her first, pre-Boris, clinker husband talks about herring)—are characteristically interrupted by the sight of a flock of charming sheep on the battlefield. The shot comes right in the middle of brilliant military photography and corresponds emotionally to the shot of the bewildered Pierre at Borodino in the Soviet "War and Peace." Boris's dislike of killing comes from his dislike of tangling with absolutes, though he reserves the right to be wrong about the nonexistence of God. As he says to Sonja, suppose he blew his brains out and then read in the papers that there was something up there. Pressed to murder for Russia's sake, he asks himself what Socrates would say. The thought of Socrates leads him back to the safe terrain of nonviolent illogic: "A: Socrates was a man. B: All men are mortal. C: Therefore all men are Socrates." Boris must spend a lot of his life climbing out of the pit of false syllogisms: it is probably the exercise for which Sonja marries him, and lives with him in a shack in the snow, dedicated as she is to having arguments with him about St. Thomas Aquinas when she isn't cooking economical sleet recipes.

Woody Allen and Diane Keaton have become an unbeatable new team at pacing haywire intellectual backchat. Their style together works as if each of them were a less mock-assertive Groucho Marx with a duplicate of him to play against. For such a recklessly funny film, the impression is weirdly serene. The feeling comes not just from the photography and the editing and the stately Prokofiev music but, more fundamentally, from the cast of Woody Allen's mind. He is the only wit alive who could manage with such easy style the skiddy topics of some of the movie's best jokes. Comedians who deal in sexual uncertainty can be dire, like comedians who trade on pretending to be cowards, because both sorts profit by affecting to have qualities that they secretly despise; but Woody Allen makes haplessness about love seem one of the conditions laid down for loving, much as he makes fear of death seem one of the conditions laid down for living. No one who wasn't petrified by mortality could make a comedy that was so palliatively funny about the straits we inhabit. God, if he exists, is described as an underachiever, presumably because of the Deity's failure to put an end to the anguish that comedy tries to see us through. In a monologue addressed to the audience, Boris says that he is going to run, not walk, through the Valley of the Shadow of Death, so as to get out of it faster. At the end of the film, he has been incredulously executed by French troops, and appears to Sonja outside her window, standing beside Death. Death is a well-built, well-fed figure, a lot taller than his victim, dressed in a white sheet that covers his face, and carrying a scythe. He seems quite affable, given his facelessness, but Boris finds him terrible company. He tells Sonja that the state of death is worse than the chicken at a restaurant they both know. Then there is a long shot of him, through a colonnade of plane trees by a river, doing a Maypole dance with Death. It is a scene of peculiar carnival respite, like the experience of watching the whole movie. "Love and Death" strikes me as majestically funny: the most shapely piece of cinema that Woody Allen has yet made, and one of comedy's hardiest ripostes to extinction.

JUNE 14, 1975

"Annie Hall"

There was once a child of three with red hair who lived in a big house at the end of a long drive in a cold part of England. She had been given a toy wheelbarrow for Christmas. The wheelbarrow, she decided, was bound to have a purpose. Every winter morning, while her nanny was sitting over a cup of tea in the servants' hall, the child would go out into the bitter air to collect a few of the stones in the drive in her wheelbarrow and dump them in a heap in the wood alongside the drive. Her task, as she saw it, was to clear the drive of these impediments. She would mutter "Find more stones" to herself, overheard by the head gardener, as she trudged up and down the drive with the wheelbarrow at her self-allotted work.

The young Woody Allen, also redheaded, is shown in the brilliantly funny and rather racking "Annie Hall" as a character who might well have embarked on a job like this. You feel he would have had, at a very early age, the same teleological approach to toy wheelbarrows. The hero is called Alvy Singer, but biographically and neurotically he could pass for Woody Allen any day. Alvy was brought up in Brooklyn: a small, skinny boy in spectacles whose growth seems to have been impeded by his bearing the millstone of the world on his head. At some moment, the boy's family, whose heart lies mostly with chicken soup, says that he is depressed by having just learned that the universe is expanding. Alvy's worries are not small ones. In his adult life, he explains to a girlfriend that he has been jumpy since he gave up smoking. That was sixteen years ago. He treats his physique and his psyche rather like second-hand mechanisms for which engineers still hold out hope. It has been a full fifteen years since he went into analysis. He falls desperately in love with Annie Hall—Diane Keaton, of Allen's "Play It Again, Sam," "Sleeper," and "Love and Death," and one of the most dazzlingly and beguilingly funny girls in movies in years—who entrances him by her braininess. She also reassures him by having a set of phobias in a lighter vein than his own. Hers are minimal—an absolute inability to learn to drive, for instance ("We can walk to the curb from here," he says once, after she has parked)—whereas he buys any book with "death" or "dying" in the title. After they have split up, and have divided the books, she says firmly that the copy of "Death in Venice" he gave her was something he chose only for the name. Some of his other characteristics, which are obviously going to be as lifelong as his therapy sessions,

160

include a fear that anti-Semitism is lurking everywhere ("D'you?" always has a dark and menacing other sound in his ears) and a mania about seeing a film from the absolute beginning to the absolute end, which drives him somehow to Marcel Ophuls' "The Sorrow and the Pity" again and again instead of going to whatever other film he has planned to see. When Annie arrives two minutes late to join him for Bergman's "Face to Face," he flatly refuses to go in. It would only mean missing two minutes of credits in Swedish, she says reasonably. But no. "The Sorrow and the Pity" it is again.

No "Face to Face," these two, but certainly side by side. Allen and Marshall Brickman, who collaborated on the script, have created a movie that slips in and out of a dual first-person narrative, using snatches of spoken thought by two characters of wry intelligence and a mock-fierce horse sense peculiar to Allen's humor: in him humor masks an extreme decorousness, courtesy to women, and fear of lobsters. It may be that in Woody Allen's imagination lobsters are a vastly magnified form of spider. Tackling the insanely difficult, Alvy masterminds the cooking of live lobsters, when steaks would at least have been quiescent; one of the lobsters behaves like a spider crawling up a bathroom pipe, and scuttles behind the fridge with the alarming Hitchcockian high-heeled noise peculiar to a lobster in a tantrum. "Annie Hall" perfects a sort of humor that can best be described as psychoanalytic slapstick. It has a Geiger-counter ear for urban clichés, and a hatred of Los Angeles which is appealing to all who share it. Annie Hall falls in love with a Hollywood citizen, played by Paul Simon, who gives the sort of parties at which the hot Christmastide sun shines down on people dressed with self-conscious casualness who will talk about "Grand Illusion" as "a great film if you're high." Woody Allen listens, and pukes. He has come only to rescue his girl from all this, and heaven knows if he can do it. When he meets her at an outdoor café, he bravely orders alfalfa sprouts and a plate of mashed yeast. They tell each other—in the jargon the film bitterly notes—that they are doing the mature thing by splitting up. The movie dialogue deliberately exaggerates the habit of speaking in quotation marks which often seems now to be strangling simplicity.

"Annie Hall" goes further than any earlier Woody Allen film in the purity of its romanticism. This is a love story told with piercing sweetness and grief, for all its funniness. The hero is intelligent. That is one of the points. He is also debonair. That is another of the points. Like Buster Keaton, Woody Allen has made one of the rare comedies in existence about a well-heeled hero. Woody in "Annie Hall" is strongly like Buster Keaton in "The Navigator" when Keaton is chauffeur-driven across the road with a bouquet to court his girl. Adrift on the empty liner equipped for a thousand, Keaton alertly boils eggs for two by a self-made Emett contraption; like him, Woody Allen is spry, courtly, and alarmed, with a definite touch of the aristocratic about his small frame. In "Annie Hall," Woody Allen technically pushes far ahead of anything he has done in the cinema before, playing with ideas in film which he has been experimenting with in prose. His ear for metropolitan speech has never been finer, his approach to character never so direct, his feeling about hypocrisy never so ringing, his sobriety never so witty.

APRIL 25, 1977

Her Own Best Disputant: Diane Keaton

"I hate these chairs," said Diane Keaton of two of her own chairs in her spotless, natural-wood-and-white living room. "They're so uncomfortable. I got them by mail order and I like what they look like, but they're no fun to sit in. I'll do something about it. They're too angular. We could sit in the kitchen and have tea—yes?— where the chairs are more ordinary. These are definitely a mistake. I have a tendency to get a little severe about taste in chairs until I've sat in them. Oh, well."

We were in her apartment, on the East Side of Manhattan. She describes it as being like a railroad car. About the kitchen, one sees what she means, but only about the kitchen. Everything else has a sense of space and liberty. Diane Keaton herself is very open. She is not at all like the many actresses who have skimmed some mannerisms off her and done insultingly mild imitations by relying on "Well"s and dither. Miss Keaton, the Oscar-winning co-star of Woody Allen's "Annie Hall," is not a whit like the flustered ingenue she was cast to play. "I've noticed people saying 'La-di-da' like Annie Hall, and I don't like it, you know?" she told me. "It's not a good idea to be identifiable, though it's reassuring. It feels safe in most ways, and that's bad, because it means that you're accepted, and once that happens that's where you stay. You have to watch yourself. I'd like a life like Katharine Hepburn's in terms of work. She matured. She made the changes. Like Martha Graham."

We went to her gym class. She goes every second day, and also goes to singing classes and acting classes. She got ready for the gym class fast: she had on a black leotard and black tights under her other clothes. It was a long class, and the woman leading it was merciless. Some people dropped out. Miss Keaton kept at it till the end. She is very supple, with an apparently boneless back, like a cat's.

"You seemed to anticipate what the woman was going to get you to do next," I said when it was over.

"Well, after all this time I'd be an idiot if I couldn't."

"Do you do ballet?"

"When I was nineteen, at Martha Graham's school. Her floor work was fantastic."

"What are you doing now?"

"I'm not working. I like that. I like to have time to myself. What are you doing?"

"Talking to you."

"Yes, I guess you are. Well, I bought some books this morning. Max Ernst and Rothko."

"Do you draw?"

"Do you?" She saw the rhythm of question-allaying she had slipped into, and said, "I draw *very small*."

She took me into a big room—big enough to be a bedroom—that she uses as her darkroom, for photographs she likes taking and then keeping from public sight, for herself alone. Everything very neat. "You see, it doesn't have to be more furnished than a kitchen. I like it better than my actual kitchen."

In her bedroom there is a basketful of rubber stamps that she has had made. She printed a page for me: an entry in old-fashioned medical typeface from some old encyclopedia, and a dental drawing—oddly, not at all macabre—of an X-ray of teeth and their roots. "You wonder whose teeth," she said. "It's like home movies or blue movies. You wonder what those people are like now who were young then."

Diane Keaton, famous as Woody Allen's co-star and in her own right, is one of the most comedically pure and brainy actresses in our midst. Her prodigious comic gifts are sometimes hidden. She tends to hoard these gifts, as if she were an impostor guest at a banquet tucking away food for friends under the challenging eyes of a portly butler, or as if her talent might run out in some world energy crisis. Like many of us, she dreads departures and endings, though she undertakes them with the debonair gaiety of a silent comedian setting off into nowhere. Equally, she sees herself as someone who puts off encounters and beginnings.

"I could just take classes indefinitely," she said to me at my place in New York. "Don't you ever get surprised when you're paid to do something you like doing?" she asked another day, when we were at her apartment. She seemed amazed that a paying cinema audience should ever choose to watch and listen to her. "My mother, now, who taught me a lot about print work, has occupied her life by doing chores. Now that I'm not working, I'm still very interested in print work. And I like to spend a lot of time making collages. It's nice to be by myself, thinking, looking into store windows." She was wearing the clothes that she had made her own. One or two of the things she wears with especial fondness were given to her by Woody Allen, her ally in anxiety: he shares with her, as with Annie Hall, a terror of live lobsters that have been bought for an intimate dinner and that roam around distressingly behind the fridge, like distraught women in stiletto heels. She has a romantic love of the big hats that one associates with boating and picnics on the grass. Allen found her one in a thrift shop. They perfectly suit her thriving and reposeful face. This costume look of hers, which has become identified as the "Annie Hall" look, often consists of men's pants and waistcoats, a floppy tie vaguely tucked into the belt of the pants, and little-girl sandals; or a skirt and shirt and pullover, and heels daringly high for someone already tall. She has a stride hard to define until one realizes that it has to do with not being crippled by carrying a bag in the hand, which inhibits so many women's gait.

Diane Keaton grew up in southern California, in Santa Ana. Her family are Methodists. The family name is Hall, but her mother's maiden name was Keaton. "I was encouraged by my teacher in junior college to think I was wasting my time in 'Bye Bye Birdie.'" She raised her eyebrows at herself and said, "I suppose it all started with singing. It was always one of the predominant things in our family. I used to go out onto the back porch and sing. There was one less successful thing than 'Bye Bye Birdie': a church recitation when I was six. I started to cry, and my mother had to come up and get me. The audience applauded me, which was terrible. I was in 'Little Mary Sunshine' when I was eighteen, and that was also terrible, because I wasn't being what I was supposed to be, which was the comedy lead. I always auditioned in junior high, and everyone knew I'd been around for years trying, but I didn't seem to have much drive. I still don't really have it."

Miss Keaton studied for a time at the Neighborhood Playhouse, in New York, but now she finds herself more and more drawn to cinema. "I want to be close to things," she told me. "You get disappointed if you see everything in medium shot in a theatre." We spoke of how well her namesake Buster Keaton understood that. Her family were encouraging but were remote from the arts. "My father is a civil engineer. I have two sisters and a brother, and I was born in 1946, which I guess would give me time to have had around ten children if I'd really worked at it, but I'm not like my mother. She spent a lot of time on us. She has a lined face. American Gothic. Gray hair parted in the middle and pulled tightly into a bun at the back of her head, and this rectitude. She's straight—

very straight." Miss Keaton made a characterizing gesture of up-rightness with her hands.

She came from California ten or twelve years ago. Quite a bit later, she lived with Woody Allen for a year; now her apartment is about ten blocks down from his. She found it hard to leave her family in California. "But sometimes one knows how strong the impulse to *do* is. I didn't know how really strong until a lot after-ward. I have a deep feeling for America. I'm definitely a product of this continent. I hadn't worked east of New York until we shot 'Love and Death' in Paris and Hungary. The workers in Hungary are poor, really poor. Outsiders would say, Well, at least they've got a regular income, whereas artists don't know where the next job's coming from. But I guess we're the privileged ones. I often dream about California. There's an opulent copy of grass, called dichondra—soft and velvety and green—that confers great pres-tige. I can't stand it at those Los Angeles parties when people cover up the real grass with plastic because they think it's going to wear out by being trodden on. Well, a lot of things get worn out by being trodden on, or even just stepped on—especially people—so why choose grass to protect? I can't stand people who keep things from being used."

I was reminded of the convention of antimacassars: "Things like doilies made of lace and hung over the back of armchairs to keep men's Macassar oil off."

"Aië, aië, aië," she said. "Those people don't want to let time be shown by living, do they?"

"What's the difference for you between the West Coast and here?"

"California is where my roots are. I like the weather. The desert. Being much more in touch with nature. Camping. I don't like be-ing out in California for what I do professionally; I just love the southern part, where I come from. As far as New York goes, it's fine, but I can't live in a fancy world too much. Though I love the buildings here. I love walking. I love the feeling that I have to do things. Everything goes so fast. You go to a supermarket, and no one says 'Thank you' or 'May I?'—which is honest. It would be all right if they meant the courtesies, but they wouldn't. You can fool yourself in California, but you can't do that here—not like L.A., not just by making it seem nicer and prettier than it really is. I suppose the truth is I'm in love with Arizona and New Mexico as well as the puttering around New York. When I'm here, I love to go to those old medical bookstores and places that have drawings of machinery."

"Annie Hall" was Diane Keaton's fourth film with Allen as her co-star. The first, directed with a matching neurotic laconicism by Herbert Ross, was "Play It Again, Sam;" after that, she played the goose-brained girl of the twenty-second century in Allen's own "Sleeper," then Sonja in Allen's "Love and Death"—a Russian lyric beauty, with her hair drawn back in an early feminist coil, as fascinated as the Allen character is by words like "epistemological," which they discuss in what seem to be very chilly places indoors, wearing heavy fur coats and fur hats at meals. The edginess she displays as Sonja during their sophomoric discussions in "Love and Death" is an edginess that both enthralls Allen's own recurring film character and seems to infect him with an intellectual's equivalent of hives. This edginess is a quality she can adopt or drop at will. There is no trace of it in the serenity of her apartment or in the serenity of her cats. The apartment has polished wood floors, no carpets, a white-on-white painting by a Californian named Bruce Nauman, with the word "VISION" picked out in the whiter white. There are big wicker baskets, and a cactus inside a galvanized-iron trash basket. The colors, apart from the cactus and its cage, are rusty brown and white. These are also the colors of her cats. One, called Buster, is a red Abyssinian of talkativeness and poise; the other, Whitey, a long-haired beauty of a mongrel.

She said, over the head of Buster, that she didn't know why she had been chosen to be in "Hair" on Broadway, which came before her close friendship with Woody Allen.

"Because you were the best who was being auditioned?" I said.

"That's probably right. There might have been plenty of others out on the street who were better but didn't know there was a producer's call."

She sang in Pasadena night clubs a while back. "I got bad reviews. It was terrible: every time someone applauded, I said 'Thank you' and apologized. I apologized a thousand times. When I was on the Johnny Carson show, it was always geared to laughs, and he played off me, because he thought he could make me frantic. I hate that." Sometimes she will leap into a sudden attempt to explain her own habit of apologizing, at the same time sheltering behind a Scotch terrier's growth of fringe over her forehead; she uses it, perhaps, as some women use dark glasses.

She would like to leave the chic part of the East Side where she lives. "All the boutiques and dogs in clothes . . ." Again she chipped away at this question of the railroad-car aspect of her present apartment.

"I like train journeys," I said.

"But not to live in," she said. "It's ridiculous to be in an unmoving vehicle. The apartment may be mostly white, like yours, but this is an *empty* train. I can see that your place is somewhere you have people to. My place isn't really finger-marked enough to be convincing, you know? It's my own fault that I haven't anyone to cook for. Of course, I'm a lousy cook. But it is a fault. I'd have to order those things you're always supposed to have by you."

"Kitchen staples."

"Yes. Well. Do you have staples? I can't seem to need them. Flour, milk, tea, tomatoes, bacon, bread, coffee, onions. I buy them all the time, but they're always going bad."

"Not tea or coffee or flour, surely?"

"Flour? *Roaches!*" Roaches seemed to be in the lobsters-behind-the-fridge category. There are fifth columnists of cuisine everywhere. For a moment, I thought she was going to say "La-di-da, la-di-da"—Annie Hall's way of bidding goodbye with a blithe wave of the hand to an impossible subject, the Annie Hall who was probably based on idiosyncrasies of her own behavior which she has now left behind—but, naturally, she didn't. She says it most famously in "Annie Hall" itself after she has first met Woody Allen, as Alvy Singer, on a tennis court. Hero worship on sight. She greets him with a "Hi, hi," covering the most love-struck embarrassment, meets an embarrassment equal to her own, then ends the impossible silence between them with "La-di-da."

"Why did you use to say 'La-di-da'?" I asked.

"People had fixed it on me. It originally meant hoity-toity, didn't it?"

She has a way of lobbing people's questions back at them which is rare in an actress. She seems to do it not because she wants to elude the hard questions but because she wants to know other people's answers.

"You like America, don't you?" she asked. "Yes?" She pursued it.

"It's interesting. Not consoling, not like Europe, but very interesting."

"Would I like England?"

"It treats you in the way you said you like. It lets one get on with one's life. There's time for meandering."

"I suppose some of the most interesting ideas have come up through people meandering. Did Leonardo meander his way into the idea of the flying machine?"

I tried to restore question-and-answer to their proper alternation, and asked, "Who are the, say, three people who've influenced you most in your life?"

"Who are yours?"

"I suppose one real person and two characters in fiction. Someone in Jane Austen and someone in Dostoevski. But you?"

"Well, now, there's Buster Keaton. I thought he was visually thrilling, and very sophisticated: more about women than about men. He lets you read a lot into things. You're left with so much to decide. And then there was a woman in Santa Ana, an incredible woman, an artist. She was mysterious. She loved a lot of things that weren't yet open to me. And then, gosh, a woman I met once when I was looking for an apartment who claimed that her husband had invented the tea bag . . . Well. And then my family. We're very close to each other. My sister Dorrie looks like an Eskimo. And then Woody, of course."

"Would you like to direct a play?" I asked.

"I prefer acting in movies. I prefer to work behind a camera. It's uninterrupted, undistracted by an audience's reactions." (She meant "in front of a camera": interesting that she sees the camera as a protective wall against gaze.)

"You said just now 'behind a camera.' As if you were half in the mind of the director when you are acting. Wouldn't you like to make a film?"

"Well. Could it be in black and white? I miss the use of black-and-white cinematography. I also like black-and-white still photography very much, as you saw from the darkroom. It takes you right *there*, into the past. You dwell in it, you get into that world, don't you?"

Again and again, she transmits a strong impulse to be a director-writer-actor. "I write things, just vignettes, in journals, since you ask." She sees things whole, in clear air, as a director or a writer must, with a benevolence toward idiosyncrasy. She seems to have a writer's instinct to record thoughts that are passing through her head and to store them away in a drawer. Many of her meditations are caught in the still photographs that she has taken but never shown around. There is something of the true photographer in her: in her ungarrulous conversation, in her sympathy with the gesture-language of people muted by circumstance. She did a brief mime for me on the way people had looked and walked in Hungary. It was a visit that had obviously impressed her very much. She takes photographs for no reason in particular, stacking them away, probably never to be seen. This leads one to the feeling that she herself would sometimes like never to be seen, or even heard.

She spoke often of singing. "I was never able to sing high. I don't know why I can't sing high. Maybe I'm afraid to sing high?"

She has taken photographs of herself as a mysterious Mata Hari girl in a black felt hat and dark glasses, with her face practically smothered in a high turtleneck collar. The photographs are an insignia of this beauty who would like to disappear into a dimity skirt and an oversized waistcoat: an image of the famous actress who would care most to be invisible, perhaps leaving behind only her singing voice, which is soft, though robust, and always questioning. In the company of Diane Keaton, one has the feeling of being with an alert and sympathetic carpenter who may be apologetically called to other pressing business at any moment.

Miss Keaton loves her revered actor namesake partly for his poetic and engineering grace. Watching one of his films, she says that she feels ungainly—this girl who moved with a lightness unexpected in tall women. She never tries to minimize her height. She uses it to achieve a certain elegance, which is courtly, though entirely modern. When she is not moving about—is confined to a chair or to a conversation—she seems less sure of herself. The Annie Hall clothes are a show of confidence. Once, when we met, she was wearing four-inch-heeled shoes with pointed toes, heavy white socks, a white blouse tucked into a long, full skirt, a black waistcoat, some gold jewelry. Her appealingly muddled hair was piled up onto the back of her head and clasped there with a clip.

Her own attitude toward work is much like Buster Keaton's. She likes practicalities. When I was watching her on the sound stage of "Sleeper," I never heard her fuzz a line with one of the hesitancies that she has been saddled with. She likes a text to be bare and clean.

"What set you on the way?"

"I suppose we are on the way—are we? Every time I turn on one of the talk programs, I think we've lost the power of speech. Well. I can't talk at all. I think I took to films because I don't like the conspiracy there is in a Broadway comedy. The conspiracy between the audience and the cast—the audience that has paid all that money to laugh. Personally, if I'm going to laugh, I'm going to laugh by myself."

In spite of being stopped for her autograph everywhere she goes, she is perfectly in earnest when she says how glad she is not to be famous. "Think of being on the cover of every magazine," she says. "I'd want to be violent to the readership, I suppose: violent because they weren't recognizing my own stupidity in being on the cover. Though I'm not sure that violence tells us all these things people say it does about the blood-and-guts nature of America and the go-get-it frontier mentality. I mean, there were also gentle and settled things. Dusters and quilts and cranberry sauce." She will embark on a thought like this one, and then stammer and consider what to do about it—apparently most attentive to a mark on her skirt, and visibly wondering whether to take cover—but at length continue to the finish, still seeming in some part of her mind to be looking for a dry cleaner. So. Violence. She comes back to it. "I can't stand violence. Which is a really original thing to say, isn't it? Though it's getting to be a bit un-American to say it, as though one were rejecting the red corpuscles of the country. Well, if I'm going to hit something, I like an inanimate object, such as an elevator. That's my sort of violence." She made up an American-musical theme tune for the line. "That's *my* kind of violence, that's *our* kind of . . ." Pause. "I'd quite like to hit the New York climate, for instance. In winter, it's a question of layers. In summer, I don't know how to cope."

"Flowered shirt and baggy trousers and pink leather shoes," I said.

"Oh, the man swore these were plastic." Pretense of disappointment.

"Do you think plastic superior to leather?"

"Not necessarily, only the salesman did, and he *emphasized* that these were plastic."

She seems like some New World Romantic who actually promises us habitation in quite another world from the dishwasher-spirited world of modern acquisitive fact. Her imaginative world, though it is totally modern, seems grounded in the farsightedness of centuries of European thought, which she has gathered partly through reading and partly by temperament. She said she was going to a department store, and would I come? For once, shopping took on the mood of a spree. Exchanging a coffee strainer: though she apparently lives in a realm of undefended confusion, she actually deals with it very efficiently. Diane Keaton, for all the "You know?"s and "Well"s, is no foolish bird. Born thirty-two years ago, she seems to be a distillation of the troubles and the acquaintance with pre-natal world history which are the inheritance of her generation. She has lived, in her thought, just as much through the Spanish Civil War and the Second World War as through the time of Vietnam. This girl from California, geographically so far removed from Europe, has a sense of non-isolationism which is alert. It seems to reinforce her deep friendship with the Jewish, Brooklyn-born Woody Allen. She speaks very sensibly about "success" and about the job of acting, which in general attracts a great deal of Western Seaboard nonsense from sophisti-

172

cates warning of the dangers of fame-chasing in the midst of chasing it themselves. "If you're an actor," she said, "you have to make your effort in front of other people. Then you have to say to yourself, because there's such pressure, 'Jesus, I'm never going to be allowed to do anything else wrong, ever, I'm just supposed to do it right again and again.' And then you have to say, 'Nuts. You must go on, I can't go on, I'll go on,' like the man in Beckett."

DECEMBER 15, 1978

"Interiors"

Let us now praise famous men. Woody Allen, whom I have seen cause small boys to fall down in mock faints in his honor, has turned from making people laugh to making people assess their lives. He has always been someone who made people think. His has never been the sort of dragonfly comedy that hovers on the surface of things. It has been a sort of comedy rooted in the temperament of someone serious. His new film, "Interiors," is a serious film rooted in the temperament of someone funny. And it echoes.

Near the beginning, there is a closeup of Diane Keaton's profile and her hand on a windowpane, the fingers stretching for a freedom that her life has not afforded her. She plays one of three daughters of Arthur (E.G. Marshall) and Eve (Geraldine Page). Near the beginning, too, there is a held shot of the back of E.G. Marshall's head as he stares out of a window. All the characters in this film look at the world as if it were partitioned off from them, as if it were separated from them by something as transparent as glass, and as unbreakable by people in control of themselves. But the control these characters exercise is shaky. It is a control that has been learned, not one that is native to them: we are inside the skulls of people who have had restraint drilled into them by the specifically middle-class discipline of psychoanalysis. The discipline would not work for anyone with a less educated vocabulary.

173

It depends on a degree of articulacy. The characters in "Interiors" all express themselves very well, but this prevailing discipline has put a leading rein on them. The figure in the film who is on the tightest rein is Eve, the mother, played by Geraldine Page with particular splendor. She is an interior decorator and is obviously near a crackup. She cherishes her convent-white schemes without knowledge of what they might impose on nonmonastic inhabitants. She moves lamps and ornaments as if they were chessmen that had to be precisely in the middle of their squares if the player were to be able to think clearly. While she is positioning things, her thoughts visibly wander: to the past, which she ennobles with more happiness than it probably held, and to a future that she speaks of with a hope that bears no relation to reality. Her husband, a stolid man, dreams of a world of fun, a release from this tightness, a change from the careful aesthetic spaces that she so compliments herself on, communicating by her very emphasis on isolation in them the suspicion that she is never going to be helped by others. She thinks that she has to stand erect, on her own, even if her back is breaking; she doesn't know the strength of being able to lean on friendship.

Arthur announces to Eve at a family meal, where she is flanked by two of their three grown daughters—Joey (Mary Beth Hurt) and Renata (Diane Keaton)—that he wants to leave her. She clings to the words "trial separation" as if they were a promise that nothing actual was happening. She is a woman who lives by the sound of words, and not their meaning. It is hardly bearable to her—or to us, because this is a consuming film about family life—to contemplate that the words stand for an actual state that is going to lead to actual divorce, actual remarriage by her husband. Easier to fix her mind on ornaments, on how she sees herself: in her chosen ice gray, with her hair done up on the top of her head in a tight bun. She is the victim of a society that places an unreasonable premium on being "creative." She has to be a "creative" person, endlessly having floors rescraped and changed, just as Renata has to characterize herself as a poet, just as Renata's husband, Frederick (Richard Jordan), has to try to be a novelist and drinks himself into the ground for lack of any deep-seated wish to do the work that his society finds so admirably "self-expressive." What a harsh trick, this film silently says, for a land to put so high a price on "self-expression," when more lenient expectations would let many of these self-enforced creators be content as housepainters or dog walkers.

One of the best performances in the impeccably cast film is by Maureen Stapleton as Pearl, Arthur's new love. The time that Arthur chooses to break the news to Eve of his wish to be free to remarry is when he and Eve are sitting together in a New York church, of all places, and sightseeing, of all things. Eve has been looking at the treasures in the church as if beauty and antiquity were mementos to be collected, objects to be carefully set on the mantelpiece of her mind and pointed up with cushions in coördinated colors. She suddenly goes berserk when her thought permits the invasions of the truth that Arthur is presenting her with. This trial separation isn't something leading to a reconciliation; it is a sharp separation leading to what she sees as the end of her life. In one of the very few violent scenes in this stilled, attentive film, she sweeps her arms across a row of burning votive candles in the church and runs shouting up the aisle.

Eve's three daughters have reacted differently to the sorrow she has otherwise so strictly buried. Flyn (Kristin Griffith) has said the hell with it and become boisterously social. Renata—a role in which Diane Keaton gives the performance of her career—is an observer, hardly able to bear the bitter asides she hears between people who really wish each other well, and trying to nullify the sulks of Joey, a model daughter in spectacles who refuses to adapt or forgive. Joey is furious with Pearl, the woman whose spirit and sense of fun have so attracted her father that, at sixty-three, he has derailed his life. Pearl is someone who would probably have been—tenderly—called a vulgarian in a Chekhov play. At her wedding, where Joey is purse-lipped in angrily dull clothes, Pearl wears a cheerfully ill-bred flowered satin dress rather too tight for her. She does card tricks, like Charlotta in "The Cherry Orchard." She lifts the fog of sobriety in which the family are wrapped, looks puzzled when they talk with such depression of intellectualized things, dispels their subtle glooms with her showgirl gaiety. She seems exempt from guilt, and this exemption is one of the innocences celebrated by the film. The activity and play that are natural to her are beyond the reach of characters like Frederick and Joey, and most of all beyond the reach of Eve, who lives on the cliff edge of a rage that she has subdued or redirected at a cost to the whole family. In a crisis about something quite other, she turns on Joey and says furiously, "Will you please not breathe in so hard?," making the repressed girl stoop more than ever. The sisters, tied to their mother, are also bound up in vying with each other in talent; it is a puny game, and the emotional profile they present is cadaverous. Only the gay woman who purveys such ease among constricted people, who seems to them a vulgarian, has the key to abundance.

Apparently about local frailties, this film—which Allen wrote himself—is universally recognizable. It's as true a tragedy as any that has come out of America in my memory. The end of the story speaks about parenthood as clearly as "King Lear." There is an inspired nighttime moment at the peak of events in a beach house when the real mother has been in hiding in the shadows and Joey calls "Mother!" and her stepmother—this figure whom she hates, this figure of prodigality who loves her—answers "Yes?"

The director of photography, Gordon Willis, has made the film look as simple and concentrated as the script. There are many compositions that remind one of Bergman, many quick cuts in scenes without dialogue which say something about the varied thoughts of this family and which are entirely original. Most of all, one should salute Woody Allen. Straight after "Annie Hall" and this giant stride away from what people expect from him, he is now shooting his next picture. So much for the bystanders and foot-draggers of the industry, who make such a grandiose fuss about what to do in 1979 or 1980, hovering between an adaptation of a Broadway hit and an adaptation of a best-seller. Woody Allen simply goes from one job to the next, taking risks that he has won the right to take, because he speaks to a great many people. This droll piece of work is his most majestic so far. The theme its characters express is very Chekhovian. It is pinned to the idea that the simplest, hardest, and most admirable thing to do is to act properly through a whole life.

AUGUST 7, 1978

"Manhattan"

Isaac, the undersized and festive hero of Woody Allen's "Manhattan," is played by Woody Allen. The character has two ex-wives. He is practically underwater with alimony demands. He has visiting rights to his child, a small boy for whom he buys too expensive toy yachts when his offspring, being Manhattan-bred, begs for acquisitions. In the most wry way, to anyone who knows the Manhattan of potholes and poverty and rudeness, the picture is a fable—written by Woody Allen and Marshall Brickman—about a city of smooth rides and riches and thoughtfulness. The picture gives us a view of New York as from a chauffeur-driven car. Harlem is invisible, as though covered by a carpet from Sotheby Parke Bernet. A friend—an American woman—said to me as the audience came out, "It makes you want to go to London." That is, in fact, one of the points of the picture. Again and again, there are references to the civilization of England and the Continent. They are the subtext. The text has to do with a most charming notion of love between people, though the love is often betrayed, and of love for Manhattan. What a pleasure to see a film in black and white, incidentally, reflecting the fact that Manhattan is a town of little color apart from the red-light signs saying "DON'T WALK." Never was there a city of so many injunctions.

And what a pleasure, too, to see such an intelligently hilarious film. It is reared on the American references we all know: Bogart, for one; its Gershwin score, for another; and, most important, its doting Manhattan humor. Woody Allen is a Manhattan treasure, though he is travelling beyond that. He did in his imperially funny film "Interiors," which some people of less wisdom than he abused for its "seriousness" and Europeanness. The "seriousness" derived from thought, from amplitude of mind about beloved European accomplishment. The "seriousness" spoke eloquently of an exuberant love of past and foreign achievement. Underneath that, of course, there was invaluable sense and wit. Woody Allen is one of our most majestically comic citizens.

177

In this film, the man he plays—Isaac—is conceived as if to make a quiet nonsense of all the people who complained that in his last film, the aforementioned "Interiors," he didn't declare his Jewishness. In "Interiors," it was of no moment. But "Manhattan" is a fond and specific narrative of a city where Jewish intellectualism is characteristic. Isaac, aged forty-two, is having an affair with a seventeen-year-old girl of some unkindness (Mariel Hemingway), called Tracy. She clearly does a great deal of the blessed hairwashing that has been bred by TV advertisements. She is a girl incapable of travel in her head, of knowledge of the past, of dwelling in other cultures. Isaac has beautiful manners. He suffers a good deal from Tracy, who has good bones, as they say, and is never going to hanker after a face-lift. He sweetly lets her do the arithmetic of their comparative ages when he is trying to explain to her that he will be practically a geriatric case by the time she is grown up. There is a touching moment when he lifts her swooping glossy hair off her forehead to talk to her. He has always had terrible luck with women. Years ago, he wrote a short story about his mother called "The Castrating Zionist." One of his ex-wives (Meryl Streep) is now living with another woman, of all things. Isaac doesn't think much of this as a setup for his son, but he is polite about it. The ex-wife has floppy blond hair, too, and is writing an autobiographical book called "Marriage, Divorce, and Selfhood." Movie sales are spoken of. Her girlfriend (Karen Ludwig) is a grumpy woman with dark curly hair who doesn't speak much but would, at anybody's guess, be truculent if Isaac were to oppose the selling of the film rights of the certainly overbearing book. She would be truculent, probably, to the extent of pouring boiling oil onto Isaac's head. The books in progress in this film are enough to ruin hardcover publishing in New York for good. An impossibly languid, tall Wasp man called Yale (Michael Murphy) is going to finish his book on O'Neill when he has finished buying his Porsche. Allen's cameraman, Gordon Willis—extraordinarily talented, now almost a member of what marvellously seems to be becoming the Woody Allen repertory company—undoubtedly photographs Yale straight on, but one has the sense that the character is being seen from the legs up. He bespeaks generations of Ivy League and orange juice and squash racquets, and has not much care for anyone. Isaac, on the other hand, will not cease defending his friends. The friends include his son and Mozart. They most definitely do not include his son's mother, whom he is resolute in regarding as having treated him horribly. He stands by Ingmar Bergman as a genius. He encourages Tracy—who has bought him a harmonica, which he turns over and over as if it were an indecipherable Sanskrit sandwich become stone—to go to London to learn acting. His true intellectual fellow is the fast-talking character played by Diane Keaton, a hapless but determined and clever girl whose analyst clings to her and telephones her at three in the morning. Isaac, quitting his job in TV, for very upright reasons, moves into a cheaper apartment, in a sequence that condenses all the jokes that have been made in the last couple of decades about Manhattan housing problems, though the jokes in this film, unlike most of the kind, are not knowing. Isaac keeps his dignity in spite of being confronted by sullen workmen twice his size and with the faces of gargoyles. He is not a complainer about trivia. When he has to give the Diane Keaton character a glass of water that he correctly says is brown—rusty pipes—you feel that his mind is on his dependable ally Mozart, or on worries about whether his son is going to have the chance to grow up to love Willie Mays and Groucho Marx and Marlon Brando as much as Isaac so excitedly does.

The script celebrates devotedness. It also celebrates the still existent enthusiasm of New York City, which used to be talked about by visitors as being like Benzedrine, and it is endearingly in love with late-night television. It abhors culture-vultures. There is a marvellously funny study of concealed fidgetiness at a classical concert. "Manhattan" is, among other things, a questioning of the bogus, and a definite putting down of the foot about pill popping, cigarettes, and liberated ex-wives writing exposés of their marriages at the cost of baffled children. The son in this film is much buoyed by the companionship of his incomparable father.

APRIL 30, 1979

179

IV

POWER ON FILM/FILM ON POWER

It is often said that politics are death at the box office. The remark holds about as much truth as the Sam Goldwynism that satire is what closes on Saturday night. Some of the greatest work in film has been done about politics, which is not, of course, a matter of showing the process leading up to dropping a note into a ballot-box. Fine and subtle things have been shown on film about the politics of Algeria (by Pontecorvo); about the means of sexist exploitation (by Godard, especially); about the changes from Batista's to Castro's Cuba reflected in the mind of the hero of a wonderful film called "Memories of Underdevelopment" by the Cuban Tomàs Gutierrez Alea; about the taste on the tongue of a staled leftist in Alain Resnais' "La Guerre est Finie."

And vice versa: power on film. The setting up of films is inevitably concerned with power, often wielded in England and America (where the money for all English-speaking films generally comes from) by tax-shelter idiots of no conviction or by boneheads with enormous empty desks whose occupation it is to get their secretaries, who speak like records, to say that their bosses have stepped out or are in conference. It follows that any filmmaker will know a lot

183

about power, and have a lot to say about it in this most powerful of all mediums. Every now and again, in the English-speaking countries, a few meditative and subversive films will slip past the money-men. Quite recently, in America, there have been some spirited examples: "Norma Rae," about women's trade unionism roots; "The China Syndrome," which predated the nuclear near-catastrophe at Harrisburg with the prescience that art so often has. Film is power's most potent means of expression: one wants to salute the men and women who manage, in some way or another, to use it to comment in their own singular voices on the financial and coercive powers that, purblind, think themselves to be manipulating their more intelligent apparent victims, the creators. It is a matter of slipping under the ropes. A Polish friend of mine, now dead, the filmmaker Andrzej Munk, told me in Poland that he always inserted into his films passages that he knew would stand out to the censors as mandatory cuttable material, so that he could get past them the sequences he actually thought more important. Artists and audiences are generally more subtle than money-men and censors.

Roberto Rossellini

History has been a long time maimed in the cinema and the theatre. There was Nahum Tate's revamped "King Lear" in the late seventeenth century, to bring up an old injury, with Cordelia surviving to marry Edgar, and Lear restored to the throne. There were the histrionics of Irving and Bernhardt, and the latter days of the Old Vic soon after the Second World War, when bawling actors' Adam's apples moved up and down like bubbles under amateur-laid wallpaper. We are still in the over-jocose reign of outdoor Shakespeare in New York's Central Park and London's Regent's Park, interrupted by the noise of politely ignored planes and police sirens, the gentle plop of marijuana smoking, and the fake camaraderie of braved-out drizzle. We are still suffering historically set rock films about ancient and very spoiled martyrs in the desert who behave like movie celebrities with introductions to the local consul. We still have a vein of exceeding piety when we are making films about famous men of art. ("Ludwig," says Schubert's stepmother to Beethoven in a loopy film about composers made a few years ago, "I'm very worried about Franz. He can't finish his symphony.") As presented in the cinema and the theatre, history doesn't often look as if it had ever actually occurred. Clothes are pristine; great names are freely dropped ("Michelangelo, are you or are you not going to finish that ceiling?" says the movie of "The Agony and the Ecstasy"); unreal emotions are stirred; paintbrushes are flung down in a pot; a Middle Ages monk lifts his arms to the heavens to say that he foresees great changes ahead, leaving us to discover a short pair of nylon socks under his robe.

It has taken filmmakers and playwrights engaged in projects of real intellectual purpose to dramatize history as if it were happening now: as it seems to in Brecht's theatre in East Berlin, for instance, and in Peter Watkins' B.B.C. film "The Battle of Culloden" (shown here at the end of March), and in Roberto Rossellini's new films of historical reconstruction. The hero of early Italian neo-realism, the director of "Open City" and "Paisan," among others, has set himself an immense task of extension. In movies mostly made for Italian television and now filtering through here, he takes on a lot: nothing less than the intellectual record of three or four continents, shot as if it were our contemporary. He calls it "an alphabet book of ideas," in a tonic mood of modesty about the complicated. The endeavor is being marvellously carried out in well over thirty films that give you, in each case, a realistically imagined account of some crucial shift in man's conscience, in his use of power, and in his progress with art, architecture, city planning, and science, by people buoyed up to pursue the long combat between religious obscurantism and early humanism. Rossellini is equipped for the job not only by his well-known skill with nonprofessional actors, not only by his grasp of the drift of events, but also by his lucid ear for hypocrisies, for claims of novelty, and for edgy laggards. Throughout his films, we hear the breathlessness as dawdlers pant to keep up with a changing age. His heroes, like

Brecht's, often come in the shape of opportunists who are able to clear some hurdle of outworn custom through politicking or accidents of circumstance. They effect change because they are born into a particular place, with particular parentage, dowry, or need, or because they are in conflict with their times. Rossellini's new films deal with our stumble out of the Dark Ages back to the very places where we had been before the spread of monotheism. Again and again, one recognizes as credible his view of long-dead mortals who seem at this moment engaged in the Renaissance and in the conflict between the bribery of religion, the graft of secular power, and the pull of forbidden rationalism. The war is always between a man and his time. The heroes of Rossellini's new films tend to be sustained by reason, but they are often undercut by reigning vestiges of the mystic, and they are never shown as innately heroic. In the director's glorious "The Rise of Louis XIV," for instance, one looked at the Sun King and prepared to be blinded by the glare; instead, one saw a quail-shaped boy, endowed with a languid Volumnia of a mother and living in a world of barber-surgeon quacks more skilled in eavesdropping and scornful cringing than in medicine. In the same way, Pindar long ago spoke of the townsman as an ordinary fellow; it took a Macedonianized and, worse still, a Romanized Greece to show him as a giant. It is not the physical but the ethical weight that revives us in the presence of certain Masaccios, in a way that Michelangelo himself seldom equals.

Now, made in the same spirit as "The Rise of Louis XIV," there is a Rossellini three-part history named "The Age of the Medici," each part running eighty-four minutes, and a separate film named "Pascal," all just seen at the New York Cultural Center, along with "Augustine of Hippo." They will be shown this autumn at the First Avenue Screening Room as part of a Rossellini retrospective. His new kind of filmmaking sees the history of art and thought as more concerned with problems than with personalities. Most historical movies are informative: his are kindling. What matters, he says, is not the existence of heroes but the noble option of asking new questions. The works endorse and tune humanist inquiry, like the paintings, architecture, inventions for measuring perspective, and ambulatory debates shown in "The Age of the Medici."

The Florentine influence on the rest of Europe must rank as one of the most worthy penetrations of any culture in history. Rossellini shows us Florence as a smallish, gabbling, discursive town of cash-mongers, usurers, artists' workshops with the doors open onto sunny streets full of passersby powdered with dust, and noble, well-read rulers with the patron's thirst for posthumous fame. The Medici enforce alliances, receive emissaries, commission paintings and churches and villas, conquer rivals, and dun debtors. Cosimo opens up his bank to the Pope, and at the same time gives expedient hospitality to the Patriarch of Constantinople in an effort to reconcile the Roman and Byzantine Churches. The scholarly money-grubber's religious negotiations have an obvious parallel in his efforts to store in his own city the texts and the architectural records that were the achievements of Rome and Greece. "Not our Florence. The *Republic* of Florence," says this undisputed, arrogant, contradictorily visionary prince. He was filled with the typical Renaissance ambition for glory and immortality, but it was coupled with the cunning of a modern and finite diplomat. He also had the aesthetic adventurousness to defy moribund peasant piety by encouraging the representation of Jesus as human. (Christ is seen through a man's mind, so he has a man's image; if an ox could draw, it would draw him as an ox.) The country people are scandalized but fascinated. They still come to pray in the great churches that we now know as faded, and that were then also faint, because the murals and ornaments were barely sketched in.

Under Cosimo, we witness portraiture becoming more than a matter of making effigies. Horses like the heavy-fetlocked nags we see pulling the papal studded trunks reattain the role they possessed in classical mythology, which symbolically had them as the steeds that bore souls aloft. The time abounded in devices to make spectators take stock of themselves. Though it was full of the humanist dread of death, the dread was mixed with a strange exaltation at the idea of dying well which was characteristic of the Renaissance and which Rossellini also finds in Blaise Pascal.

Not every city in Italy welcomed Florence's amazing activity. In a complex scene of mistrust, politesse, and veiled ambitions going on in an architectural workshop, we see the ruler of Rimini commissioning a church from Leon Battista Alberti which Alberti insists must be only the casing, aware of a rival local architect standing at his side who is responsible for the designs of the chapels within, professionally despised by the great visitor. The lord of Rimini wants a city built for battle. He wants as a living-place a commanding villa with the attributes of a fortress. Alberti, a long-nosed, skeptical man who is, with Cosimo, one of the two viewing points of the film, dryly suggests a villa at the very top of a hill looking down onto a town split up into unconnected regions without arches across the streets. The notion fits his precept of functionalism—a tyrant must have a tyrannically planned city to look down upon, just as a farmer must have housing that also suits his animals, "and not forgetting his wife"—but it fights sorely with his concept of an amiable conglomerate like Florence, in which the unit is the family multiplied. The Florentine idea was destined to gleam through the despot's wishes, and Rimini found itself landed with some still extant creations of a loveliness more playful than even the mother city would have allowed itself to cherish in this time of its most severe and fevered invention. Even Rome was then Florence's suburb, glossed over and swarming with brigands. We see planners in crypts dripping with damp and covered with lichen trying to imagine the lost or buried glories of ancient Rome. Like human hair retaining its color on a corpse, the stage thunder and monumental ornamentation sometimes evident in Roman antiquity kept a sepulchral animation in the period before it was restored. But Rossellini is resistant to melodrama. It is typical of him that his wonderful Medici films should be so full of the low-toned, urgent, abstract discourses of Florence, and of small-town energy and rows and droppings-in. The atmosphere that he catches is full of easy perambulations from one local figure to another: gossip about Brunelleschi or Donatello, a resentful mutter from Ghiberti about not having won the competition to do the cupola and lantern of the Duomo when he had vanquished other contestants so magnificently in the contest to design and make the bronze Baptistery doors, a visiting Englishman whining in a grandee voice about the state of the mere wooden roads and houses in London. Rossellini's town skims with familial fights and excitable exclamations, overriding the Medici canniness about loot which made the great events of thought and art possible. His sage Renaissance Florence has the mood of a hamlet on the verge of a longed-for wedding feast that is not going to be marred for the bride or the guests by the machinations of in-laws or matchmakers.

"Pascal" is self-contained, like each of the three Medici films. It is set two centuries later, naturally, but the domesticated, easy style and the fascination of the discourses are the same. (Rossellini wrote the films in collaboration, using contemporary sources.) The dubbing of the Medici films is bad, but "Pascal" is subtitled. The structure of all the films is a matter of accurate balance and proportion. It seems no accident that Rossellini's father was an architect. The director-architect son here shoots in long takes with unagitated camera movements, so that the intellectual debates about aesthetics, learning, and religion seem to sail. Young Pascal, working among geometrical instruments, using a pair of bellows, a syringe, and a pipette of mercury to demonstrate his newfound theory of the existence of the vacuum, is a red-eyed, urgent, pallid young scholar who embodies in his far from strong flesh the conflict between science and religious dogma. His notion of the vacuum offends the Church. A vacuum is nothing; therefore it cannot have been made by God; therefore it cannot exist. Pascal has proved that it does. Indeed, he would dearly like to make his own soul a vacuum to be filled by the self-knowledge that he thinks of as coming from God—though he suddenly becomes a sharp rationalist about his sister's swooning lack of charity when she announces that she wants to become a nun and to desert him for the Jansenists in spite of his illness and their father's recent death.

The film is full of physical and metaphysical conflicts that have to be reconciled: good fortune, servants, four-poster beds shrouded in beautiful brocade, patrons ready to support the pursuit of knowledge in return for a little fawning; on the other hand, no medical information, cruel remedies, unrelieved cold, no patronage for any scientific research considered heretical. The male Pascals are independent spirits who wonder in spite of the Church. But the Church is a dangerous enemy. We see clerics trying a woman for witchcraft in a context of argument that is intellectually from a world completely different from the witch-trial scene in Ken Russell's hysterical "The Devils." It might have been written by Shaw. It perfectly supports Pascal's suspicion that a man is living in perilous times when people are full of opinions and void of knowledge. The film is like "The Age of the Medici" in its gifts. All of Rossellini's new movies are intellectually elating, benevolent in their detail, and remarkable in the time they allow for dissertations more complex and beguiling than anything else in the world's popular cinema. For these films are profoundly populist: no one could mistake as anything else their view of the possible unity of thinking, art, and horse sense.

MAY 13, 1974

Retorts to "The Birth of a Nation"

Black American films have often been insults, pieces of burnt-cork condescension, stale jokes played on ground-down people. They have also served as cheap babysitters, models of glamour and bravery, and sermons on the theme of the all-American tenet of wishing to be middle-class. The common notion of the black American film—as it was until lately, before "Claudine" and "Sweet Sweetback's Baadassss Song"—has compounded Stepin Fetchit, Mammy, jazz, God, a villian who comes to a bad end, women intended to do laundering, and drink intended to bring forgetfulness. A pretty heroine was seen as a scrubber or as yet another cripple to be left behind on the frantic crawl up the scale, not as a worshipped flower-faced Gish girl wrapped in tissue paper like an orchid; and liquor was an anodyne to be swigged alone, not Moët & Chandon to be shared with friends. Life held very little courtliness, very few friends.

Independent black cinema, which struggled to be different, was born of the shift West to Hollywood after the First World War.

Black independent filmmaking, in reality often dependent on white backers, seized on the emptied studios in New York and Philadelphia and Chicago and Kansas City to make films for the ten million-odd audience of blacks unspoken to. More directly, independent black movies made the necessary riposte to the great but bigoted "The Birth of a Nation," with its D.W. Griffith vision of slaves run amok, the flickering masterpiece against which the six-year-old N.A.A.C.P. wanted a court injunction. In 1918, three years after the Griffith film was released, the Birth of a Race Photoplay Corporation released "The Birth of a Race" as its own counterblast, starting with money that was raised by the black middle class to refute Griffith. The capital was ultimately white, and the film dire for lack of money, confidence, and experience. Battle spectacles are juxtaposed with cut-rate footage, and the social lesson taught is the craven one that was to become familiar: fit in with the existing, white-regulated order.

In the boom years of the twenties, the flailing imitations of Hollywood multiplied. They were about the hope of moving up which has made so much of modern life a matter of elbowing away the neighbors and banging doors into followers' faces. In Hollywood-infected black films, the nub of things was to push your drunken father under the carpet and to leave Mom to scrape her knuckles on a washboard—or, more recently, to fob her off with a washing machine that she sits in front of to watch pajama legs go round and round as if she were a cat mistaking the machine for a television set. Even the independent twenties films are about passing for white; about leaving girlfriends behind in the struggle; about aspiring to be a doctor or a lawyer or a landowner, or anything but one of the Hollywood black stereotypes of the rolling-eyed buffoon, the uncontrollable villian, the faithful servant. The limits of possibility are a low ceiling in a cell too small to stand up in. People crawl on all fours, as if they were in a Beckett play: and don't most of us, black and white, though it is taking us a long time to hear the others who are gasping for air? Move first one leg, now one arm, now the other leg, now the other arm. On the knees, can't get up; a wounded bull in the ring.

Before the Second World War, there were about seven hundred ghetto movie houses. They were nearly all owned by whites. There is something unspeakably sad about the wood-shaving films that were being sold in them as food for ten million people. It is not only that the blacks who made the films were barred from knowing anything about film technique and distribution, and were dependent on tenth-rate white personnel who took no trouble except to make a fast buck, and were forced to haul prints around in the backs of old cars to be shown in churches or schools or revival-meeting halls. It is also that the rules of social strata were usually held to be binding and immutable, and that ignominy at the hands of other breeds led to the dealing out of disrepute to your own. The black women in the films have to be bashed about to get them to show proper respect: "To make a woman love you, knock her down," says an advertisement for Oscar Micheaux's "The Brute" (1920). So much for aspiration. In the Colored Players Film Corporation of Philadelphia's "The Scar of Shame" (1928), which has been showing at the Whitney Museum as half of a two-part program about early black independent filmmaking, a pretty mulatto girl gets married to a dandy who fancies himself as coming from an unreachable higher class and refused to take her home to meet his family. "Caste is one of the things that Mother is very determined about," says the hero, so driving his wife back to the dog days, to live now with a raffish racketeer. When the husband finds her with the racketeer, the two men fire at each other, and she is accidentally shot in the neck. She recovers, and starts to work in a speak-easy as an entertainer, wearing a pathetic tulle bow tied at the side of her neck, like a kewpie doll. "Caste is one of the things that Mother is very determined about": yes, indeed. Today, one is struck by the gallantry, anguish, and startling merriment that underlie the making of these films. The hopes held out were little to live on. Fatalism reigned. Louise's "scar of shame" (which "marred her beauty," says a subtitle) was the inevitable product of a broken home, according to the film's deep-breathing introductory titles. In the black films made until very recently—even in the independent ones—white mores held sway but God decided that everything was against their realization. The aspirations were white but blackness was a fact that made them stillborn. The most you can hope for, these black pictures say to us, is to emulate white table manners, white aesthetic standards, even white accents; though every now and again, even in films made long ago, black idioms break through. There is a subtitle in the silent, improvised "The Scar of Shame" about ways not to have "miss-meal cramps." It is the phrase of a tenth of the nation with much more than a tenth of the national troubles and much more than a tenth of the national inventiveness. There is scathing additional cruelty in the fact that the talkies, which did so much to inhibit black independent moviemaking, were first made famous by Al Jolson, a white man in blackface.

It is a sad fact of history that the Negroes themselves agreed on a visual code of villainy: the wicked in Negro films were the most black, the good were the most nearly white. Mulattoes could "pass." All the same, determinism ruled them. They couldn't go any higher than they were born. Which reflected—still reflects —an appalling truth. Warner's "Hollywood Hotel" (1937) breaks ground by showing a jazz group that mixes whites and blacks; but in the South the sequences with the black Lionel Hampton on xylophone were cut. It was all right to be a black popular musician, but only if you were performing with blacks. Other professions were more difficult. The great Lena Horne recalls that she sorely wanted to be an actress in her youth but that she opted to sing; she had a better chance that way.

In "Broken Strings" (1940), an affecting social melodrama being shown at the Whitney—written and starred in by Clarence Muse, directed by Bernard Ray—we see the violinist hero suffering suddenly from a left hand that is neurologically crippled. He has to have an expensive operation. His young violinist son earns hospital money by playing swing. But the father threatens him with a beating for his love. The father, black, has white musical ambitions: he is a classical violinist, and swing is for colored people. Conventions cruelly sedate the rebelliousness that could have been expressed

193

then in the movies. A white film man is quoted by contemporary records as having said, "We're crazy about our colored associates. We find them willing, eager, accomplished, and always gay. There's never a dull moment when a Negro film is in production." This about people who in a film (Micheaux's "The Exile," of 1931) or in life itself could be doomed by having a sixteenth of a sixteenth Negro blood in the veins. This when films showed the deserving weak triumphing over the unjust strong but when deserving picture-making itself was limited to making ten-thousand-dollar movies to be shown in segregated and wretched cinemas that had in no way triumphed.

The triumph is in things like the life history of, say, Oscar Micheaux, by all accounts a born storyteller and a cheerful con man who exercised his boon gifts from the bottom of a very cheerless ditch. He was his own copywriter and salesman. He would even somehow float stocks to get films finished, and persisted in refusing to show his movies in churches, perhaps because of the history of his knavish father-in-law, a minister. Micheaux started adult life as a Pullman porter. From 1919 to 1948, he wrote and distributed over twenty features. He seems to have been not only some sort of visionary but a director breathtakingly tough on his actors, who worshipped him. Evelyn Preer, a star of his, recalls that for one scene he got her to walk through a pond that was supposed to be only up to her waist; but the water, she reports with some awe, was over her head, and she nearly drowned. One of the pictures Micheaux made with her was "Within Our Gates" (1920), which he boldly advertised as a preachment against race prejudice "full of details that will make you grit your teeth in silent indignation!" In 1928, he went bankrupt, but he bounced back. We can learn more about him from a forthcoming book by Pearl Bowser, of the Chamba Educational Film Services, who was called in by the Whitney Museum to put together the current program. In the meantime, his approach to his life still comes to us as a clear voice through air chattering with accents less blithe.

MARCH 29, 1976

Record of a Rascal Hunter

He crouches over his newspapers and *Congressional Records*, the great and irreplaceable I.F. Stone, political maverick and unique muckraker. His spectacled eyes and pen-sharp nose are as close to them as Toad to the steering wheel in "The Wind in the Willows" when Toad is spiritedly studying the road and honking an ancient motor horn, much as Stone has sounded alarms in handprinted broadsheets and rapscallion articles unmatched in English-speaking political affairs for two centuries. The marvellous nuisance-man of Washington hunts down fallacies in newsprint which even editors miss from one week to the next, and finds rascals in bound volumes that bore other reporters into a doze. He consumes print with an intensity as maniacal as Toad's in burning up the road, partly because of a deafness that led him to read instead of listen. Stone seems to grasp at this disability with tacit and stirring thanks for the way it focusses his senses. Head down, he quickly tears out scraps of the dozens of newspapers and magazines he regularly reads, being too impatient to use scissors, and orders them by a system that looks more like piling than filing. Yet he can find a reference in ten seconds—or immediately if it is in his mind, where it is usually stored.

An unobtrusively deft documentary called "I.F. Stone's Weekly" records the way he works. It was made by Jerry Bruck, Jr., with a lot of Stone's own fanaticism. The film commands a moved respect for its hero, who has been a loner all his life yet who has sustained a contagious sort of conviviality in his reporting. When people started subscribing to the newsletter called *I.F. Stone's Weekly*, which was a single-man job if there ever was one, they felt among friends because of his company. His voice carried. He sounded always as if he had air, repose, and comrades around him, even in the McCarthy days, when no newspaper would employ him. He had long since been forced to resign from the National Press Club for trying to entertain a Negro judge at lunch there. He was one of the first to go into the high-level lies about the Tonkin Gulf. No man has ever been more adept at hunting down bland whoppers, at detecting the hidden hush money for pressmen that is implied in their dining with canny political figures whom they might otherwise be free to bombard tomorrow, and at reporting world affairs with a mixture of scrupulous worry and the guttersnipe humor that is the sinew of America. The mixture is heartening, rare in life, unequalled in the history of modern lone reporting, and, above all, brave. Jerry Bruck shows us this modest man racing through bookshops for foreign newspapers and magazines, picking up books and dropping them again in the same movement as he looks for another to add to his pile, getting his newsletter off the presses (with a voice-over interpolation from the printers about his paying bills almost before they are sent). At an unaccustomedly swanky ceremony, to give Stone the Polk Award, he thanks people for "my first establishment award" and promptly goes on to talk exclusively about the forgotten achievements of George Polk in reporting the Greek struggle against "our first Vietnam."

The famous *Weekly* began with a tiny circulation. Until it was discontinued, in 1971, the circulation manager was Stone's wife. She is seen saying briefly in the midst of feeding the Addressograph that if her husband stopped to organize his files he wouldn't have time to do his reading. There is a shot of Stone sending requested back issues of the *Weekly* himself, walking to the mailbox laden with batches of them. Another week, one sees him darting excitedly for records that a young assistant, later worn out by Stone's energy in research, admits to finding boring. Stone must have fatigued junior helpers by the dozen into taking to their beds. He has always been virtually alone.

Jerry Bruck, in putting his film together, shows much the same stamina and much the same style of seizing the point. (The movie is now showing in Chicago commercially, and at campuses all over the country. On April 24th, it opens in Texas; in mid-May it will play in New York.) When Stone is talking about the dread consequences of lunching with power for any impartial reporter, Bruck quietly cuts in a sequence of Ron Ziegler playing tennis at an athletic club with men who know how to deal with a social bribe even better than how to deal with a ball. Stone's own happy croak alternates with narration by Tom Wicker. Stone tells an audience about the day when he started tracking down a lie about underground atomic testing which "really began in the mind of that scientific screwball and real nut Edward Teller, because as we got close to an agreement with the Russians, he began to say, 'Suppose they test underground, or suppose they test on the dark side of the moon. . . . How will you know?'" Stone got his regular *Times* the next morning. As he puts it in the film, the *Times* wrote that underground tests the day before conformed "to the expectations of the experts, meaning Teller and Latter . . . that the tests would not be detectable more than two hundred miles away." But somewhere else Stone got a city edition of the *Times* with a shirttail saying that Toronto had detected them. In the late city edition, he found other shirttails, one from Rome, one from Tokyo, saying that *they* had detected them. "I thought, gee, I wish I had enough money to cable those places and find out what's going on." But he hadn't, so he stacked all the stuff in his basement, this elating man who can detect casuistry thousands of miles away yet hasn't the cash to send a cable about atomic testing. He waited. Events developed. The great powers came close to a test ban. The U.S.S.R. offered listening posts about five hundred and eighty miles apart. "Two days later the Atomic Energy Commission, which is in my opinion the most mendacious government agency in Washington," released to the press a report saying that tests could not be detected more than two hundred miles away. The obvious purpose—obvious to Stone, that is—was to make a liar out of Harold Stassen, who was negotiating with the Russians for President Eisenhower, and to undercut agreement. Stone says that he said to himself, "I've never been on a seismology story before," and he discovered by telephoning around town that the Commerce Department's Coast and Geodetic Survey had a seismology branch. So he jumped in his car and went down there. "And they were so glad to see a reporter. I don't think they'd seen a reporter since Noah—since there was a tremble from Mount Ararat when Noah's Ark landed and there was a wide squiggle on the seismometer." We are glad to see a reporter, Mr. Stone—all the rest of us, who have read you all these years—and we thank Mr.

Bruck for this footnote to your nobility and funniness, though I don't suppose that you would want us to dwell on compliments.

Now Bruck is investigating ways that independent filmmakers might distribute their own films, circumnavigating the present vagaries without having to join tennis clubs or send cables. Bruck really does modestly exist in the footsteps of the indispensable I.F. Stone. On to the next piece of research, and the next discovery drawn from records devotedly stacked in the basements of good men's minds.

APRIL 22, 1974

A Filmmaker's Meditation on America

While I was watching Peter Davis's "Hearts and Minds" for the second time, at a noon public performance at Cinema I, a woman of about sixty-five came alone into the three-quarters-full theatre. The other people in the audience were nearly all men, also unaccompanied. The woman hurried to the row I was in. She stood stock-still beside me for a few minutes, looking at the screen with festering surprise. Obviously, when I thought about it, the title had misled her: she had escaped from the rain outside to see what she expected would be a love story; instead of that, there was a screen showing wounded Vietnamese, wounded G.I.s, assured United States policy-makers in offices spouting upholstered bombast, confused and skeletal Vietnamese sorrowfully quitting the debris of their American-bombed homes. The woman, who was wearing a plastic mackintosh and carrying an umbrella, a book, and two shopping bags, moved to stand in front of me with her back to the screen. She said softly, "Oh dear. I hope it isn't a war film." I said that it was an anti-war film, about the effects of Vietnam, and that I believed she'd be interested. She shook her head wanly but pressed onward and over me to sit two seats away. A three-dollar ticket is a three-dollar ticket, and it was wet outside. I glanced at her now and then. She took in everything, looked startled, cried. At the end, she went on sitting in her place, with her eyes still on the now blank screen, and said to me, without turning round, "I didn't know we'd done that." Pause. "I liked what the American woman said about a mature person's being able to make a mistake, so why can't a government?"

It would be a million pities if the inapt outburst by Bert Schneider (the film's co-producer with Peter Davis) in reading aloud a cable from the Provisional Revolutionary Government's Ambassador to the Paris peace talks, Dinh Ba Thi, which he did in the heat of accepting an Oscar, were to debase the film into seeming a simpleminded broadsheet or a piece of penny-in-the-slot cant about the woes of imperialism. I say "a million" because before the outburst and the passing hubbub of complaints "Hearts and Minds" had every chance of reaching the minds of a million Americans likely to react with anger to a picture thus falsely branded as didactic but with interest and warmth to the reflection upon America that this picture really is. The Academy Awards incident was a red herring for a number of reasons. In the first place, it was ex post facto, and as irrelevant to the content and meaning of the film as the clothes that someone might wear on the Academy's platform; the picture itself is what critics and audiences need to address themselves to, and that was completely edited and finished in July of 1974. In the second place, the matter and the intention of the film are Peter Davis's, not Bert Schneider's: Schneider played no part in either the shooting or the editing, and, according to Davis, was generous enough to refrain even from trying to have any political effect on the tone of the picture. In the third place, Schneider's speech added editorial comment to a film that Davis had been very careful to allow to speak for itself. As to Davis's credentials as a reporter—and it is vital that we trust him to be a good witness—there was courage and probity in his TV program "The Selling of the Pentagon," which had a more trenchant and maybe less fully adult structure, and I am persuaded that the even temper, the heed for justice, and the charity of spirit that flood "Hearts and Minds" give it the right to be considered not only a true report but also a work that has the individual point of view possessed by art.

Before making the bulk of the film—he had already shot some footage—Peter Davis went in 1972 to a lot of America's national parks. He wanted to clear his own head by asking people there whether they felt differently about their country then from the way they had felt at the end of the Second World War (or, if he was interviewing someone too young to remember that, at the time of Korea). Only the last of his series of questions was about Vietnam. He chose to do his reconnaissance in national parks because he thought the people there would be in a reflective mood, with America on their minds. The broad range of their responses has been assimilated into the film, along with much, much else, for "Hearts and Minds" is not at all adequately defined if it is taken to be a mere piece of adversary journalism speaking up against the war. It is an extremely troubled and contemplative picture about some of the origins and some of the consequences of the American involvement in Vietnam. Impressive that a work so coherent and mature can have been completed when the book is even now not closed. I don't mean that the happenings since the time when the footage ends, in July of 1973, have made it obsolete—not a bit, unless a sense of history is something to be pulped when it is less than two years old. It is from the attitudes and actions depicted in the film that the present terrible debacle has flowed. The film's antennae are very alert, and the information received is not editorially interpreted: it is merely passed on to us, which is why it can powerfully affect minds as open as the mind of the woman who was sitting near me in the cinema.

Without commentary, "Hearts and Minds" emphasizes the psychically cogent fact that the Americans on combat duty in Vietnam were often fighting a battle with the invisible. When a high-flying aviator let loose a load of bombs, his imagination declined to saddle his conscience with visions of the almost impossible to take in, and decided that what his eyes couldn't see didn't exist. A veteran from Oklahoma describes "the thrill you get when you see something explode," and goes on to say, "You never could see the people. You never saw any blood. You never could hear any screams. It was very clean. I was a technician." Earlier, he likens bombing to "a singer doing an aria." Not at all a bad man. But he couldn't manage, at the time, to put himself in the position of the people on the ground who were the audience of that lethal aria. The film takes on the task in his stead. Ruined peasants, robbed of everything, speak with tragic brevity. An aging Vietnamese standing without anger in the wreckage of his bombed home says, pointing to a pile of rubble, "I used to raise pigs here." "Where was the kitchen?" asks an American voice offscreen. The man gestures to a bomb crater. And a very old woman, toothless, is asked about her dead sister of seventy-eight. "What did she die of?" "Bombs," says the woman simply, as if bombs were a natural malady. There is only one outburst against the Americans, and that is good-humored: "First they bomb as much as they please, then they film." (Peter Davis was rather good-humored to use it.) One sees footage of Nixon, and contrasts his gobbledygook with the victims' eloquence. "Throughout the war in Vietnam, the United States has exercised a degree of restraint unprecedented in the annals of war," the film shows him idiotically saying. Back in Vietnam, peasants look at fragmented bodies and at splinters of pretty crockery lying in the mud. A Vietnamese woman, crazed with grief, tried to climb into a grave. Straight afterward, General Westmoreland says soberly, "The Oriental doesn't put the same high price on life as does the Westerner. Life is cheap in the Orient. As the philosophy of the Orient expresses it, life is not important." The cut between the two scenes is not a piece of easy pointmaking. Both things happened, and their weight doesn't lie in their juxtaposition. If all the sequences in "Hearts and Minds" were to be thrown up in the air and put together again in random order, the meaning of the film would still be the same.

Practically everyone we listen to in "Hearts and Minds" seems to be in the dark. For Americans, here or there, the war made no sense. We see an American in his own country saying, "I think we're fighting for the North Vietnamese, ain't we?" An American soldier in combat says, "They say we're fighting for something. I dunno." Everyone had to find shelter somewhere. The Vietnamese found it in religion, in doggedness, in making coffins if they could afford the wood. Most Americans found it in distance. Some of these—Daniel Ellsberg and Clark Clifford, for instance, who both speak in the film—found it in a change of opinion so violent as to amount to an act of self-ransack. Americans in Vietnam found it in willed ignorance, or in flag wagging, or in the offering of small kindnesses, or in conduct so callous that there was no chance that life in Vietnam would relate to anything they knew. We see them behaving unspeakably in a brothel. A G.I. in a street scene, after a scornful appraisal of the worth of a whore whom he assesses through a semi-curtained window, responds viciously to the price she asks. "Too much," he says. Too much to pay for *her*. A repatriated American stiffneck who has been imprisoned by the North Vietnamese finds his particular solace in not budging an inch from the mindless chauvinism he set out with. Back in America, heavily still in uniform on a rabble-rousing lecture tour, he says of the look of Vietnam, "If it wasn't for the people, it would be very pretty." This occurs in a Catholic grammar school, what's more, and in answer to a question from a child, what's more. The future, if it is recoverable, lies with other sorts of mind. Perhaps the most passionately searching scenes in this most searching film are the ones that put on record the changing thought of some returned G.I.s. We are aware of their trying very hard to take in the unassimilable at last. If they can do it, it will be an expression of some pliant natural genius. A start has been made. The same chilling aviator who talked of himself as a technician at the beginning of the film appears with a new view of things near the end. He is asked by an unseen American if he thinks we've learned anything from all this. He says, with his head down, "I think we're trying not to." Then he looks up, and grins through tears that he struggles for a painfully long time to shed. "I think *I'm* trying not to, sometimes. I can't even cry easily— my manhood image."

"Hearts and Minds" isn't really so much a film opposing the American intervention in Vietnam as an inquiry into the effect that the Vietnam war has had on Americans. It is about America's view of itself, which has been knocked into a still inchoate new form. In its essence, "Hearts and Minds" is a complex tale about possessing apparently infallible power and then finding that it doesn't work. Peter Davis has thought hard, and he sees the Vietnam war as the vehicle for that sense of power in America. After the Second World War—when America's military force had been used on a side that was, for once, simply and visibly the right one—the nation's strength seemed mighty enough to have been God-given. Now, for a growing mass of the population, the notion that any military power can be God-given has crumbled. With it has gone a crucial tenet in the established dogma of Americanness, which had come to include an almost religious notion that there was rectitude in winning. The belief developed from this unconscious popular formula in logic:

We have triumphed in the past by might.
In the past we have been right.
∴ Might will go on being right.
∴ America will go on being right.

By extension, since God's will is right (=triumphant), America is divinely selected to be right (= triumphant).

∴ America and the Almighty will go on triumphing hand in hand, equipped with the fire and the sword.

Davis's film takes another look at this edifice of fallacies. He gazes particularly hard at the step that equates blessedness and winning, and concludes that it will just about do to nourish the fervent souls of drum majorettes. The picture shows us an array of majorettes on a football field, looking as awkwardly missionary as a parade of topless waitresses about to be decorated by the First Lady on the twelfth anniversary of Toplessness. Quietly emphatic on the same obvious but crucial topic of winning, Davis catches a hysterical football coach yelling victory exhortations in a locker room, where athleticism and a sense of deified purpose oddly mingle; he also includes footage of a fatuous minister urging high-school boys to win a game ahead. "This is serious business that we're involved in, and that's religious, and God cares," the minister says, as if football were a dummy run for what he would probably call "the great game of life itself." He does actually say, "May you be winners in the big game, but, more importantly, winners in the biggest game of all, which we all play. Let us pray."

But the theorem about the divine right of winning has now been disproved as thoroughly as the divine right of kings once was, and more traumatically, because there are a greater number of decent, shamed, confused citizens here than there were ever despotic monarchs in Europe. Americans have had to cope for years with an instinct that something terribly important was happening in Southeast Asia, though there has never been a comprehensive attempt by a President or a TV network or a major film company to vindicate their instinct. They have had only their nerve ends to judge by; and the knowledge of the risks run by draft dodgers, who must have been empowered by a very strong idea; and the evidence of brave, prophetic independent films, like Eugene S. Jones's "A Face of War" (1968) and now Peter Davis's thematically more complex picture. Television news has sold the public short with its method of tucking shots of faraway suffering between commercials for hair shampoos and parish-pump stories about this week's Con Edison mishap. Treated so, the repeated pitiful faces on the screen have been reduced to nothing more than the insignia of suffering, for we have been given no sense of cause and effect.

"Hearts and Minds" is endowed with that sense. We have been sorely in need of it, because the once-supportive theorem about power has been in visible collapse for years. The film recalls the way President Johnson, poorly grasping the need to turn the impossible war into a police action in the public mind, subconsciously undercut the effort by falling into the trap of continuing to say, "Make no mistake about it. . . . We are going to win." The urge to "win" in the traditional bellicose style has revealed itself to be a dud impulse, and Peter Davis shows us that the revelation has cruelly baffled many veterans and many civilians. So far, only a few voices in the Republic have been raised to express a point of view as ample and poised as the one that underlies "Hearts and Minds." Davis understands that, by the criterion of "winning," the "loss" of

Vietnam—which never belonged to anyone but the Vietnamese anyway—has dealt a body blow to a long-entertained American notion that "sincerity" is enough not only in the holding of a belief but also for insuring conquest by the use of force. Sincerity has proved itself *not* to be enough; so has the parallel American ethic of diligence and its due reward. Simple shows of devoutness and industry on the part of Presidents and their advisers aren't any longer adequate. The acts of going to church with the family on Sunday and of working on tropical holidays solve no complicated international crises. Nor does American might, which has turned out to be not at all a sacred virtue bound to succeed: it hasn't triumphed in any sense in Indo-China, and its profane exercise there has caused far more suffering than all the other unholy Holy Wars put together. But a lot of Americans still seem haplessly eager to remain superstitious, even if they are not devout and abjure belief in an afterlife. Faith in America's power used to be capable of deputizing for faith in God, because it helped zealots to dismiss the power of other political systems with as much beatific security as monotheists dismissing heathens. Now that the power has been found wanting, it is the superstitious here who have been most painfully affected. It is for these very people, perhaps, that there is the greatest sanity and balm to be had from "Hearts and Minds." The film takes a far kindlier and longer-sighted view of the capacity of the American national character to receive and absorb tormenting new information about itself than most citizens now do in this shaken, guilt-freighted land of the fortunate.

APRIL 28, 1975

"The Poor Don't Care What They Look Like"

Remarks made to me lately in answers to questions about Latin America, quoted because of the new Constantin Costa-Gavras film

"State of Siege," which is nominally about Uruguay but concerns the whole continent, and also paternalism, foreign investment, questions of public responsibility, processes of change:

Brazilian Unpublished Novelist of Seventeen, Just Arrived in North America, with a Bad Cold: South America needs strong governments, because it is underdeveloped and we have to wake up from our primitivism. Military governments are strong governments. They are the only ones strong enough to fight big powers who have education.

Uruguayan Laborer: The Tupamaros are our guerrillas. They come from the middle-up class. They come from universities.

Wife of a Millionaire Plastic Surgeon in Venezuela: We're going to leave Caracas. There are no more patients for my husband to treat. The lepers? Oh, the poor don't care what they look like.

Brazilian Intellectual in His Forties: Brazil is the most imperialist country in Latin America.

Argentine Waiter and Shop-Owner: Brazilians have never seen anything, so they expect nothing.

Argentine Café-Owner: I don't think the Peronist government is good, or the best, but I like a change. The military did nothing for Argentina.

Young Argentine Mechanic: Yes, the military did nothing for Argentina. What the Peronists are trying to do is become more Socialist, but they have no plans. The unions are very strong, and the Peronists control the unions. The military asked for key positions in the Peronist government. If it doesn't get them, it may overthrow the government as before, and perhaps that would be civil war, because many members of the military are for Peronism.

* * *

BRAZILIAN BOY OF EIGHTEEN, BUTCHER'S ASSISTANT: Under the military we have always been very much a colony of the United States, but now the people are enlightened by our boom. Brazil will soon be the biggest country in the world.

LATIN-AMERICAN ECONOMIST: The boom is from American investment and American markets.

BRAZILIAN COFFEE-BOY: Military governments tend to be leftist. Strong governments are leftist governments.

YOUNG URUGUAYAN TRANSLATOR: We are a very small country between Brazil and Argentina, but our guerrillas are serious. They know the truth about charity from big countries. Charity is guns. We would rather have choice.

SCOTTISH NURSING SISTER IN NEW YORK: A.I.D.? Assistance for Industrial Development, isn't it? Of course, in Scotland it means the Artificial Insemination Donor plan, for cattle and so on. I don't know why a beautiful country like America needs to inseminate anyone. Look at the mess England's made of converting Ireland ever since Cromwell. Wicked waste, all that I.T.T. money.

GEORGE STEVENS, JR., DIRECTOR OF THE AMERICAN FILM INSTITUTE, IN WASHINGTON, ABOUT THE CANCELLATION OF SHOWINGS OF "STATE OF SEIGE" AT THE NEW KENNEDY CENTER MOVIE THEATRE: I cancelled the showings entirely on my own judgment. Nothing to do with losing Nixon's money for the Institute. Though there were a lot of congressmen getting ready to support me on the cancellation. It was a question of taste, not of censorship: this picture rationalizes political assassination. I'm not against pictures people might call anti-American. I took "West Side Story" to Moscow. If it had been "The Ugly American" the Institute staff had picked, that wouldn't have been an ideal choice but one could have lived with it.

* * *

COSTA-GAVRAS: There is no connection between the assassination of the Kennedy brothers and the assassination of Dan A. Mitrione in Uruguay by the Tupamaros—Mitrione was the head of the public-safety division of the A.I.D. mission—because there is no evidence of concerted effort and political thinking by an intellectual group in the terrible Kennedy killings. As to what the film shows about A.I.D., my fellow-conspirator is a European—Franco Solinas, the writer of "The Battle of Algiers"—and you know more than we do, because you are in America. It is for all of you here to judge whether we did right in using the facts we have found out about Mitrione when he was supposed to be representing A.I.D.—his knowledge of Brazilian torture cases when he was in Brazil, the F.B.I. card he carried, the Uruguayan-police card he had undercover in Uruguay, the police training he went through in North America—and then whether people will understand us when we personify his story in our hero, who is by nature not such a bad man at all. It is not the facts of Mitrione's private life that are reproduced in our character. Only the public ones that we could be sure of by research.

A COLUMBIAN WHO DRIVES A TAXI TO EARN THE MONEY FOR COLLEGE TUITION: If there is a revolution in my country with people like the Tupamaros in it, I will leave New York and join it. And if there isn't one, when I finish my education I will go back and try to make one.

In the thoughtful new political film by Costa-Gavras, the third of a near-trilogy with "Z" and "The Confession," the character based on the assassinated Mitrione is called Philip Michael Santore. He is played by Yves Montand. Especially since "La Guerre Est Finie," Montand has contained exactly the nature of a certain kind of jaded, intelligent left-wing European. Hopes unfulfilled by events seem to be lying emptied in the dead air of his head. Montand can make idealism and radicalism look like habits of long ago. Nothing new here, he seems to be feeling, but still nothing to be given up. Life is full of a taste like sour wine, and of sleep lost on the undertaking of missionary tasks with vanished purposes. Whether Montand's quality has anything much in common with Mitrione's seems doubtful, for Montand is such a European. (So was Mitrione, actually, in a pedantic sense that is not to the point: he lived in Italy until he was two.) The experience of watching the film is like looking at the story through a prism. A Frenchman is playing a Latin-American-trained United States immigrant who is in naïve servility to a big proselytizing power that could be only America or a Communist force or an embattled Vatican. The prism does nothing unhelpful; in fact, it puts any propaganda content of the film at a useful distance. This picture is much less dizzying than the earlier ones. But it has the same narrative energy and the same whipping cuts; unless you see a Costa-Gavras picture two or three times, and if you naturally respond to more reposeful filmmaking, it is easy to find things in his movies glib. Terrifying political topics go by with a swiftness that seems meant not to trouble, and to make the problems look soluble. I don't think these bits of crabbiness are deserved, though, especially about the new film. One is simply in the presence of a director and a writer who prepare slowly for production but who value speed on the screen, and who are more interested in the sweeps and causes of events than in character. The Brechtian anti-typecasting of Yves Montand speaks for the director's and the writer's priorities. The chunkily debonair Renato Salvatori here plays no one to swoon about. He is a goonish A.I.D. hireling of forty called Captain López, flawless in hypocrisy, evasive under journalists' catechisms, and impeccably sad at official funerals.

It is August "in Latin America," says the script, but obviously Uruguay, though the place isn't stressed. The weather is wintry. One feels the particular chill of a flunkey nation. Police barriers everywhere. A man is frisked on a bus. The computer voices of messages transmitted on car radios control police movements. A man with the look of a foreigner peers into López's room. Then the corpse of Yves Montand is seen in a hospital. Medical notes are barked out. The body has been brought in from the back of a Cadillac with Montevideo license plates. The car was reported stolen the day before. Parliament votes for a national day of mourning. The Santore whom Montand plays was an A.I.D. "functionary." There is a pompous funeral procession. Courage sometimes prevails in the obsequious circumstances: "It is regrettable that the places reserved for the university president and faculty are empty," says the voice of a TV reporter, unseen. And the archbishop has refrained from giving the funeral oration for a man whom he knows to be another country's hireling. Cameras study the face of the widow. Her husband happened to be a likable man. It was his job, including training in torture, that made him humanitarianism's enemy. How much did his wife know about his job? Was she ignorant? Or his ally? Or even an accomplice? Perhaps she didn't ask questions. But one is at fault not to ask questions, suggests the picture.

Already, even before we are party to any of this, the utterances of officialdom have the ring of lies. What is meant by calling Santore in his eulogy "a victim of terrorism and violence"? It sounds like a don't-ask sign. Flashback to the kidnapping. The Tupamaros have been appropriating cars for it. Journalists question officials. "Will the terrorists demand ransoms?" "Or, as in Brazil, the release of political prisoners?" "We have no political prisoners here," a representative of law and order answers with dignity. "Only common criminals." "Don't you think the terrorists must have had huge numbers of supporters?" says one journalist. And another: "Is Brazil massing troops at our borders?" The state of affairs is said by still another journalist to be intolerable to the government. It is more intolerable to the country, retorts a correspondent with a wider view.

We see something of the city: ordered, ducal-looking official mansions with guards and quick escape routes; thousands of poorly dressed people going to work. Emergency powers are in operation, voted to last sixty days, now two years old. The word "Tupamaros"—the recognition that a guerrilla force even exists—is officially banned. Linguistics to deal with overwhelming reality. The journalists weren't aware of Santore's existence. He had no official position. Everything is clouded. Costa-Gavras has a growing respect for ambiguity, like the scriptwriter Solinas. Santore is described by the lofty A.I.D. director as "a specialist in communications." Captain López says to weary-looking, sage journalists, "Yes, A.I.D. collaborates with our police. . . . Safety measures affecting traffic." No, says the picture, it collaborates on coercion and torture.

Flash to another place. Santore is being questioned by young Tupamaros with gray-brown masks over their heads, showing only tired eyes, and mouths that look oddly made-up and pretty in the petrifying surroundings. Santore admits he was in Brazil and Santo Domingo, yes. His smile is not unsympathetic, and his ironies are unaggressive; he feels himself to be in command. "In 1964, Goulart's Brazilian democracy was overthrown by the military," says a young Tupamaro. Parliament was abolished, political parties, freedom of the press, trade unions. But you, you still stayed. . . . Johnson even sent congratulations a few hours before the *Putsch.*" "Political expediency," answers Santore casually, to which the inquisitor says, "And morality was guarded by Spellman's blessing." Another Tupamaro, very young, unmasked, intervenes, and simultaneously wishes he hadn't thought of the remark: "The American God is *putschiste.*" The interruption is over in a second, but the Tupamaro's regret stands for the film's benign over-all eye for muddle, for mistakes, for brave measures wrongly undertaken, for the paradox of a privately kind man like Santore countenancing torture by the Brazilian police, which he suavely calls Communist propaganda.

One begins to sense a curious intimacy built up hour after hour between Santore and the Tupamaros, like the tie that can bind torturer and victim as it was located by Sartre in his introduction to *The Question,* Henri Alleg's book about Algeria. Now and then in the film there is an offer of a cigarette, an exchange of current news when the inquisition for the day is over. Stretchers are used gently for wounded hostages threatened with assassination unless demands are met. A seized Brazilian diplomat in a little next-door room marked off by a curtain is less frank than Santore about his role as torturer. And there follows a dogfight in Parliament about foreign influences, foreign investment, the right to use the unmentionable vital word "Tupamaros." We are in a small country with colossal problems, tenacity, and will—a place where cops are often produced by hunger, and not only by some richer nation's masquerade of having a vocation for peace. Other people, out of the same hunger, become thieves. Hunger doesn't leave people many choices. Even Santore, who thinks he is the boss, is the lackey of his own catch phrases. His situation becomes piteous through the compassionate vision of the film. He realizes all too well the truth that, once captured, he is more useful to his government dead than alive. The local Minister for Foreign affairs is concerned to protect what he calls "sovereignty," which is like the sovereignty of "other interested countries;" the diverse countries are all of the same stripe when it comes to the question of individualism.

"State of Siege" is not about morals so much as about politics. It is not at all a romantic film but a grievous one. Cant kills. The picture deliberately hacks away all possibility of plot suspense. The grip of the story is in the possible twists and turns that casuistry can take, and it has two fine, inquiring minds controlling it.

ELECTRICIAN FROM URUGUAY: Ech, you have heard of the Tupamaros? But you have not been to Uruguay. Well, you know what is a peon? The Tupamaros are necessary because we are a peon country.

APRIL 14, 1973

Notes on Reporting and Fiction

Cloaked Identity

Constantin Costa-Gavras, director of "Z" and "The Confession," and Franco Solinas, writer of Gillo Pontecorvo's "The Battle of Algiers," have lately made a movie called "State of Siege." It was unwisely banned by the American Film Institute for its Kennedy

Center opening after being officially invited, but it is now in theatres all over the country and they are packed to the gunwales. Costa-Gavras's whipping cuts probably play more part in its popularity than Solinas's level-headed traditional Marxism, which shows us a Uruguay that believes itself to depend on United States aid but that actually contributes vitally to the United States economy every time a Uruguayan uses American toothpaste or swallows American aspirin.

The central character, an A.I.D. worker whose actions are villainous in the picture's terms, emerges as more hero than sinner, because he is played by Yves Montand, who irreversibly seems a rather exhausted good guy, carrying the sour taste of a jaded Europe on his tongue like cigarette fur on an all-night driver's. He doesn't seem to belong at all to the clan of energetic good-lookers who carry out the late President Kennedy's plan for benevolently collaring underdeveloped countries before Communism gets its foot in the door. His name in the identifiable affairs depicted was Dan A. Mitrione: an A.I.D. man assassinated by young Tupamaro guerrillas in 1970. But his name in the film is Santore. Why the change, when Solinas and Costa-Gavras insist on the social veracity of their sources? Shakespeare's "King Lear" obviously couldn't be accurately biographical, but there are verifiable cases, like Mitrione's, where future students are apt to be vitally misled by the bequests of our artists. "Hamlet" and "King Lear" merely pose as biographical; fiction of this sort has a freedom that journalism can't properly allow itself. The result of the name change in "State of Siege" is that a knife-blunting job is done on A.I.D. and on the involvement of big powers in the sovereignty of little powers. The casting of Yves Montand further dulls the blade. One is looking at Uruguayan events across reflecting cutlery: in what is specified only as "a real South American country," though it is identifiably Uruguay, one sees a very European and benign Frenchman playing a wicked American. It is like casting, say, Henry Fonda as Neville Chamberlain. The edges of the story don't bite. The Pentagon Papers would have meant nothing if they hadn't been about what turned out to be documented historical facts. "State of Siege" allows itself not the liberty of art but the cloaked name-calling of the New Journalism.

The Vehicle of Urgency

Any journalism is a powerful engine. Daniel Defoe—son of James Foe, a tallow chandler who lived in Cripplegate—often used the classic form of journalism for fiction. He used it in his *A Journal of the Plague Year*, which is written as if it were a contemporary chronicle. No one would believe from its sober, factual, brick-on-brick style that Defoe was actually only four when the Great Plague broke out, in the winter of 1665, and that he was using the instinct of a novelist in electing to end the book not with the real, purging climax—the Great Fire of 1666—but with citizens praising God for an abatement of the plague. Chekhov, greatest fiction writer of all the Russians, chose to work instead as a reporter in his *The Island: A Journey to Sakhalin*, which gives a firsthand account of the Czarist penal colony on Sakhalin Island. As for "State of Siege," you wonder why Solinas, in particular, didn't use the method of reporting, which implies not the Olympian omniscience of fiction but the "there are things we don't know" element in newspaper stories, which helped to make "The Battle of Algiers" so remarkable. A work using journalistic methods is a quick nail to drive into a subject, not a slow fuse, like a novel. The intellectual technique of "State of Siege" gives it an inapplicable stately look of factual dependability, for all the whirring style of the editing.

The Half Nelson of Semi-Biography

Cinéma Vérité about real people—"Salesman," "Marjoe," the Leacock and Pennebaker films, "Chronicle of a Summer"—often tells semi-truths, because the unadmitted presence of the camera forces more or less unreality on behavior, depending on how native the style of showoff is to the characters. Entertainment hucksters and, indeed, salesmen thrive on it; subjected to it, perfectly nice children tend to turn into little Shirley Temples. Girl models and ballet dancers, who are anyway used to inspecting themselves in looking glasses all the time, aren't modified by the presence of the camera, but most ordinary people are. So what looks like truth—a housewife with a shopping bag being interviewed on TV in the street—actually has less veracity than the same chronicle would probably have if it were played by an actress. Even drum majorettes get shy of a camera in a way they don't of a football crowd. In the Maysles brothers' "Salesman," the scenes of the Bible peddlers in people's front rooms ring sometimes dead false. The Richard Leacock film about the police at a convention in Hawaii, called "Chiefs," itself, for the same reason, has some of the hollowness of the backslapping he is trying to show us. In Howard Smith's and Sarah Kernochan's "Marjoe," the young evangelist of the title thrives on exhibitionism but seems—correctly, as it turned out—to be taking part in a story of conversion which is being told with hindsight. On the other hand, Jean Rouch's and Edgar Morin's interviews in "Chronicle of a Summer" are done in a probing, psychiatric style that forces confidences out of their subjects by pressing questions and cameras so close to them that sometimes they almost cry. Vanessa Redgrave's Isadora probably comes closer to the truth of Isadora than the real Isadora would have done if she had been trying to draw herself; it is a difficult thing for nonprofessional actors to convey an essence of themselves, as the cast of Straub's dramatized and slow, slow "Chronicle of Anna Magdalena Bach" did. If "State of Siege" had veered more from Uruguay, Mitrione, and the concrete-looking but unknowable facts (who can tell what Edward IV or the Duke of Clarence actually thought about when he was alone?), it might have come closer to the vividness of fictional truth, instead of giving us the passing color of fake reporting flashily done.

Primers of Revolutionary Method

Even more than Godard, Brecht was the master of revolutionary handbooks. In "Galileo," for instance, we are shown an unscrupu-

215

lous man of the senses who claims credit for the invention of the telescope when it has already been invented (by a Dutchman). The Pope's own astronomer confirms Galileo's round-earth findings, but the Inquisition forbids their publication. So for eight years, to the chagrin of his worshipful apprentice Sarti, Galileo remains mute, then recants after breaking silence, and meanwhile writes his great "Discorsi" in secret. He ends by knowing himself to have been a traitor to his profession, a man who has made science the servant of authority, a criminal whose cowardice has been signal. Yet he stands on the central plank of Brecht's revolutionary platform, the plank of the antiheroic. ("Unhappy the land that breeds no hero." "Unhappy the land that needs a hero."—Brecht's "Galileo." And, from his "The Exception and the Rule," "Next to you someone is thirsty: quickly close your eyes! Plug up your ears: someone is groaning next to you!")

Brecht is energetic, sardonic, a writer of broadsheets in urchin poetry. In his didactic plan of things, though not in his often sweet-spirited and gentle view of people, the poor are stingy and the rich are ruthless. After an increase of income, the sufferers immediately turn into rapacious businessmen. Like Brecht's "The Mother," freely adapted from Gorky, "State of Siege" intentionally neglects the psychological and particular. It is about the theoretical and communal, and it is written in an arid style with a rasping eloquence. Even so—as with Brecht's plays, in spite of himself—the central figure emerges potently as a dignified, sly human being. But there is an essential difference between Brecht's work and "State of Siege." Play after play of Brecht's shows us the horror *before* revolution, whereas "State of Siege" happens *during* what is very nearly a successful overthrow of a stolidly brutal government by students, trade-union leaders, professional men and women, and workers conjoined in learning to master the mechanics of revolution, as the people of Dubček's spring were. The repeated wording of a referendum that is conducted in an undertone on a bus has the echoic effects of poetry. Like Defoe's prose, the film can perhaps best be understood by people similarly placed to the ones depicted: by people like the Uruguayan rebels, who are shrewd, matter-of-fact, philistine, to whom the methods of the pamphlet are natural.

The Biographer Polemical and Presumptuous

Costa-Gavras and Solinas would have done better to call the Mitrione character by his real name, and to come clean about where the events happen. After all, the writer and the director are dealing in polemic. Why not use the zest and liberty of the form? They could have held up Brechtian placards when they were talking about unknowable things if compunction kicked. What really stopped them? Misplaced respect for a dead man who is anyway besmirched politically by their story? A hope that a quasi-fictional method would look less patently antimonopolistic (seen in America as anti-American)? It merely seems hole-in-the-corner.

Pratfalls of Commitment

Like High Tories depicting butlers and charwomen, Communists drawing the rich are likely to take headers. Brecht's stock-exchange intrigues in "Saint Joan of the Stockyards" present a grotesquely naïve picture of capitalism. So does the procession of corporation owners and bankers in "State of Siege." Only Brecht's furious comic muscularity wards off the objection to Hitler's being represented as a Chicago gangster in "Arturo Ui," with its careful parallels to Shakespeare's "Richard III."

Blackening the Enemy

The most cogent pamphleteer and fiction writer of them all, George Bernard Shaw, knew the wisdom of giving good arguments to the other side. The Inquisitor in his "Saint Joan" debates brilliantly. So does the Church in Brecht's "Galileo," and so does the existing order in his "Days of the Commune," in which the pull between violence and discipline is stated but not resolved. "State of Siege" has to deal with the same problem and doesn't quite make it intellectually vivid, though it sometimes successfully shows the Tupamaros as creatures of surprising wit and whimsey, who catch by infection their totalitarian government's brutality and capacity for committing torture. They are dressed in hoods that make them look like Ku Klux Klansmen, with nothing but pairs of eyes and alarmingly pretty pink-lipsticked mouths showing through their brown wool masks. The armed guerrillas are mostly escorted by girls carrying handguns. (The abundance of pretty girls equipped to kill seems to make the hackles of the film's detractors rise.) But when the young men take off their masks they look tired and scared. We have the sense, after their kidnapping of three officials in an attempt to overthrow the government, that they hadn't counted on the cold-bloodedness of A.I.D. Nor had the Montand character, who wrongly reckoned that he was more valuable to authority alive than dead. The decision of the government to let the ultimatum about his execution go past without a move is shocking to the Tupamaros. Their position is suddenly and rather piteously impossible. If they give in, they will seem impotent through weakness; if they hold out, they will seem impotent through cruelty. This Marxist understanding of the characters' predicaments is one of the best things in a coolheaded picture, written with gravity and seriousness. If the big-power opposition had been less caricatured—in the scene where American diplomatic wives are indoctrinated and warned against local water, for instance—"State of Siege" would have been comparable to Shaw, though still culpable for lack of biographical truth. In two hundred years' time, one wouldn't like putative students of our benighted period to find this film in the biographical file about Mitrione; its shrewdness about A.I.D. is a different matter.

MAY 12, 1973

A Mind Pressed Against the Window

"Finality is not the language of politics," said Disraeli. "A Woman at Her Window" leans its thought against the pane of the future, as if to cool its forehead, just as it cools ours. This most intelligently written political film is made in a tense that might be called the future indefinite—as, indeed, political dramas of any truth are bound to be. It is set mostly in Greece in 1936, the year after a coup d'etat has set King George II back on the throne; in another coup, General Metaxas has established a military dictatorship in the name of the King. Margot (Romy Schneider), the selfish estranged wife of the secretary to the Italian ambassador, toys with a staid, rather likable right-wing French industrialist named Malfosse, who is played by Philippe Noiret with his usual snuffling humor, like a boar hunting for truffles in the woods with oddly hell-bent porcine intent. She is also allured, in her parodic woman's way—I assume the filmmakers to be making a point here—by a Communist named Michel Boutros, who is played with glinting mind by Victor Lanoux. The film has a certain amount of picture-postcard stuff of Delphi and Epidaurus, but the dialogue—by Jorge Semprun, the Spanish novelist and poet who wrote, among other scripts, "The Confession" and "Z" for Costa-Gavras and "La Guerre Est Finie" for Resnais—has stature enough to match the landscape. One doesn't often hear political talk of this sort in a movie. We might be wandering in the agora at dusk discussing the possibility of democracy, except that everyone knows that this is 1936 and that we are soon to be in an unlit world darker than any night that has ever dropped.

This is no primitive left-wing tract. Boutros, the political militant, thinks that it is as insane to love the Parthenon as to love a dead woman, but the reason is partly that life has gone stale on his tongue, like the taste of cheap cigarettes after a night of driving across frontiers. The industrialist says, in the mode that seems uniquely European—discursive, with time to spare—that he is sure that Russia has nothing like the Parthenon. Long ago, Boutros answers, men built temples to house what they valued most: their gods. What men build today is not comparable. But it is not for lack of architects; it is for lack of gods. So? So we shall have to build for men. In that, we are so far very inexpressive, very clumsy.

The industrialist speaks of Oedipus. At the exact moment when Oedipus realized he was guilty of incest, the sunset vanished and

219

the light turned gray. As might be anticipated, Boutros prefers the "Antigone." Malfosse had expected that Boutros would side with Creon and the ethic of the State. Stalin's trials are underway: against Kamenev, Zinoviev, others. What if they're guilty? Well, what is guilt? The implication in the talk is that revolution requires guilt, and on both sides—that Stalin required the guilt of absolute power in the same way as the tyrants in Sophocles and Shakespeare. But where, says Boutros in effect, did a small, rich middle class win its right to impose an orderly, tolerant culture on a mass of disorderly men raging for change? Robespierre and Napoleon come up, and the truism that revolutions possibly have to devour their children to calm them. But this is not to say that truisms are always untrue. The choice confronting revolutionists, we have learned, often lies between the better course with the greater bloodshed and the repressive course with the lesser. One thinks of India, of Ireland. The fallacy is that the longer the oppressive measures go on, the greater is the bloodshed in the end.

The talk in this film is succinct. There is mention of a man who always pretends that inevitable events are his choice; the remark calls up a character in a sentence. The Romy Schneider figure is a beauty, beautifully dressed, with a beautifully witty turn of mind as long as it is turned to her own beautiful sexual advantage. She is a clinger with the dismaying appearance of self-reliance which often goes with great good looks. She has done with her husband. She uses every device of a Mata Hari to help the left-wing Boutros, whom she has now fallen in love with: she exploits for him her grace, her title (she is a marchesa), her husband's friends, to go with him in the guise of a tourist to Corfu and then to Ragusa to slip the knot closing around him. The staid industrialist, who is almost the husband figure in the story, sees his affair with her disappearing as if he were watching a boat leaving the shore. Thirty years later, long after Margot has disappeared, there is a "surprise" ending: an ending entirely necessary, life on course.

No doubt this film will be promoted as a love duel between two men for the heart of a great beauty. It is something much more unusual than that, and something we are more than ready for: a sophisticated picture about war, politics, power plays, people with a contemplative turn of mind. It is also about cause and effect, and the blind eye that most of us choose to turn to them. There are splendid ironic scenes of golf matches and champagne-drinking and shady hats, with dialogue such as we hardly ever hear in English-language films going on above the velvety lawns. A disagreeable Austrian named von Pahlen (Carl Mohner) has an argument with Malfosse. But the French won the war, Malfosse says to Mr. von Pahlen, who responds triumphantly: and France has lost the peace, by sitting on the Versailles powder keg. Politesse: are you interested in the Versailles Treaty? Anger: I have to be; my country is a result of it.

The director of this admirable French film is Pierre Granier-Deferre, who made Simenon's "Le Chat," with Simone Signoret. Semprun, who adapted Drieu La Rochelle's novel *Une Femme à Sa Fenêtre*, has a political mind that is unique in films in being so closely allied to sensibility about character. No drums are banged to force a point. Moderation has seldom been so painstakingly put forward: one thinks of E. M. Forster. The gradations of elitism in the film are clearly visible. The Communist is not altogether sure that he likes his disguise as a chauffeur. There is something noble in the mixture here of grand political scale and attention to human minutiae, and rarely have epic subjects like the growth of a police state and the burgeoning of a world war been treated on film with such powerful thoughtfulness. These are the sorts of topic that are generally left to novelists. It takes filmmakers with an exceptional sense of both scope and detail to bring off a picture of the calibre of "A Woman at Her Window." In every story of true endeavor, perhaps there is a particular character who signifies courage: in this film, I am not sure that it is not the Romy Schneider figure, who risks her life and eventually loses it not only because she loves a man but because she sees injustice being done and noxious fog gathering in people's minds. Will there be the final crisis of the world's populace? No, there will be only politics.

JUNE 12, 1978

Vivid Doldrums

Racked by acrimony, shuddering with curses, alive with snipings at élitism, an Italian yacht plows its very Latin way through a magnificently even summer sea. The weather is calm and lucid, but the temper of the people sailing is obstreperous and hectic. Lina Wertmüller's new film, called "Swept Away by an Unusual Destiny in the Blue Sea of August," is about a set of rich hedonists who argue violently over Stalinism-versus-capitalism while the members of the crew sullenly reheat coffee that they undoubtedly long to throw in the upperdogs' faces. The boss is an ill-natured bottle-blond beauty—the wife of an industrialist—who flounces as much as anyone can in a bikini, complains that the crew's T-shirts stink, and roars her route through an endless argument with a guest about Communism. She is, of course, against it. She is also capable of the full downrightness of the very wealthy in capping an idiocy about Stalinism with just as inadequate a riposte about the proficiency of Hiroshima. Settling everything. As she spouts polemic against Socialism and the smell of the crew, her swimming guests tread water in the warm sea and answer back hard, revived by a row as only Latins can be. She expresses blistering disdain of a friend's shorts, which are indeed rather long and baggy. But it is, after all, a holiday. "These happen to be very chic. Bermudas," he says, not at all unmanned.

This is the highly Latin situation between the sexes which Lina Wertmüller's wry Italian film proposes, like her earlier "The Lizards," "Love and Anarchy," and "The Seduction of Mimi": that the viragoes of so much Mediterranean sexual comedy will always meet their Petruchios. The termagant here is played by Mariangela Melato. The sailor whom she has tried most energetically to subjugate—played by Giancarlo Giannini—slowly becomes her buoyant master when they are marooned. She has told him that he looks terrible, that he should change his shirts more often, and that he is no sailor. She has demanded to be taken by him in a yellow rubber dinghy to join the other guests, who have gone to a grotto for a swim. There is no fear in her of sex rearing its festive head. Not even when the outboard motor goes dead. She simply sleeps, adrift, without seeming to miss food or drink, apparently fortified by natural resources of contempt, wakening with the dawn to use her parched lips to provide a good breakfast of abuse for the poor man, who is without a compass but not without either mechanical ingenuity or masculine fury.

Having seethed about the idea of eating raw a pilchard caught by the hero with his bare hands, having even thrown it disgustedly back into the sea, the glamorous loudmouth starts to waver, and to wish for some of the lobster that he cleverly catches on the desert island where they land. Her wealth, which is immense, comes from industry, and she still can't take in the fact that safety, servility, and comfort aren't up for sale. Habits of authority die hard. Difficult to believe that the ancient coinage of rule has no currency in a new civilization of two. Sometimes, against custom, she starts to behave with grace. She predictably grows to worship the casual ability to stay alive of the mysterious lout whom she no longer employs but still feels to be her rightful property. This is a very Marxist film, beneath its complexion of comedy. Who belongs to whom? Is it the now unpaid wage earner to the rich employer separated from any bank? Or is it the burdensome complainer to the amused survivalist? The tenaciously habitual in arrogance to the newborn in command? The one who feels the greater need to the one who feels the freer?

Neither belongs to the other, says Lina Wertmüller, with characteristic political skepticism about emotional combat. (She wrote the screenplay.) The heroine falls in love with the underdog master and relishes being vanquished, but only for a time. During the long episode of desert-island life, she is quelled by her own eroticism. Yet the instinct of the privileged remains, latent, after her serf seems to quash it: she is made to say "Mister," made to say "please," made to wash his sailor pants, made to regret her haughty recoil from the sight of a rabbit that her lover has caught for them to eat. "I feel like that poor little rabbit," says this floundering malfeasant of women's lib, limp with longing, identifying with the skinned, speared, about-to-be-roasted rabbit, but still enough of a born overlord to despise the naked sight of the food she regularly respects when it is clothed in sauce. She learns, but only for a time. In the rubber boat, when she was haranguing her lover about the uses of dieting to cleanse the system, and recommended it for women in the south of Italy, he said, "They're on a constant diet. It's called poverty." Watching her situation now, he loves her, teaches her a lesson, knows how hard it is to be the one knuckling under, and finds his sympathies keeling. Only a primal, untaught Marxism upholds his resolve. Every now and then, he remembers how rich she is in the outside world, how likely she is to revert, how the rich burn food to keep prices high.

Lina Wertmüller's fine film is apparently a simple parable about a social irony, like J.M. Barrie's "The Admirable Crichton," in which the butler in a shipwrecked party of aristocrats is eventually called Gov because he is the most capable person. But "Swept Away by an Unusual Destiny in the Blue Sea of August" is about more than token amusements of paradox. It is about certain things' being swept away. The man, cast socially as a servant, regains in his native state his born worth, but he loses his heart; the woman, cast socially as the boss, is forced to admit her subservience, but as soon as she rejoins her husband and friends she loses her acquired pliancy. In other words, the hero is swept away by her. And what she learned from him, which caused him to love her, is also swept away: the broom of social groupings has brushed naturalness under the carpet. Back in what the film would sarcastically call civilization, the hero sends her a topaz ring bought with the total stingy reward that her husband gave him, and tries to arrange to return with her to their desert island. She half promises on the telephone that she will. He simply sits on a quay and waits for her. An expensive helicopter rises. Leave it behind, after all: a nasty incident, an aberration, a joke.

SEPTEMBER 22, 1975

Church-Step Farce

"The Seduction of Mimi," written and directed by Lina Wertmüller, is a handsomely comic and political-minded farce that in
Italy, where the characters live, has deadly-serious roots. The plot
is a round robin of illegitimate babies, pride in motherhood, and
pride in fatherhood. It is full of reckless Latin fury about cuckoldry,
and gives prime place to omertà. People who know Italy might
broadly define omertà as an agreed-upon male conspiracy of silence
which covers up acts of vengeance.

The hero is a poor Sicilian called Carmelo Mardocheo (Giancarlo Giannini), a solemn-looking, intense buffoon with a center hair
parting and an expression that he nobly tries to convert from constant alarm to a promise of male prowess which will be fulfilled any
minute. He is nicknamed throughout the film Mimi, imputing a
sympathetic simplicity to his actually very tangled sexual dilemma.
He is banished by the Mafia from his Sicilian surroundings of
black-clad aunts and a reproachful wife named Rosalia (Agostina
Belli). Rosalia is dressed in raven clothes forty years too old for her,
so that she seems to be in mourning for her life—like Chekhov's
Masha in "The Seagull"—and perhaps for her husband's, as much
as she is capable of entering into any man's temperament in this
sexually divided society. An old man, grumpy but excited, is having his legs scrubbed before going to vote in a rigged election. It is
the Mafia's anger at Mimi's not voting according to their directions
that obliges him to leave. While her husband is away, in Turin,
Rosalia changes. She learns to dance and to smoke. She works in a
factory. In the meantime, Carmelo sets up a second household in
Turin. He becomes a keen metallurgist and, against all the odds, an
intent trade unionist. His mistress, Fiore (Mariangela Melato),
whose face looks like a Cranach, has a beloved baby by him. ("Later, your daddy will buy you a blender," he says lovingly before she
has the baby. "He isn't even born yet, and already he is a member

of consumer society," Fiore answers, grateful enough but intellectually bothered, you feel.) When the baby is born, it is smuggled away very noticeably in black clothes and dark glasses, which are more than startling on a minute infant. The sepulchral babe is accompanied by its parents, in a car with muslin curtains. The conspicuous illicit family has now been drastically moved by the Mafia from Turin to Catania, very near Mimi's wife's home. Worn out with lovemaking and commuting, the man is in a state more of collapse than of guilt when he sees Rosalia. Local rumors spread that he's impotent, so he has his friends in to see Fiore's baby as proof of his manhood. But Rosalia's proximity keeps obliging him to go through the motions of resuming life with her. His marital worry, not quite keeping pace with his left-wing political convictions, is that no one would marry Rosalia if she divorced him. "Would *you* marry a divorced woman?" he asks a friend. "An *American* woman, perhaps," says the friend fiercely. "A woman of *substance*." As soon as the men of the town know about his baby, Mimi is rather envied. A metallurgical foreman with a car, a wife, a concubine, *and* a child! Perfect! "A Communist doesn't behave like this," says a friend. But, after all, a man . . .

Rosalia has her revenge. She has a baby by a uniquely boring tax officer. She explains proudly to Mimi that she resisted him, "but the more I resisted the longer he sang." She gets pregnant in a crane on a work site, to the secret admiration of the community. Mimi spiritedly braces himself to make love back to the tax officer's colossal wife, a scuttling woman with five children who is pitifully far too plain to give any credence to his cries of passionate love for her. The dialogue here is very funny and not at all cruel: Latin bedroom-and-churchstep farce, written for a woman who is not a beauty but one of life's larger foothills, and for a man who is not farce's conventional intimidated lover but someone with the spirit of a Don Juan.

Lawyers present hopeless ways out of the complexities. Incensed clients run about with knives. Babies abound. But after all his years of toil Mimi is still a poor man with left-wing ideals. Neither the Mafia nor the women of his community can batter his hopes for society. He is, as he says, a metallurgist, which means that he is a civilized individual. He has not yet quite worked out that having illicit children out of vengeance hardly squares with his liberalism, but perhaps he doesn't see having the children as an act of vengeance. Perhaps he loves them all. His idea of honor has suffered many changes. "Honor is when a man plays at war and then hurts himself," he says. Wrongly jailed for a Mafia murder, he is told by a member that the brotherhood of thugs managed to get him the minimum sentence. But the Mafia has always been his enemy. "You'll come, because in your position you need money," he is told coolly. Still declining, he serves out his sentence, and emerges from jail to find Fiore and his growing illegitimate son abandoning him: vanishing shapes, infinitely beguiling in bright colors, visible in the back of an open truck. "They're all cousins!" cries Mimi, running after them, insisting on a hope impossibly hard to maintain in jealous southern Italy, eventually giving up far behind and throwing himself down onto the sand. Lina Wertmuller has made a wonderfully funny sexual farce that becomes a cry for another scheme of things.

JUNE 24, 1974

Swiss Pride and Prejudice

It is a truth universally acknowledged, to misquote Jane Austen, that a Swiss man in possession of good fortune must be in want of a car and a watch. Alain Tanner, the writer and director of "Charles Dead or Alive" (1969; running at the New Yorker Theatre), is Swiss himself. His Charles is a gentle third-generation watchmaker whose loathing of watches—and indeed of cars—has unexpectedly reached an intensity of tonic derision that lifts him away from the familiar and makes him seem to dangle above the world of his factory's greed and of its foursquare, stalemated egoism as though some astonishing dialectic foresight had suddenly picked him up by the nape of the neck so that his feet no longer touched the floor of the present. The only way a man can ever make the next thing happen is to look at today with the eyes of the future. Yes. True, probably. To be tested. Charles, this man of fifty, who has a funny revolutionary daughter, Marianne (Maya Simon), and a dreadful son, Pierre (André Schmidt), pasty with moneymaking, begins to unravel himself as if he were an old cardigan.

It is the hundredth anniversary of the firm he heads. TV is doing a report on him: the usual fatuities. It grows difficult for him to believe in his own palpability. Hauntingly played by François Si- mon (son of Michel), he keeps staring at himself in the looking glasses of cloakrooms. He seems to feel as if he were living in parentheses. Words rot in his throat and go dry in his stomach. He breaks his spectacles in a washbasin one day so as to see less clear- ly. Above, there are the Alps. Below is the anarchic world, with Switzerland, "righteous and eternal," in its lap. The prospect doesn't please him, and the thought of himself least of all.

The TV people talk about his family. His grandfather came from the Jura with nothing much but a toolbox; he was a watch- maker above everything. Charles' father was a mixture of a watch- maker and a businessman. Charles' son is purely a businessman. "You've left yourself out," says the TV reporter testily, not seeing any particular significance in that, and entirely missing the fact that this parched and subtle man is practically eliminating himself from existence by his own wish. "Our subject was to be the spirit of family enterprise," holds the nettled TV interviewer. The hu- man temperament is always messing things up. The same unruly humanness makes Charles go off the rails of the topic again and remember family talks long ago of Bakunin and Kropotkin and Malatesta. Later, alone, in one of the Brechtian swivels of this technically engrossing film, he starts putting the TV interviewer's questions to himself. When he lies in a bath, you can see him brooding about allies in speculativeness: Socrates, maybe; people can drown in a bath, he tells himself. The left side, the one with the heart, is turning into a rock. The other side earns an honest living. I am a notary or a grocer. Order reigns, according to everyone else. My daughter will pass her philology exams, no doubt, on the money I make from watches that I certainly sell too dearly. I am much better without spectacles. I can read advertisements perfectly. Advertisements for cigarettes called Tops, in king-size or super-king-size boxes. Ah, spinach.

He flees his wife and family, and takes to a hotel under an assumed name, lying on the bed and listening to radio descriptions of himself: said to be disturbed, last seen wearing a dark-gray suit. The chambermaid gets cross about his undecided plans and treats him briskly as a thing that complicates bedmaking. At midday, he will lie awake with his eyes closed. Some news on the radio makes him grin. Young leftists in hordes have blocked the roads in and out of Geneva and Zurich as part of a political demonstration; the outraged motorists, having had a go at the young with the usual barbarism of the bourgeoisie when property is threatened, are now making portly complaints to the canton officials. Charles seems pleased. The news nourishes his own hatred of cars, which is a thought-out and solemnly held political position. When he eventually musters himself to go out to a café, and makes friends there with a casual young couple who virtually adopt him—a bearded sign painter called Paul (Marcel Robert) and his pretty, larky mistress, Adeline (Marie-Clair Dufour)—Charles expounds his dogma. The position that the driver must sit in is very bad. It interferes with the digestion and fattens the heart. Motoring is a system of accumulation without exchange. The people concerned never meet. Method of social dispersion. Everyone in his little box. The young couple seem to be of a mind to agree. The girl talks about preferring the suburbs to caterwauling city life. People in the city are ignoble in summer, she says. With a characteristic high-hat gesture to the absurd, Paul shoves Charles' car down the side of a giant gravel pit. All three of them seem very much elated. What a stroke!

The couple take Charles into their amiable muddle of a house. Marianne comes on an accomplice's visit and decides in the kitchen to write down a maxim for each day. (Tanner's films often have a tang of Godard.) You are to learn the maxims by heart, she explains, and then you begin to notice their relationship with what happens. Paul smiles. "And after that I'll be intelligent?" he says, this agreeable, horse-faced man who is such a misfit in orderly Switzerland but also such a product of the tradition of modest surrealists and anarchists and thinkers who—like Tanner himself—have found a place for themselves there. Monday: Be realistic, demand the impossible. (Anonymous.) Tuesday: There are no stupid people, only stupid jobs. (Proverb.)

Charles and Paul go sign painting together and talk off the tops of their heads. The thing is to know what you want. Does *Paul* know what he wants? No really. Only that there are some things he won't do. You feel that he is faintly accident-prone, in spite of his bearish sturdiness: a muddler of great probity, embracing a mediocre system that he regards with a beguiling sort of passion as unchangeable. He worries about Charles. The man's situation isn't normal. No, Charles agrees, but it's more normal than before. An exemplary shock is more difficult to achieve than an exemplary success, says the film. Living in a society of meagre understanding, little curiosity, and uncertain temper, Charles-the-mad has administered to himself his own shock treatment.

Charles' stodgy son tracks him down through a detective, mostly because the heir needs to cope with the problem of his father's signature on checks. He commits Charles to an asylum to be rid of the paperwork. The sirens wail. But Charles has his own resolves to support him. He reads Saint-Just in the ambulance, adding to his keepers' certainty that he is out of his mind. The thought he is concerned with is that the times have changed so much that the notion of happiness and unhappiness now supplants the antique notion of destiny. This is one of the central ideas of Tanner's unsuperstitious picture. It is a sage and affectionate movie, which asks hard questions with a unique dry warmth and a native distance from the usual wish to incite audience identification. "Charles Dead or Alive" is a more schematic film than Tanner's ravishing "La Salamandre" (now running at the Paris), which he made a year or more later, but it is unmistakably created by the same modest, grown-up man. He knows a lot about being a fugitive. He went to England from Switzerland as a total foreigner in the mid-fifties and made a fine, gay, abrasive short film about Piccadilly Circus called "Nice Time." He has worked for B.B.C.-TV and in Swiss television. His technical command is delicate and lucid, like his mind. "Charles Dead or Alive" is a poem, a broadsheet, a fable. It is wry and sometimes very beautiful. It has the character of prophecy.

SEPTEMBER 2, 1972

A New Russian Classic

In the traditional silly season of August, a glory has arrived: a Russian picture of the greatest filmic invention, called "A Slave of Love." It was directed by Nikita Mikhalkov: great-grandson of the nineteenth-century Russian painter Surikov, grandson of the Post-Impressionist Konchalovsky, son of the poet Sergei Mikhalkov, brother of the filmmaker Andrei Mikhalkov-Konchalovsky. It is quite a heritage—and quite a bequest that we have from the director of this film. It flickers with a life and an energy that would have captured D.W. Griffith. One is often parched for such vivacity in the current movies of the Western world; now we have it from a quarter usually thought to have been made moribund by bureaucracy and propaganda. The task that Mikhalkov set himself is noble, and the achievement dashing.

We are in the Crimea just after the October Revolution. White Russians are holding out in the south. A film of absurd melodrama is being made by people who cannot accept the revolution. They want the past restored to them. The director of this film-within-the-film (Alexander Kalyagin) is a plump man who wears a hat at a jaunty angle. He promises himself that he will get thin, but he

231

wants to eat, too. "I want everything at once," he says. It seems that he has little talent, apart from a great talent for disarming. He calls the script brilliant when it is clearly poor; but at the same time he bosses the writer, asking for alterations. He is a man who veers and is incapable of seeing contradictions. In one shot, this would-be thin man tries to hoist his legs onto a tree branch that he is clutching: the Russian sense of the casually odd and beautiful detail has not been lost. It is near the end of the shooting of the film. "It is unlikely we shall ever meet again," says the director, almost to himself. He plays the piano, saying that he wonders whether he and the cast are still alive. He senses something of their deadness in vital times.

But his star—called Olga, and played by Yelena Solovei, who has a huge-eyed face that makes you want to clasp your hands around it as if it were a goblet—is very much an alive being, even if she does go along with the preposterous triviality that rules on the set, making inert people yearn vaguely for something else, and despite the walled-off atmosphere of the film-within-the-film. Her alertness glimmers. We see her in magnificent closeups—"A Slave of Love" was photographed by Pavel Lebeshev—often in a big white hat that blows in the wind as she holds it, and makes the screen itself seem to flutter. She laughs, again in closeup. In one sequence composed in many whites, she holds a bunch of white flowers. The conviviality she emits is infectious. The film conveys a gaiety that we usually think lost to contemporary Soviet filmmaking. In a shot of Olga in a car, she claps her hands with a very Russian sort of joy—joy of a kind that I remember reigning at the Royal Opera House, in London, when the Bolshoi Ballet company advanced to the footlights and applauded the audience for its welcome. Olga is an impressive woman, a woman of character, in spite of the fact that the melodrama she is working in is garbage. All around her, in the revolution, there is a cause. "How wonderful to be wrapped up in a cause," she says. She longs for a cause as if she were longing for a trip to Moscow. Not for nothing does she bear the name of one of Chekhov's three sisters. She seems to have a fragile sense that she is not keeping a promise to history, but the promise eludes her, and so does any mood of purpose.

"A Slave of Love" is about people out of step with their era. It begins with the sound of fun-fair music, and it maintains its sense of play to the very end, but what it is saying is something serious and to the heart of the matter. The scenes from the melodrama are shown to us in black-and-white, of course, because of the period. The surrounding picture is shot in a color that sometimes looks powdered. There is an astounding sequence, with the sound track full of the noise of crackling leaves, in which the cameraman of the film-within-the-film, an undercover Bolshevik named Pototsky (Rodion Nakhapetov), drives it home to Olga that a new country is being born. An epoch is being lost—an epoch that, from the camerawork, looks as if it were something already remembered: shown like old photographs found in an album in an attic, there are scampering children, sailor suits and straw boaters, balalaikas, slumberous flirtations. Juxtaposed, there are more black-and-white shots—as if in a newsreel—taken secretly by Pototsky, of the real world of political upheavals which the actors of the film-within-the-film are so cut off from. The makers of the melodrama plan dreamily to go to Paris, but they mean to send the reels of their film to Moscow, perhaps as a talisman. There is a shot of Olga saying desperately through glass, "You must remember me." It is a completely metaphoric shot of the past calling to the present. The closing sequence is startling. It seems to come out of nowhere. Olga is in a trolley car, which is on the move and has no other passengers. It is a beautifully yellowed scene. There are backview shots of White Russian soldiers galloping after the trolley. Olga is shouting, "You'll be cursed by your country, soldiers!" She seems now to be someone who will discover the future with intelligence, on her own. Yet the sum of what she has been told by her director at the end of the film-within-the-film is "All I want you to do is smile." What we do is smile with pleasure in a magnificent film, and think.

AUGUST 28, 1978

V

EXILE

An author of fiction—any sort of fiction—is often curiously though painfully aided by exile from the country he was born in and the language he dreams in. So, three distinctions here represented:

1. *Exile from language.* Vladimir Nabokov, of course. I met Nabokov first in the early sixties. (It was on the long train journey in Switzerland to spend time with him that I wrote the last scenes of "Sunday Bloody Sunday," directed by John Schlesinger, with Glenda Jackson and the late, great Peter Finch. In those closing scenes I wanted to set up a natural way of using the resources of theatrical soliloquy on film.) Nabokov was chasing butterflies in the High Tatras. We spoke together in several languages and he drew me some joke drawings in a mood of high seriousness. He revelled in jokes and word-games. He was a living example of the literary good that can be done by exile, whatever the ache. We tried together to find a good English translation for the title of his Russian-language novel of 1936 that he eventually decided to call "Despair." At the time we contemplated "A Howl." I think he was startled and gleeful to find someone out of the blue who spoke Russian and was

engaged in similar technical problems. A wise man—George De-
vine, founder of the English Stage Company—once said to me that
all problems are technical.

And then there is the remarkable "The Passenger" by Anton-
ioni, about an Englishman in flight to Africa from a numb life as a
TV-news journalist. It is the most gentle and humane film Anton-
ioni has ever made. The hero is an alien in this new world he has
chosen. The demotic talk is strange to him. His vocabulary of be-
havior is as unrecognizable to others now as his old language. He is
a stranger in a society where he elects to be lost. "The Passenger"
is a different matter from "Blow-Up," which reflected the myth of
swinging London that foolish American magazines had spread.
"The Passenger" is a masterpiece about a dredged human spirit
refilling itself with water from canals dug with difficulty and re-
solve.

2. Exile from the metropolis. Fellini's wondrous "Amarcord."
The snobs in Italy are apt to retreat into comments about "8½"
being no good because Fellini is not a Roman: wherein lies the
wealth of feeling for character in "Amarcord," its humor, its affec-
tion extended to the idiosyncratic, its festivity.

3. Exile from history. Fassbinder is a most interesting example of
the crop of West German directors too young to have recall of the
Nazis. They put acquirable knowledge out of their minds. They
know nothing of Brecht's great Berliner Ensemble in East Berlin,
would apparently know nothing of what such men as George
Grosz were telling us in his caricatures of Berlin people in the
thirties. For such gifted men as Fassbinder (and Herzog, and many
more), their films absolve them, at first glance, from any chance of
responsibility for the war by the mere act of not being old enough
to remember 1939–1945. The directors and writers appear to be
trying to assert no knowledge of the past, but the unadmitted ac-
knowledgment of need for repayment is there, all the same. The
recompense is secreted in the films, which are openly at sea,
kind to the bizarre and out-of-step, and underpinned by a convic-
tion that the effort to build a new Germany of lost souls is a great
deal more admirable than some economic miracle. Fassbinder is
particularly concerned with the predicament of characters of his

own age who seem to have been called upon to be made stupid or hermetically sophisticated in order to forget what they know in the lobotomized part of their minds.

Nabokov

"Is the Queen pregnant?" said Vladimir Nabokov.

"I don't believe so," I said.

"When I saw her on television at the World Cup watching football she kept making this gesture." He did a mime of smoothing a dress.

"She always does that."

"Oh, I see. A queenly movement. Permanently with child. With heir." He chuckled and looked interested.

We met in a distant part of Switzerland. I had said to him on the hotel telephone, sounding to myself ludicrously like a character in *Sherlock Holmes* but assuming that he wouldn't know it, that he could identify me downstairs in the lobby because I had red hair.

"I shall be carrying a copy of *Speak, Memory*," he had said back. (*Speak, Memory* is his autobiography.)

His ear for the idiom was instant and exact. It turned out that his father had known Sherlock Holmes's creator, Sir Arthur Conan Doyle. ("Though Conan Doyle was much more proud of his intolerably boring books on South Africa.") Nabokov has a writer's passion for the physical details and likes Holmes's habit of passing half-a-crown through a chink in the cab to the cabdriver. He also has an intentness on the nuances of speech—Holmes's, mine, anyone's who uses English—that is made much more urgent by his exile from his own language.

Twenty-nine years ago he abandoned his "untrammelled, rich, and infinitely docile Russian tongue," which he had already used to write novels unpublishable in the Soviet Union and so not published at all, for an English that he learned first from his governesses. Perhaps his command of it now is partly due to the obstacle, as a man will often think more swiftly who speaks with an impediment. Nabokov now writes a dulcit and raffish English that has found more of the secret springs of our language than most writers born to it can ever get under their fingers. For instance, he knows precisely the mechanism of an Anglo-Saxon use of bathos and rudeness, which will plant an anti-climactic word or vernacular insult in a suave context where it goes off with a peculiar mixture of self-mockery and shabby bombast. For all that, his distress about losing Russian is obviously gnawing and will never be appeased. In the preface to *Lolita* he writes briefly about it as if he were an illusionist robbed of his luggage, performing on a stage where his plundered trickery has to be practiced without any of the apparatus of association.

It occurs to me that perhaps this is exactly what makes him write better about love than any other novelist in modern English. The afflictions of exile carry a taste of theft that is the pang of intimacy itself. The tricked focus in the experience of loving, the one that hideously connects rapture with mortality and causes lovers to hoard the present as though it were already gone, bestows a psychic foretaste of loss that is close to the one that gave the privileged Russian children of Nabokov's age a genius for recollection. They lived their Russian youth with the intensity of the grown-up in love, mysteriously already knowing too much about losing it. The ache that clings to good fortune or great accord is one of time's ugly gags, like the grasping housewife already secreted in the rapturous frame of little Lolita.

Humbert Humbert is in love with a booby trap. His whole situation hoaxes him. *Lolita* is an account of the passionate involvement of a man constantly ambushed by *dépaysement* and consigned to the plastic exile of motels. *Dépaysé*: de-countried: we need a word for it now in English far more than we need "deflowered." It isn't at all fully expressed by "alienation," or "rootlessness," for like the comic agony of love in *Lolita*, it is a concept of loss that includes the knowledge of what it can be to possess. Before I met Nabokov I had wondered sometimes how it was possible for a writer to live permanently in hotels, as he has done since 1960, mostly in Switzerland; but it was a stupid speculation about a great novelist of *dépaysement* who carries his country in his skull. His landscape isn't Russia, but Russian literature.

His permanent address now is a hotel in Montreux that he described as "a lovely Edwardian heap." We met in the Engadine, where he and his wife had come for the butterflies, in another Edwardian heap with spa baths in the basement. He is a tall, loping man whose gait and way of peering reminded me faintly of Jacques Tati's.

"I am six foot," he said. "I have very thin bones. The rest is flesh." He picked at his arm as if it were a jacket.

In his autobiography he describes himself as having the Korff nose, passed on from his paternal grandmother's side: "A handsome Germanic organ with a boldly boned bridge and a slightly tilted, distinctly grooved, fleshy end." He wears spectacles, but switches to pince-nez after six to alter the ache in his nose. His accent is neither Russian nor American: I think it originates in the upper-class English undergraduate speech of immediately after the First World War, when he went to Cambridge. ("Cambridge, Cambridge, not Cambridge, Mass.," he said.) His French is delicate and pure. He hears it as dated: "The slang goes back to Maupassant." His Russian is the authentic sound of pre-Revolutionary St. Petersburg. He did a mischievously expressive example of the boneless accent of standard *Pravda* speech now. I don't suppose that either he or his wife can detect that their birth in itself is a distinct and commanding fact about them both; but then the upper-class people of Europe never do. It is only the rest who can see the difference, and the well-born truly believe themselves to be indistinguishable.

The Nabokovs think of going back to America to live, perhaps in California. They are looking for what? A climate; and far more than that, a language. "We were in Italy, but we don't want to live there. I don't speak Italian. And the *scioperi* (strikes) . . . Véra found a château in France, but it would have cost a lot of money to convert it. It had drawbridges. It had its drawbridges and drawbacks." He has a habit of going back over what he has said and correcting it that is rather like the way he immediately uses an eraser on his notes. "I don't much care for De Gaulle. I fear things will happen there when he dies. I would go to Spain but I hate bullfights. Switzerland: lakes, charming people, stability. All my publishers pass through from one festival to another."

He had been up since six, as usual, and had a bath in the curative basement. "I discovered the secret of levitation," he said. "One puts the feet flat braced against the end of the bath and rises covered with bubbles like a fur. I felt like a bear. A memory of a former state."

We had a drink rather early in the morning. The whiskies looked small as he asked for soda. "Make the glass grow," he said, and then muttered: "The grass glow."

His books are written on index cards so that it is possible to start in the middle and insert scenes as he wants. He writes in 3B pencils that he says he sharpens compulsively. They have India rubbers on the ends which he uses to exorcise mistakes instead of simply crossing them out. My own error in writing with a pen struck him as technically cardinal. His pocket notebooks are made of paper squared like an arithmetic book. The formal pattern that might distract most people obviously stimulates him. I could understand this: it must be a little like seeing figments in the black-and-white tiles in public lavatories.

"Some of my best poems and chess problems have been composed in bathrooms looking at the floor," he said.

At some stage we started to play anagrams. I gave him "cart horse" (the solution is "orchestra"). He took the problem away on what was meant to be a nap, and came bounding into the bar two hours later with an expression that was a very Russian mixture of buoyancy and sheepishness. The tartanned paper of his little note pad was covered with methodically wrong steps. "Her actors," he said, in try-on triumph, eyeing me, and knowing perfectly well that the answer had to be one word. Then he started to laugh at his picture of the creature whose property the actors would be. Bossy women stroke him as irresistibly comic: they trudge through his books, absurd, cruel, creatures of inane placidity who see everything in the world as a mirror of their womanliness and who will speak sharply about something like Bolshevism as though it were an obvious minor nuisance, like mosquitos, or the common cold. I believe his woman producer also amused him because he finds the theatre inherently funny when it is earnest: something to do with its thickness, I think, compared with the fine mesh of novels he likes.

When he taught in America he lectured on *Anna Karenina*, Tolstoy's *The Death of Ivan Ilyitch*, *Ulysses*, Kafka's *The Metamorphosis*, and Jane Austen's *Mansfield Park*, which was suggested by Edmund Wilson. The precise butterfly-pinner discovered that Tolstoy made the two families in *Anna Karenina* age on a different time scale, so that more years have passed for one than for the other. He also says that Joyce left out any reference to Bloom's coming back from the cemetery.

"I know Dublin exactly. I could draw a map of it. I know the Liffey like the Moskva. I have never been to Dublin but I know it as well as Moscow. Also, I have never been to Moscow."

He and his wife both lived in St. Petersburg, but they first met in Berlin in exile. They could have met many times when they were children; at dancing class, perhaps; it bothers them and they go over it.

"Véra's coming down in a moment," he said. "She's lost something. A jacket, I think. When she loses things, it is always something very big." He started to shake again. His sense of humor is very Russian, and the sight of its taking him over is hugely pleasurable. There is a lot of the buffoon in it. He is one of the few people I have seen who literally does sometimes nearly fall off his chair while laughing.

"Véra has been doing 'cart horse' as well," he said. "Eventually she suggested 'horse-cart.' She hadn't much hope."

In the lounge there was an Edwardian mural of naked lovers, except they were not naked and seemed to have nothing much to do with loving. The woman was vulgarly draped and the man wore, as well as a tulle scarf across his groin, a vaporish example of early Maidenform around his chest. After days of looking at the picture Nabokov still found it mildly interesting. It happened to be a rather obvious demonstration of the intimacy in art between silliness and prudery. The high-flying Philistinism of protected art tastes strikes him often as richly foolish. Long ago the Empress of

Russia gave him pleasure by being an eager admirer of Ella Wheeler Wilcox. *Invitation to a Beheading,* one of his early Russian-language novels, has a sulphurous passage about an imaginary book considered to be "the acme of modern thought" in which world history is seen from the point of view of an elderly and apparently sagacious oak tree. Nabokov detests literature that has sweeping social pretentions. He also loathes prurience. The bad art of the past that has lost its power to bamboozle will often reveal that a large share of its badness consists in failing to go too far, which is the only course that is ever far enough in aesthetics. The streak of blue nerve in Nabokov's work is part of its quality. It has an effect that is close to the exhilaration of flair and courage in real conduct.

In the actual world, the vice for which Nabokov seems to have most loathing is brutality. He finds it in tank-shaped political bullies, "swine-toned radio music," the enjoyment of trained animals, the truisms of Freudianism, the abhorrence of Germany between the wars. (There is a German in one of his books who believes "electrocution" is the root of "cute.") In the world of art his equivalent loathing is for mediocrity, which is perhaps only the aesthetic form of the same brutality. There are celebrated writers in whom he detects a naïveté that he obviously finds almost thuggish. He detests Zola, Stendhal, Balzac, Thomas Mann.

Nabokov spoke eagerly about the descriptions of the fish in Hemingway's *The Old Man and the Sea* and about the jungle passages and close physical descriptions in Graham Greene's *A Burnt-Out Case.* "The avant-garde French novels that I've read don't stir my artistic appetite. Only here and there. Even Shaw can do that." I asked him about Genet: "An interesting fairyland with good measurements." Ostrovsky, the Russian playwright, he described as having "a streak of poetry that he unfortunately put down because he was so intent on writing about the merchant class." Tin-eared translators torment him. "*Vive le pedant,*" he writes defiantly in one of his prefaces, "and down with the simpletons who think that all is well if the spirit is rendered (while the words go away by themselves on a naïve and vulgar spree—in the suburbs of Moscow for instance—and Shakespeare is again reduced to play the king's ghost)."

The English translations of his Russian novels have been done by Nabokov himself, generally with his son, Dmitri, who is a racing driver and a singer. Nabokov has just finished doing a Russian translation of *Lolita*, typeset in New York. "To be smuggled in, dropped by parachute, floating down on the blurb." His attachment to words is urgent and moving. A copy of the unabridged Webster's dictionary is carried about in the back of Nabokov's Lancia; in his hotel room on holiday it was open among the M's, halfway through, which is the way he leaves it so as to save the spine. In his autobiography he speaks of turning even now to the last page of any new grammar to find "that promised land where, at last, words are meant to mean what they mean."

"In Massachusetts once I was ill with food poisoning," he said. "I was being wheeled along a corridor. They left the trolley by a bookcase and I drew out a big medical dictionary and in the ward I drew the curtains around myself and read. It wasn't allowed because it looked as if I were dying. They took the book away. In hospitals there is still something of the eighteenth-century madhouse."

"Pasternak?" I asked. At once he talked very fast. "*Doctor Zhivago* is false, melodramatic, badly written. It is false to history and false to art. The people are dummies. That awful girl is absurd. It reminds me very much of novels written by Russians of, I am ashamed to say, the gentler sex. Pasternak is not a bad poet. But in *Zhivago* he is vulgar. Simple. If you take his beautiful metaphors there is nothing behind them. Even in his poems: what is that line, Véra? 'To be a woman is a big step.' It is ridiculous." He laughed and looked stricken.

"This kind of thing recurs. Very typical of poems written in the Soviet era. A person of Zhivago's class and his set, he wouldn't stand in the snow and read about Bolshevist regime and feel a tremendous glow. There was the *liberal* revolution at that time. Kerensky. If Kerensky had had more luck—but he was a liberal, you see, and he couldn't just clap the Bolsheviks into jail. It was not done. He was a very average man, I should say. The kind of person you might find in the Cabinet of any democratic country. He spoke very well, with his hand in his bosom like Napoleon because it had almost been broken by handshakes.

"Yet people like Edmund Wilson and Isaiah Berlin, they have to love *Zhivago* to prove that good writing can come out of Soviet Russia. They ignore that it is really a *bad book*. There are some absolutely ridiculous scenes. Scenes of eavesdropping, for instance. You know about eavesdropping. If it is not brought in as parody it is almost Philistine. It is the mark of the amateur in literature. And that marvellous scene where he had to get rid of the little girl to let the characters make love, and he sends her out skating. In *Siberia*. To keep warm they give her her mother's *scarf*. And then she sleeps deeply in a hut while there is all this going on. Obviously Pasternak just didn't know what to do with her. He's like Galsworthy. Galsworthy in one of his novels gave a character a cane and a dog and simply didn't know how to get rid of them.

"And the metaphors. Unattached comparisons. Suppose I were to say 'as passionately adored and insulted as a barometer in a mountain hotel,'" he said, looking out at the rain. "It would be a beautiful metaphor. But who is it about? The image is top-heavy. There is nothing to attach it to. And there is a pseudo-religious strain in the book which almost shocks me. *Zhivago* is so feminine that I sometimes wonder if it might have been written by Pasternak's mistress.

"As a translator of Shakespeare he is very poor. He is considered great only by people who don't know Russian. An example." His wife helped him to remember a line of Pasternak translation. "What he has turned it into in Russian is this: 'all covered with grease and keeps wiping the pig iron.' You see. It is ridiculous. What would be the original?"

"Greasy Joan doth keel the pot?"

"Yes. 'Keeps wiping the pig iron!'" He expostulated and looked genuinely angry. "Pasternak himself has been very much *helped* by translation. Sometimes when you translate a cliché—you know, a cloud has a silver lining—it can sound like Milton because it is in another language."

"Isn't that what happened to Pushkin?" said Véra.

"He had translated the French writers of his day. The small coin of drawing-room poets and the slightly larger coin of Racine. In Russian it became breathtaking." I remarked that someone had once said to me that the first man who compared a woman to a flower was a genius and the second, a fool. "And the third, a knave," said Nabokov.

We went for a drive in the new Lancia through the mountains. Mrs. Nabokov drove, rather fast, mostly in third gear on a tricky road, in the faces of jibes from her husband about sheer drops that she had chosen on other days as suitable places to turn.

"Sometimes my son wishes I wouldn't joke so much," he said with melancholy.

I sat on the back seat, which was still insulated in cellophane, and took off my shoes to keep the cover intact. A hat for butterfly-hunting and walks was on the back shelf.

"You could cover your toes with my hat," said Mrs. Nabokov.

He looked for good meadows for butterfly-hunting and memorized promising paths off the road. His feeling about nature is communicable even to people who don't share it. He is the only man I have ever heard who responds to mention of Los Angeles not with abuse of the city but with glory in the vegetation. He wrote once that when he hunted butterflies it was the highest experience of timelessness, a way "to picket nature" and "to rebel against the void fore and aft." I think it is also an expression of the great writer's passion to define.

We had lemon tea and cream cakes in another hotel looking out across the mountains. He was charming to a waitress who had seemed to have heard the order and said peacefully after a long wait: "I can tell by the nape of her neck that the cakes are coming." He has a comic affection for girls' bodies that is rather like his tenderness for gaffes, as though the naked toes or napes of girls absorbed by other things fall unknowingly into a category of farcical and touching blunders.

I asked him whether Lolita would have turned into a boy if his own real child had been a girl.

"Oh, yes," he said at once. "If I had had a daughter Humbert Humbert would have been a pederast."

I thought perhaps that he might cherish a little hatred for *Lolita* now, as writers often do for books that have had more attention than anything else they have written, but his feelings seem not to have swerved. The book remains his favorite, though he says that *Pale Fire* was more difficult to write.

"I had written a short story with the same idea as *Lolita*. The man's name there is Arthur. They travel through France. I never published it. The little girl wasn't alive. She hardly spoke. Little by little I managed to give her some semblance of reality. I was on my way to the incinerator one day with half the manuscript to burn it, and Véra said wait a minute. And I came back meekly."

"I don't remember that. Did I?" said Mrs. Nabokov.

"What was most difficult was putting myself . . . I am a normal man, you see. I travelled in school buses to listen to the talk of schoolgirls. I went to school on the pretext of placing our daughter. We have no daughter. For Lolita, I took one arm of a little girl who used to come to see Dmitri, one kneecap of another."

He says in his preface that the book originated in a story in *Paris-Soir* of an ape that had been taught to draw: its first drawing was of the bars of its cage. The brawl around *Lolita* and the fierce humor that stylizes all of his work often seems to obscure the extreme tenderness that impels it. His sensitivity to suffering and the exploited makes the attention paid to the plot facts of *Lolita* seem even more brutishly literal-minded than usual. When he was in Hollywood to do the script, the producers asked him to make Lolita and Humbert Humbert get married: apparently this would have pulled some knot of embarrassment for them. The idea of the book being classified as obscene—as it still is in Burma, for instance—is much more gross than anything in most pornography, for it is a book that extends exceptional gentleness to the yearning and the out of step. Elsewhere, in his *Laughter in the Dark*, a murderer thinks "impossible to kill while she was taking off her shoe": it is a modern equivalent of the moment in *Hamlet* when a man can not be murdered at prayer. In Nabokov's work sexuality stands for tenderness, and tenderness is the remaining sanctity.

In the car again I asked him about something he had once written about the author of *Alice in Wonderland*.

"I always call him Lewis Carroll Carroll," he said, "because he was the first Humbert Humbert. Have you seen those photographs of him with little girls? He would make arrangements with aunts and mothers to take the children out. He was never caught, except by one girl who wrote about him when she was much older."

He started to answer something I was saying, and turned it into an imitation of Edmund Wilson saying, "Yes, yes." Nabokov and Edmund Wilson are old friends, but they have recently conducted a waspish public fight about Mr. Wilson's knowledge of Russian, involving claims that seem fairly foolish in the face of a Russian-speaker. Nabokov's private feelings seem affectionately caustic. The imitated "Yes" involved a head-movement like a man trying to get down a pill when he is gagging on it. "Apparently consent with him is so difficult he must make a convulsive effort," said Nabokov warmly enough, and came back to *Lolita*.

"It was a great pleasure to write, but it was also very painful. I had to read so many case histories. Most of it was written in a car to have complete quiet." He says in *Speak, Memory* that "in a first-rate work of fiction the real clash is not between the author and the characters but between the author and the world." This is the force of *Lolita*. The most unsparing love-novel of our literature of glib and easy sex is about an obsession that is locally criminal, written by an alien attacking the numbness of a culture from the inside of the machine that best represents its numbness.

DECEMBER, 1966

Antonioni

Michelangelo Antonioni's august and delicate "The Passenger" is the story of a man trying to fly the coop of himself. He has come to a critical moment of alienation from his English life and work. His identity and his past both seem to him matters of dislocation, and the resulting laxness has nearly consumed him. Not quite. With the courage of an almost beaten man attempting a probably final throw of the dice, he seizes the opportunity to pretend himself dead and to assume the character of a man facially very like him, victim of a fatal heart attack, whom he has met in a remote part of Africa by chance. For the first time in the Socialist Antonioni's career, a declared causal connection is made between a character's distress and his environment. This man's failure of resolve, gently understood by the director, is the political consequence of a dulled life in England and of a fleeting and parasitic job as a TV-news journalist. It is significant that Africa and a movement to change an African government—together with the love of a strange girl who is ready to see him as a new man—are the things that resurrect him for a time.

The film is superficially a thriller. It includes chases, narrow escapes, false alarms, danger in broad daylight while the hero is doing mundane things like renting a car. But not even a newcomer to Antonioni, let alone anyone who has seen his other films, could experience "The Passenger" as a piece of Hitchcock plot-making. Its philosophical foundations and its perceptions of a man's essence are far more interesting and subtle than any narrative. Narrative is the foot soldier of the dramatic arts; Antonioni's points fly in this picture so fast that their meanings are caught only on the wing. "The Passenger's" ambiguities are not a thriller writer's red herrings but the double meanings of a metaphysician who happens to be a Marxist. Before this, the aristocratism of Antonioni's painterly eye and the radicalism of his complex intellect often seemed to be at odds. Here they work in unity. Besides giving us a triumph of technical invention that stretches the wizardly vocabulary of film as he has never stretched it before, Antonioni takes us into the dense world of Camus's "The Stranger" and of the left-wing Existentialist philosophers. There is none of the disquiet between the instinctive and the ideological halves of a slumbrous man in arcane agony which made his "Eclipse" and "Red Desert" seem the struggles of a dozing patient to kick the sheets about in a long, long night. A good many times, at Antonioni's earlier pictures, one felt as if one were sharing the nap of a tormented fop. They often appeared the work of a genius whose dreams were lured by limply beautiful aesthetics and whose intelligence was wasted on teasing us with deliberate obscurantism. "The Passenger" is streets ahead. Everything about it is there by necessity. For instance, where Antonioni's films have often had an unwarranted way of seeing with a foreigner's eye—particularly "Blow-Up" and "Zabriskie Point"— the method is totally pertinent to "The Passenger," because it is a study of a bleached-out man for whom everything is estranging. The man has reached a crisis where even his own past seems an alien's, so that he feels momentarily elated by shedding it to inhabit the carcass of a stranger who is at least new to him.

We are somewhere in Africa. David Locke (Jack Nicholson), an English reporter educated in America, tries to track down a story about a guerrilla hideout. He fails lamentably. Even a small child refuses to be informative when Locke uses him as a guide on a drive by jeep through the desert. A grown guide from the hideout, also volunteering no information, then takes the reporter on foot up a steep hill of sand. But at the sight of a string of camel riders presumably from the side in power the guide abruptly abandons the project and treks off alone. Locke can only go back to the jeep. Another chance missed. How many left? One? Two, with luck? Most of us think chances are limitless, but this man doesn't. His jeep gets ignominiously stuck in the sand. In a tantrum of equal ignominy, he bangs the wheels in turn with a shovel and quickly gives up, shouting "All right! I don't care!" in a position like a Muslim praying. Back at his fly-riddled hotel, there is no soap in the shower. He accepts the fact in his prevailing mood of inert despair, and wanders into the adjoining room of his new acquaintance, named David Robertson. He finds him dead. Their physical likeness is eerie. A fly buzzes. Locke idly starts to go through Robertson's belongings. He looks at Robertson's British passport, and he puts on Robertson's shirt instead of his own. Later on in the film, there is a line about being able to find out a great deal that is sure about a man from the contents of his luggage: better evidence, the film implies, than his outward behavior, just as it was suggested by a wise and quizzical African witch doctor whom Locke interviews in a flashback that the reporter's questions expose a great deal more truth about the reporter than any answers could about the witch doctor.

By putting on Robertson's shirt, Locke has begun the process of changing identity. He returns to his own room, which is a mirror image of Robertson's, and we see him switching photographs in the two passports while his tape recorder plays a conversation between him and the dead man. A time change follows, and the two men are alive together on a balcony in the past, continuing the mechanically embalmed conversation. And then, by an act of film technique as fluent and fit as achieved originality always is, the camera tracks sidewise in space and time across the end of a wall to take us back into the film's present tense, with Locke still concocting his new identity under a fan that moves like a wounded wasp. After dragging Robertson's body into his own room, he abandons his belongings as if they were owned by the corpse, just as he plays dead to his alienated wife, who is in London, by leaving her photograph with the body that is now cast as David Locke's.

The identity, the plans, and the as yet undeciphered motives of Robertson begin to fill the directionless reporter like water pouring into an empty vessel. Locke has Robertson's air ticket, made out for flights around Europe on missions as yet unknown. The route aims first for London, then for Munich. There is a Munich luggage-locker number scribbled on the ticket. Locke also takes possession of Robertson's diary, which is full of the names of far-flung cities to be visited in rapid succession, and notes reading "Daisy," "Lucy," and "Melina." He is drawn by the enterprises of the dead man as if Robertson were still alive to magnetize him, for there is nothing more attractive to the burnt-out than the spectacle of purpose. For a time, Locke follows Robertson's curt orders to himself with obsessed obedience. The designation of his new casting dawns on him slowly. Robertson presented himself to Locke as a traveller who came with merchandise: someone whom the Africans understood, he explained, because he worked with things, instead of with the fragile images and words of Locke the reporter, who had found himself growingly incomprehensible in Africa. In Munich, unwittingly watched by a black African and a European companion as he opens Robertson's luggage locker, the reinvigorated man finds a briefcase full of diagrams of guns. Meaning what? He doesn't know yet. In a hired car, he follows a white horse-drawn coach for no reason except that it is pretty and that he can see the mostly hidden coachman making hand signals. He arrives at a church, to find himself in the middle of a wedding. When the ceremony is over, he stays on alone in the church. Why? Because he is posturing as someone whose reasons for moving in any direction at all are still hidden from him. The ellipses begin to be filled in when the black African and his European friend arrive there on secret business with this man whom they have followed and whom they take to be Robertson. Locke hands over the diagrams, uncertainly pieces together the role he has assumed untutored, and finds himself cast as a highly rewarded political gunrunner in the pay of guerrillas in Africa. There is grateful talk by the two cryptic visitors of the hazards he is facing by working for the guerrillas. Not that Locke cares. It is not the danger of being taken to be Robertson that he ever tries to escape from in the film; it is the danger of being found out to be Locke extant. He wants ferociously to slip the old clutches. The familiar makes him sick at heart. His passionless wife, his adopted child, his ephemeral career as a reporter have all become stale concerns for him. He ditched them for the sake of inhabiting a new identity, which elates him by the sheer potency of the political motive it bestows. Motive to fight on which side? He doesn't care, for the moment. It takes a character who is named just The Girl in the credits—she is exquisitely played by Maria Schneider—to make such questions matter. Obedient to the edicts of the diary, he has gone on to Barcelona. The Girl, met there, is a quiet-voiced, attentive student of architecture who recognizes him as a man at the end of his tether. She quits her companions for the more important business of heeding him. Talking to him, she absorbs more within a very short time than his chilly wife in England ever did, because the wife—a brisk, coarsely pretty figure, played by Jenny Runacre—is an untender woman whose judgments are based only on the evidence of the explicit. She can call on nothing that might be sensed. It is a limitation that must have contributed to the aridity that Locke is running away from. His endeavor to disappear would strike most intimates of such a man as an obvious possibility, but it doesn't strike her until she examines her supposedly dead husband's passport photograph when Locke's luggage is returned to her in London. In the meantime, The Girl has become a passenger in Locke's hired car. She listens to him. The guidance that her own sure character can give him is offered without weight: in a remark about its mattering very much which side a gunrunner is on; in a practical plan to get a mechanic when another stoppage by a mulish vehicle has driven him into another hapless frenzy; and, most of all, in the act of hauling him out of a bog of flailing rebellion about keeping Robertson's next appointment, which is in Tangier. She says simply to him that Robertson made those appointments because he believed in something, and that's what Locke wants, isn't it? She loves him ungraspingly, and soothes him in a predicament that she seems entirely to understand.

The two characters have a typically eloquent and terse exchange about disappearances. "People disappear every day," she says. "Every time they leave the room," says Locke/Robertson. Lying on a bed in a hotel in Almería, he tells her a story about a blind man who gained his sight through an operation when he was nearly forty. At first, Locke says, the man was exhilarated. Then he started to notice that the world was poor. He felt surrounded by dinginess. Squalor everywhere. In the days of his blindness, the man had been able to cross the road with a stick. Then he grew too afraid, and he lived in the dark. The man is Locke's emblem of himself, manifestly. He tells The Girl to go. Altogether aware of some peril, she walks first into the adjoining room and then to the square outside, visible to us through the window grille of Locke's room. There is no sign of his getting up. He isn't in the camera frame any longer. Perhaps he is already dead of a heart attack matching Robertson's? The camera tracks closer to the window, looking out into the square and the walls of a bullring where foolish trumpets are sounding. The Girl is very far away: a small, urgent figure in heavy shoes, leaning forward as if she were in a gale. Cars arrive. An African whom we have seen to be on the government side, and coldly brutish about it, gets out of one and walks to the hotel. There is a muffled shot, or perhaps only a backfire from a car, and the sound of an inside door opening and closing. Is the African an assassin? Is *that* how the unseen Locke dies? It seems likely—but not positive, because not important in such a film. Then the pursuing wife from England, significantly roused to action long after it was merited, speeds into the square in a police car. The camera goes back to Locke's bedroom. His face is hidden. His wife, asked whether she recognizes the body as Robertson's, says, looking at her husband, "I never knew him." The Girl, asked if she recognizes him, says "Yes."

"The Passenger" is an unidealized portrait of a drained man whose one remaining stimulus is to push his luck. Again and again in the movie, we watch him court danger. It interests him to walk the edge of risk. He does it with passivity, as if he were taking part in an expressionless game of double-dare with life. Jack Nicholson's performance is a wonder of insight. How to animate a personality that is barely there? He does it by cutting out nearly all the inflections from his voice, by talking very slowly, by making random movements. One particular gesture is oddly expressive and impassioned. A slight flapping of the arms, as if he were trying to fly. He is sometimes hit by excitement: when he first takes the decision to be Robertson, for instance, and when he feels free of trouble, aloft in a sightseeing car that swings from a cable high above some blue seawater. He leans out of the car and makes a completed version of his flying movement, with his arms spread apart over the sea far below: like a seagull coasting, yet also with a suggestion of a man flinging himself into the embrace of suicide.

Locke is a man racked by the idea of being too distant from the center, which is a major theme of the film's syle and content. He feels doomed to live on the outskirts. The picture has a concentration on suburbs which is no accident. Nor is the oddity of a view of a striking modern housing complex in Bloomsbury, inserted bang in the middle of shots of London houses built a century or two ago. Even when Locke comes upon the familiar, he does it at the tangent of a stranger or a burglar. Disturbingly, he creeps in disguise to the front door of his own house in London after his assumed death, and listens through the letter box to a fragment of his own obituary film on TV. "The Passenger" is full of the imagery of disjuncture. One of the voices in the obituary film is out of sync with the lip movements; cars break down; Locke and The Girl, trying to make contact on the roof of a Gaudí structure in Barcelona, are cut off for a time by a barrier even when they are only yards apart. And Locke is out of joint with his job: though he is famous for his foreign reports, foreignness is his defeat. We recognize a metaphor for that when we see him ineptly struggling to make himself comprehensible in Spanish. Earlier on, trying French, he says, "Vous parlons français?" The first and second persons in verbs have begun to overlap, as his own identity is to overlap Robertson's. He doesn't even possess any longer the pure energy of a reporter on the trail of a scoop. His professional attributes have disappeared as completely as the attributes of his one-time self, so that he feels as much at odds with his past work as with his past personal life. Unalignment is everywhere. In the desert, a passing camel rider has a violently trembling leg that doesn't seem to belong to the rest of his body.

The parallel theme of ambiguity, which has often been explored by Antonioni in a mood of pixie obscurity, is clarified in "The Passenger" to become an excursion into ideas about interchangeability and recurrence. Locke and Roberson are both named David. There are duplicated images of electric wires leading nowhere in different hotel rooms, of like fans in different places, of flies and smashed flower petals on different seedy walls. Everything is done very lightly, as if a punkah were brushing by one's face. Antonioni is working here in unemphatic command of his talent, and for the first time he has bent it to the making of a film that has both the density of a thoughtful novel and the transparent simplicity of an astonishing creation in the visual arts. Besides that, he is as exact about politics as he is about questions of character. His position is stated even in the title: the film was once called "The Reporter," but Antonioni must have considered this to be misleading about who it was he meant to be the key figure, for he changed the title to "The Passenger." So the hero isn't Locke, the empty, unsure man; it is The Girl, who transmits substance and certainty, and whose temperament runs in a radical vein that is always open to ideas of change. It is a joy to find Antonioni making clean statements softly. He shows us, with compassion, a lost man whose alienation is a direct result of his society and his job. Incapable of inventing a new nature, this man can only dwell in someone else. Locke throws himself willy-nilly into a stranger's stream of cause and effect. His history is not some random study in spoilt melancholy; it makes plain a very intelligent filmmaker's political thought. This is not to speak of the serene relevance of almost everything else in "The Passenger": the beautiful and understated sound track, which uses natural sound as if it were music; the camera innovations (the director of photography was Luciano Tovoli); the uncluttered compositions, often like paintings by Veronese, but paintings brought to life. And the screenplay, which was written by Mark Peploe, Peter Wollen, and Antonioni, from an original story by Peploe, grandson of the Scottish painter S. J. Peploe. Earlier Antonioni films have often seemed studied, but not this one. Its details are easy and apropos.

APRIL 14, 1975

Fellini

Fellini once said about "8½" that he would be autobiographical even if he were telling the life story of a sole. "8½" was even more obviously autobiographical than most of his films; it was also without explicit timeliness, so that it got hard criticism for not being engagé enough. I remember walking on the Aldermaston March—the English Easter march in favor of unilateral disarmament—and trying to pass on my admiration of the film to a better athlete, who was striding away his holiday in heavy nailed boots, carrying a knapsack of austere provisions and notebooks of political jottings. He took a mountaineer's glucose tablet for energy, looking at me in a way that made it clear that an admirer of "8½" was a very minor peak to conquer, and said that the film left him unsure of how Fellini felt about the separation of Church and State, as though that wrote off the whole regiment of people in the arts who have chosen to create reveries about love and private life.

Fellini's new "Amarcord" ("I Remember") is even more beauti-

257

ful and detailed than "8½," and free of the playful toying with the ugly and the outlandish which has made his latest films seem impure products and strike the impatient as epicene frescoes intended only to shock. It is perhaps the most dreamlike film he has ever made, though it is actually no dream film. It is about a childhood obviously close to Fellini's, at the start of Fascism, recalled by a fifty-year-old man brought up in a small town. The recollections overlap, as real-life events do. Pranks, family rows, the remarks of town oddities, the coming of Fascism in the guise of something like an uplifting Boy Scout troop seem to flow into one another. The central family consists of Titta (Bruno Zanin), standing for the adolescent Fellini; a tired mother; a self-dramatizing father, wearing a straw hat that he keeps stamping on while telling his relatives not to dramatize; a small brother, who looks at life as though he had his nose pressed against a window; and a thin, unbalanced uncle, less insane than others think. This Dostoevskian character, though he has been committed to an asylum, is said to have always been more clever than his brother at school. Attenuated now into an unshaven figure with a wise, taciturn, occasionally polemic face, he has extra inches of ankle and wrist sticking out of his Sunday-best suit like the ends of sentences that impatient families have never allowed to be heard. Though apparently mad, he is perhaps less deceived than anyone else.

The season is changing. The witch of winter is ritually burned in a bonfire. Spring is arriving. Fluff balls fill the air like the feathers of molting ducks. The town unmarried beauty, who lies about her age and weeps now and then for a husband, wears her red beret at a more dauntless angle. Everyone fancies himself and indulges in grandiose fibs that take in no one. A man who is supposed to be playing in the local seaside-resort orchestra, belonging to a dated hotel that looks about to be shipwrecked, enacts the local Lothario to a surprised but grateful visitor and asks her, "Are you Polish? Only Poles have such fiery eyes." Sex is much talked about by the elderly, in tones of undiminished optimism, and tentatively approached by Titta, who makes a valiant attempt to woo the local tobacconist. A colossal amazon of a woman who wants to be carried about as if she were flying, like a Dumbo mother with the aspirations of a Zeppelin, she howls in ecstasy when the gasping boy manages to lift her off the ground. Pressed against her fluffy V-necked sweater, he twists his head round for air. There is an unmistakable Fellini moment when the excited woman, heaving with pleasure after the boy's repeated and Herculean successes in lugging the screaming sandbag about, strides ahead of him and raises the roll-up metal shop door for him as if it weighed no more than a piece of paper, saying solicitously that it's too heavy for him.

Boys at school undermine the mannerisms of their teachers. A master who talks meditatively of the Romans but concentrates mostly on keeping his cigarette ash as long as possible turns furiously on a small boy who has had the wit to bang authority's desk just when the ash is at a crucial point. Another master, pedagogically mysterious in his habits, chooses to teach in a hat and overcoat and to prowl round the classroom without looking at the boys. While an angelic-looking child manages to blow a raspberry at his schoolmaster every time he is taught a Greek letter that, according to the demonstrating master, involves placing the tongue at a particular place on the palate, the rest of the town is getting caught up in the early days of Fascism. Rows of young boys and girls and ranks of hopeful, poverty-stricken old-age pensioners wait for the arrival of a Fascist general. Their salutes, like his arrival, are obscured by a cloud of smoke. The only dissident is Titta's father, head of a bricklaying firm, who tries to turn up for the occasion in a Socialist tie. It is taken off him by his infuriated wife, for reasons of civic safety rather than of pro-Fascism. All the same, an old-fashioned phonograph bravely rigged up on top of a tower emits shocking sounds of Socialist music. His employees, if they had the money, or the time to think about it, would be Socialist to the core. One of them, nicknamed Brickhead, has written a poem: "My grandfather laid bricks. My father laid bricks. I laid bricks. But I got no house." He laughs. Someone asks the name of the poem. "Bricks," he says.

Uncle Teo, the madman, is taken out for a rare spree in a carriage driven to the family's farm. Courtesies are exchanged. On the way, Uncle Teo eats biscuits and shows the family the stones in his pockets. The family arrives at the farm. Things slowly disintegrate.

Uncle Teo climbs to the top of a tree and yells "I want a woman!" over and over again. Male members of the family get a ladder and climb it to get him down. Each one in turn is hit on the head by a well-aimed stone, about which a great deal of fuss is made. "What an eye! He hasn't missed once!" exclaim the watching children in admiration, absently swatting themselves hard because of the mosquitoes that seem to send most of their scuttling elders, apart from Uncle Teo, into such a state. He has a grander spirit. He stands at the top of his tree undisturbed, uttering his oratorical cry for a woman from his crow's nest of a soul. Uncle Teo may be mad, but he would never be a Fascist. He is at last brought down by a bustling midget nun, who swiftly climbs the ladder and says, "Get down! Enough of this madness!" She and other attendants at the asylum have been called for in despair by the hysterical relatives, who have tried everything to entice him down, including a fake departure without him, though Uncle Teo is a canny visionary who wouldn't care about the trick anyway. There is a life elsewhere, he visibly thinks. Told in the carriage on the way to the farm that he can catch a glimpse of blue sea if he looks over there, he stares fraternally at the sky instead. The asylum attendants understand him. "One day he's normal, the next he isn't. Happens to all of us," says one of the male nurses. Uncle Teo's solemnity, good sense, and feeling of awe are typical of Fellini's film. They are shared by an almond seller who dreams of a wonderful harem ("Oh, what abundance!" he exclaims, red-nosed and excited) and by the wide-eyed small children of the movie. One of them, going to school with a satchel on his back in a fog, falters and halts when he suddenly sees a wonderfully beautiful, soft-nosed white buffalo appearing out of the whorls of mist.

The fluff balls are soft, the snow is soft, and the eye of the film looks softly upon the little town's ceremonial occasions. There are many excitements. There is the bonfire, for instance. There is a communal voyage in small boats to see a grand liner called the Rex. It takes a long time to get to it, but everyone makes the effort. The girl of the town puts on a white sailor suit instead of her usual red dress, and a white beret replaces her red one. We have seen her going to bed in the first one: a gesture that seems to be a mark of the town's sense of the dashing, which is uncrushed by poverty or Fascism. There are always bad things to deal with, after all. The trip out to see the liner is an event. The dolphin species is talked of in words of wisdom. "My dentist says it's a very sentimental fish," someone says contemplatively. The town girl in her sailing kit finds her longing for someone to talk to over a cup of coffee momentarily assuaged by the community spirit. The liner is overwhelmingly beautiful: it is a brightly lit continent full of the debonair and the well-off. "What does it look like?" asks an engagingly irritable blind accordionist, restlessly lifting his dark glasses and frantic for a report. All the same, he can catch the sense of Italianate fun: small-town, self-important, full of braggadocio in ways that Fellini understands and loves. What a worthwhile trip! What a triumph! Then the town is again covered with snow. "We had a record snowfall this year, excluding the Ice Age," says a character who sometimes acts as a narrator.

"Amarcord" is an economical film about small-town bravery. It often sends shivers down the spine. Fellini has surely proved himself good enough by now to be trusted by skeptical bystanders who sometimes see him taking what seems to be a wrong route. To make such an atheistic, wonder-struck, affectionate work as "Amarcord" is very difficult. It is anecdotal yet all of a piece, comic but stirringly saddening. Once in a while, one wants to shake someone by both his hands and say "Well done."

SEPTEMBER 23, 1974

Fassbinder

The pang of exile. The late Russian novelist Vladimir Nabokov and the English-based Czech-born playwright Tom Stoppard share it. Stoppard has adapted Nabokov's 1936 novel "Despair" for the screen, and it has been filmed, under that title, by Rainer Werner Fassbinder. The three men have the same disguise of preciosity, which has to do in Nabokov's and Stoppard's case with the shams demanded of the émigré speaking a strange language and needing to seem at ease.

Early in the nineteen-sixties, before the 1965 English-language revised version of his novel was published, Nabokov and I spoke in the mountains of Switzerland of how best to translate his Russian title, "Otchayanie." We considered "A Cry" and "A Howl." At the time, he opted for "A Howl" and put it down on one of the innumerable index cards that he used like a deck of playing cards in making one of his incomparable novels. Perhaps he was attracted to "A Howl" as expressing the ache of missing Russia. The film begins with the tragic words, spoken by Dirk Bogarde as the hero, Hermann Hermann, "Russia, which we have lost forever . . ." Who is the "we"? White Russians, of whom Hermann is one? The world? Or both, perhaps? Hermann, in his urgency to adjust to strange territory, has adopted a tone of flippancy perfectly suited to Fassbinder's way of making films. Tragedy is never far behind. Hermann says that all the information he has about himself is from forged documents. In this, the saddest and wittiest performance of Dirk Bogarde's career, which exactly catches the careful and slightly-off enunciation of a connoisseur speaking a learned language that he secretly hates, we are made to sense that the hero feels himself to be a forged document, really dwelling in other circumstances, knowing other people.

We are in Berlin, where Nabokov himself took root after fleeing Russia. (He never learned German, though.) Hermann's friends and cronies are a George Grosz gallery of grotesques. He makes love to a fat wife called Lydia (Andréa Ferréol), who wanders about sublimely naked apart from little socks and high heels, and who complains about having lost her lipstick when her mouth is jammy with it. Also not wearing much—just a Victorian-looking black bathing suit, which he sometimes covers with a coat—is a bulging cousin of Lydia's called Ardalion (Volker Spengler), a redhead who belies the usual assumption that redheads have liveliness by being extremely dozy, in a very grumpy way, when he is awake. Only Hermann is meticulously dressed and alert. Also aloof. He sees the multilingual earth as leaving dirt on his shoes.

Hermann has been forced by the ignominy of circumstance to

own, of all fatuous things, a chocolate factory, as if he weren't agonizingly aware of such more crucial matters as the political upheavals in the Ruhr. Lydia stuffs chocolates into her mouth as though she were stoking a boiler. The ethical point of the film, which Fassbinder elegantly makes, is the fatuity that indeed over-takes intelligent people plundered of their origins and forced into wiles. Fatuity is also the drive of the plot. Hermann is determined to commit the perfect murder of a man whom he conceives to be his double, by changing places with him. His victim is Felix (Klaus Löwitsch), who, crazily, is not remotely his double. But Hermann, being a doomed man in a doomed land already up to its ears in guns, butter, and deadly ambition, thinks he can overcome the difficulty by growing a beard like Felix's. The life that he is leaving behind him is nothing, so he sheds it on his slithery course, which nominally has to do with cheating an insurance company but, it is clear, actually has to do with exchanging his pent-up life for any other. Dirk Bogarde is beautifully cast. His performance is full of pettiness and facial fuss that are a wall to hide great trouble of mind and great displacement of temperament. The intentional mannerisms of the performances are matched by Fassbinder's tech-nique, which indulges—as though stuffing the wretched choco-lates—in shots through decorated glass, and the ominous ticking of clocks in scenes that we know to be portentously absurd. Hermann Hermann—his two names are indicatively the same, as though he were floundering even for an identity—wants to take action, takes action, but then finds himself where he stood in the first place. All his careful émigré dressing will not put order into this disturbed world of the nineteen-thirties. The fatuous murder he commits for a change of character is an effort to make local events the events of his life, to possess at least a history when world history has robbed him of it.

Fassbinder is an amazingly prolific director; born in 1945, he has already made more than twenty films in his short career. He be-longs to what is called "the new wave" of West German directors, but he is hard to number among them. Good artists are seldom alike. He delights in pulling audiences' noses; he delights in, so to say, offering them a inch of glucose when he knows they hope it is cocaine. Fassbinder is no cocaine dealer. His concern—contradicted by the film's surface—is with the maintaining of stoicism, gentleness, and sanity in chaotic situations. He is extremely intelligent. He must be much troubled by the split Germany, and much troubled by the worldwide evidence of the receding brainpan. His best earlier film that we have so far seen in this country is "The Bitter Tears of Petra von Kant." It is genuinely bitter and also very funny, with a fierce humor that remains in the mind for good. In "Despair," some people will have their attention waylaid by the intentional facetiousness of Fassbinder's direction. Other people will take joy in the quite unfacetious English that Stoppard has so thoroughly mastered. The key and moving point of this comic film is Hermann's fib that Felix is his brother. In Russia, when he could speak without forgery, he never had a brother. He is now quite alone in the world.

APRIL 19, 1979

Rainer Werner Fassbinder's "The Bitter Tears of Petra von Kant" (1972) is a film about lesbians which Fassbinder solemnly describes as "strictly autobiographical." It is a lucid, beautiful work of innovation which hides its fondness for its characters under a cloak of august formalism. One remembers at the end that the dedication reads, "A case history of one who here became Marlene." Marlene is an apparently minor character who never speaks—of the six women in the film, she is the mute—but the story, in recall, is about the effect of its events on her sensibility. It is typical of the ricochet movement of Fassbinder's films that at the time we should regard her only as a witness. She is apparently present only as a hand on a glass wall, listening to two women talking about love. Or as an offscreen clattering of a typewriter in her employer's office-bedroom.

Petra von Kant (Margit Carstensen) is a dress designer, twice married. She wakes in her plush double bed looking like a very hung-over ballet dancer: hair pinned back, skeletal body, expressive arms. She complains to Marlene (Irm Hermann), her assistant, that her head aches. Marlene is already fully dressed for work, wearing the Edwardian clothes that one comes to accept as contemporary in this hothouse of ruffles and beads and fur trimmings. Petra demands freshly squeezed orange juice. She has had dreams that seem to weight her like pig iron.

Sit up. Grab the white telephone. Talk to her mother, fibbing about having been up for ages, affecting pleasure at her mother's going to a resort. Marlene obediently brings the orange juice. Petra smokes in bed, in a white nightdress fit for a night club. Then she gets up, starting to get dressed by putting on a curly dark-brown wig. She and Marlene dance together, to a record of "Smoke Gets in Your Eyes." Then she abruptly sends Marlene to the easel, because a costume drawing "has to be finished by noon."

There are fibre-glass figures and costume drawings everywhere in the working part of the room. We are watching a woman who is almost suffocated by stylishness, surrounded by copies of herself. Everything is ersatz. When she is on the telephone about an appointment, she forces a pause so that she can seem to be looking in her diary. When she talks to her mother, she pretends that an order to her assistant was a crackling on the line.

A woman friend arrives from Frankfurt. (The only men in the film are the nudes in the huge Correggio mural beside Petra's brass double bed.) As Petra makes up before a mirror, her reflected face moves about in stylized compositions with her friend's. Their impulsive talk runs against the grain of the deliberated images on the screen. It is a habit of Fassbinder's. They are saying that love is difficult. That expressing love is more difficult. That one would often like to say something affectionate, "but you're afraid of losing a point, of being the weaker one." Petra, completing the change in herself from a childishly fibbing daughter with a hangover to a lonely but beautiful career woman giving advice about marriage, utters thoughts that lie at the heart of Fassbinder's notion of her predicament. If you understand a person, she says, then change that person; only pity what you can't understand. She will never be

265

satisfied by what her friend says about women's trump cards: remembering marriage, she says, "I wasn't interested in conjuring
tricks." In her authoritarian solitude, she is looking for equality of
company, curiously enough; in her hypocrisies, she is looking for
probity. The real thing, that's the answer. Omniscience, that's the
answer. Knowing what's going on, not only in yourself but in others.

Yet, all the time, this creation of perfect bones and mascara,
seeking to control everything around her, has very little mastery,
which is one of the abiding and passionate themes of Fassbinder's
apparently unemotional works. The same idea runs through "Fox
and His Friends" (1975), a story of male homosexuality. "There are
more things in heaven and earth . . ." quote both Petra and Fox.
Petra speaks wisely of the uselessness of fidelity under duress, but
by the end of the film she is the one applying the duress. Fox—
played by Fassbinder himself—shows off about his winnings in a
lottery; but a man friend cruelly makes a buffoon of him about his
lack of French in a restaurant, then persuades him to buy a place
that is a folly of grandness and leads him to ruin. In all the sumptu-
ous sophistication of both Petra's and Fox's experiences, there is
much pain, much innocence. Just as Fox is robbed of his fortune by
tutelage in good living, so Petra is tormented in her fortunate
world of a room, furnished with a copy of a great painting and
bald-headed, long-necked mannequins.

Petra falls in love with a working-class girl called Karin (Hanna
Schygulla). When she is suddenly abandoned, as she has abandoned others, the nearly intolerable pain perplexes her. She calls
Karin a slut. She says that if she'd known things would turn out this
way her attitude would have been different. As the friend of much
earlier in the film said, "When you foresee the end from the start,
is the game worth the candle?" Yes, of course, says the film, because no other route is ever possible: Petra was lonely, and Karin
was company to grasp. Fassbinder is defining need without love.
"I'm so alone without you," Petra says to Karin. "Alone, without a
slut?" says Karin acidly.

With Karin gone, the white pile carpet of the office-bedroom
becomes the stage, with Petra crawling over it tippling gin and

hysterically clasping the telephone receiver. Clinging to a vestige of power, she refuses to go to Frankfurt when Karin eventually rings. In the meantime, Marlene has been unnoticed, but not unobservant. Much changed, and suffering, she packs her case. Very little. She takes with her a naked mannequin doll that was a knowing birthday present to Petra. Then she leaves, hobble-skirted. Hobble-skirted because of obeisance to femininity? Because she is beguiled by Petra's notion of love, which is a process of demands and reprisals much like the ones played out in "Fox and His Friends"?

Fassbinder's films ache, in spite of their apparent formalism. On the face of it, "Petra" is a theatrical film. Six women, no men; five acts, separated by change of dress; no change of scenery, much change of mood. The set moves from bed to corridor to carpet. In one of the final episodes, when Petra is sprawled on the floor with the telephone, the pile carpet becomes a field of razed earth.

Fassbinder shoots in very long takes. The camera seldom moves. We become obsessed with the contradiction of composed and worldly faces uttering primitive anguish. Heads in closeup will appear to touch and part breathtakingly while intimacy is abstractly spoken of. In pain, there are no mascara smudges. Lovemaking is made emblematic: by the heads of two dressed women briefly bending over one another's shoulder. Everything is terse and minimal. Noun and verb. Fassbinder is concerned here with the sort of love that rests in contest. So his real heroine is not Petra, the victimizer turned victim, but her silent assistant, who has been tortured by the sight of sadistic love's punishments.

This is a political film, as Fassbinder's always are, as well as a sage film about love. Petra believes that what she has earned she can break. In her agony of longing for Karin, the lower-class model who has made a reputation out of working for her and then found it easy to leave her, she stamps on a tray laid with an expensive tea set. All fragments. But she is only breaking a talisman of her elegant ambitions: it is no triumph, because she is not destroying her passion for Karin. The passion is born of capitalism, Fassbinder implies, for Petra still truly believes that she paid for Karin by giving her the benefit of her greater talent and income, constituting a superiority of class in the tournament. The changeover of power is shown by Fassbinder with a curtness veiling sympathy. The dialogue is sharp in a stylized set of scenes. It is often the case that extreme stylization covers extreme pity. This is so of "The Bitter Tears of Petra von Kant." In a setting deliberately made to seem shallow, his characters deepen: the powerful hypocrite turns into the loser, and the silent employee symbolizing obedience and imitation changes into the rebel and the original. We are watching a more political and more angular "Miss Julie." Fassbinder makes films with a cutting edge. Henri Langlois, director of the Paris Cinémathèque Française, during an *hommage* to him said that he represented "the beginning of German postwar cinema."

Fassbinder was born on May 31, 1945, in Bad Wörishofen, Bavaria. In *Cinéma*, in an interview with Jacques Grant, he describes his background as being "upper-middle-class and jolty." After his parents were divorced, he lived away from his doctor father and with his translator mother, who often gratefully packed him off to the cinema so that she could work. At an acting school, he met Hanna Schygulla, star of most of his films. Together they got in touch with Action Theatre, a cellar theatre in Munich which was the root of the "antitheatre" that he founded in 1968. A year later, he shot his first feature film, "Love Is Colder Than Death," with the same troupe. Like Bergman, he works as often as he can with a semirepertory company of actors and technicians. He has written and directed more than twenty features (some for TV), written and directed an eight-part TV serial, and acted often in his own and other people's films. Like many prodigal artists, he seems to correct any mistake he finds in a film by immersing himself in the next picture. No going back. The new work is the revision. "Petra" was made in ten days. He gives his films a peculiar mood of double dare; perhaps all great talent contains an element of cheek.

Fassbinder's films are not so much about the working multitude as for it. "Films directed to the proletariat aren't necessarily about the proletariat," he says in the same interview in *Cinéma*. In "Petra," which is unusually upper-class in its outward appearance, Karin is there to stand for his familiar characters: "In a negative way, she represents an aspect of the workers' consciousness, but she is an obsessional object . . . For working artists, the manual worker is a sort of obsession." About the theatre, he professes to social doubts. "The theatre, after all, is more important for the people who are part of it than for those who watch it." Fassbinder is a specialist in provocative utterance, but his work itself denies frivolity. It is deeply serious and meditative. Its surface is as formal as Gluck's music, but the texts express much tenderness, especially for the immature, the scared, and the jumped-up or hopeful heading for a fall into hell, like the hero of "The Merchant of Four Seasons," a fruit-and-vegetable hawker with aspirations who drinks himself to death. Fassbinder is not a "realistic" filmmaker, because he finds it a tautology to copy the real onscreen. He is interested in making a new reality: one that exists in our heads. An imitation of reality tends to make us stall at the point of the merely apparent, he thinks. Like Brecht, he believes in the distance that can be provided by the comic. He is troubled by the gurus of life, as he is by all master-slave relationships. The extreme formalism of his best later films tends to hide their warmth. He would like to see his characters escaping their traps. He has a great feeling for life's truants. One remembers that he ran away from home himself at the age of sixteen.

JUNE 14, 1976

"Force—it's the only way. Guns, hostages, blackmail," says an anarchist to the heroine of Rainer Werner Fassbinder's "Mother Küsters Goes to Heaven," talking to her, at the end of the film, about means of getting the German public to recognize what in truth happened to her dead gentle factory-worker husband. The husband has been represented by a magazine as a lout who in a fit of mania murdered a fellow-worker and then killed himself, and she desperately wants the record corrected. But a gun isn't the way to do it, she knows.

"It sure would start people thinking," says the anarchist.

"You can't blackmail people to do that," replies the woman, in her soft and stoic way, making one of the tonic points of all Fassbinder's films. He isn't a man to force an audience to ponder by planting a pistol in its ribs.

"Mother Küsters" was made in 1975. At the start of the film, we see Mother Küsters working at a Frankfurt kitchen table. She might be peeling onions. *Kinder, Küche, und Kirche.* But the West German economic miracle has happened, so this modest, quail-shaped woman is not slicing vegetables or rocking a baby but keeping the economy going. Screws are being put into endless numbers of identical electrical parts. Piecework at its worst. Yet Mother Küsters brings to it her own placid bonhomie. Woman's work is here, implies this far from ordinary housewife with a characteristic suppressed merriment—though her output fell by a hundred the week before, which mildly depresses her. Mother Küsters is played by Brigitte Mira, one of Fassbinder's regular acting troupe. She has a face that looks as if it were made of melting tallow, the brisk walk of the plump, and interested eyes. She regards electricity with less fellowfeeling than she would have for *Apfelstrudel,* or even for her smugly pregnant daughter-in-law, Helene (Irm Hermann). For a woman like Mother Küsters, dealing with electricity is like living in a cold-storage room, though a warm draft blows in when members of her family enter and take over some of the work from her while they talk to her, as naturally as though she were making a cake and they were beating the eggs. Her son Ernst has always wanted to be a builder. Oh, to build something, instead of fitting screws into plugs for Lord knows whose offices or houses. *Ach!* Well, on with the pile. A radio in the kitchen reports that a man in a chemical plant has run amok, killed the boss's son, and then killed himself by throwing himself into the machinery.

A man comes to the front door, a factory colleague, and tells Mother Küsters that the man was her husband. She can't take it in. Her Hermann was never a violent man. All he did was say, sometimes, "We're not getting any younger." Her face trembling, she telephones her daughter Corinna (Ingrid Caven), who is working in a far-off night club as a cheap chanteuse. The manager of the club doesn't give a damn about the news. He slouches. "Who has any family nowadays?" he says. Fassbinder deals in a particular kind of sullen nonchalance about crisis. The girl's face, apparently made up with sable eyelashes and strawberry jam, looks like a child's at a party that has gone wrong.

Once the story of the factory murder is out—interpreted by the boss class as mutinous, by the left as revolutionary—reporters are ravenous for gossip. The pregnant daughter-in-law gloats over the attention paid to her. One of the journalists (Gottfried John) promises a sympathetic story but publishes a monstrosity of sensationalism, having won Corinna into his bed by assuring her of fame from his account of her father's brainstorm.

So: On one side, the West German miracle. On the other, the Thälmanns (Karl-Heinz Böhm and Margit Carstensen), very elegant Communists, whose manners remind them to offer their condolences. They are genuinely kind and dangerously naïve. When the officious daughter-in-law moves herself and her husband out of Mother Küsters' apartment, after answering want ads on her mother-in-law's telephone, Mother Küsters finds friendship with the Thälmanns and goes to speak at one of their Communist meetings. The occasion is full not of rabid politickers but of quiet-faced kids in jeans and placidly married couples. We might be at a church social, with the Thälmanns there as the local lord and lady of the manor. It is all gracious, affectionate, imperturbable. Hermann Küsters knew that there had to be change, but he effected change in the wrong way, says Herr Thälmann with vehement banality. Good point, agrees the audience.

A little later, the anarchist advocate of guns proposes to Mother Küsters a sit-in with him and his group—a group consisting of one subdued-looking member—in the offices of the magazine that published the sensational article about Hermann Küsters. She agrees. By closing time, the sitting militants have got hungry and quit. Mother Küsters stays on, out of her depth but staunch. It is the night watchman who eventually gets her to move. After all, he says, she can come back tomorrow morning to go on with her all-night vigil, and tomorrow, and tomorrow. Meanwhile, he offers a dinner menu of "heaven and earth"—sausage and apple dumplings. Responding to the first practical offer she has had in many a long day—much more sound than the Communists' or the anarchist's—she gets up from the floor, uncrossing her black-stockinged legs, which must have gone to sleep, and leaves the deserted and foodless revolutionary picnic place.

As West Germany is torn down and rebuilt, so the wreck of Mother Küsters' life is propped up for an evening by the night watchman—a widower—who has offered her the heaven and earth. Food is not heaven, but the watchman's is probably nearer to it than anything else that has happened to her recently; the Communists' courtesy was hardly manna.

"Mother Küsters" is full of a skeptical comedy that is very much Fassbinder's. His early films were greatly influenced by American gangster movies; like Godard's, though, they implant doubt. His abiding theme is the person who wishes that he had made something of his life which he never did. Mother Küsters has this wish and discerns it in others. She even seems to have sympathy for her daughter-in-law's paltry tight-little-family goals. Mothers Küsters is a noble woman. Who is to say how much passion was expended in all those hours of putting together electric plugs with a screwdriver? People suffer most because they can't express grief.

The film—written by Fassbinder and Kurt Raab, longtime actor and designer with Fassbinder's group—is like Brecht's plays and poems in declining open sensibility, but all the same its coinage is care for people, with a guttersnipe wit about the self-deceptions that slaughter intent. Probably the journalist is not so bad a man as he seems, but he is doing something lethal to Mother Küsters by getting her to reenact phony scenes of cooking and bedmaking for his camera, because he is getting her to create a replica of the same dulled life that made her husband go berserk, and coming nowhere near the truth of what made them love each other. And probably the well-bred Communists truly mean to be kind; but one of the most touching scenes in this pungent political comedy is an overhead shot of Mother Küsters alone in their cultivated drawing room, automatically taking the stiff-backed, armless chair beside the big armchair that belongs to the master. The shot is precise, unstressed, troubling. The film has a melodramatic plot, but it is no melodrama. Any work of fiction is beyond melodrama when its logic is clear and large enough. The picture tells us that rhetoric is no escape; that a guru-disciple relationship between sexes or classes is damned; that primitivism of expression—losing one's mind, having a tantrum, using emotional bribery—makes savages of us all; that, since no film artist would hand you the keys to character, the only thing to watch is outward conduct. Mother Küsters does not, of course, go to heaven, as the title bitterly states. But she has made the best choice with her sausage and dumplings, and to have choice is, indeed, a sort of heaven on earth. The Communists were not the answer: they were hilariously hemmed in by their inherited classiness, and someone less lonely than Mother Küsters would have broken down their well-bred walls to find out what they really felt. The anarchist was not the answer, either: he seemed made for the oddly baleful fête champêtre of the magazine-office sit-in. And the pugnacious pregnancy of Mother Küsters' daughter-in-law was certainly not the answer: no new way of life was going to be born from that. The film, like Fassbinder's "The Bitter Tears of Petra von Kant," has sins of hypocrisy on its mind: play-acted phone calls, plagiarized sensitivity. Fassbinder's style paradoxically makes an ideal of theatricality rather than of naturalism. In his attitude toward his characters, he is like a burglarious child shaking a piggy bank to get out the hoard: rattling them upside down and from side to side to try to get the truth out of them.

Fassbinder is the *wunderkind* of German cinema, born in Bavaria of a doctor father and a translator mother. He went to drama school, and calls himself an autodidact apart from this apprenticeship as an actor. His first feature film was titled "Love Is Colder Than Death" (1969). Again and again, at febrile speed, he has explored the "Mother Küsters" theme of the withering of emotion between people living together, forcing them to exist in a way that fragments their spirits and often ends in death. Setting his films in contemporary Munich and Frankfurt, where new and uncertain buildings are going up on bombed sites, he generally uses as his décor the houses and wallpapers and knickknacks of the petit bourgeois. Though there is a lot of Brecht in him, perhaps it is not as much as he would like: Brecht was confirmed in his sardonic nonbelief, and one has the feeling that Fassbinder is hectically looking for what not to believe in. Certainly the answer for him doesn't lie in investigating his own grand-bourgeois family background. It is part of his poet's nature that he has jumped over his own shadow.

MARCH 28, 1977

In the child world of the prodigious young Rainer Werner Fassbinder's films, everyone is an immigrant. There is something fugitive about all his characters. They belong nowhere. Their lives seem rehearsals for death. Fassbinder (German), in spite of what one might expect from his tremendous output, was born after the Second World War, but guilt weighs on him all the same, often in the form of a fierce and tacky humor. He would like to know more about the past, you feel, but he is damned if he is going to ask. The construction of the new Germany has much to do with his outpouring, which is an economic miracle in itself, and much to do with his feckless attitude toward politics: by nature, he seems inclined toward East Germany, but a certain moral allegiance or torpor keeps him in the West. There is no question about his artistic brilliance. It is the brilliance of a layabout sunning himself in apparently crass aphorisms whose humanity he prefers to keep hidden.

Child of the Common Market, too young to recall Fascism, he takes shelter in an assumed mood of cool, and concerns himself with the plight of the self-exiled and the out-of-bounds. His sub-

274

jects are incompetent criminals, downtrodden office workers, scab laborers, noble women with no one to talk to, the children of bourgeois families that are ready to throw their kids to the dogs if they break the rules of respectability. The admirable New Yorker Theatre Fassbinder season this spring and summer is currently showing a fine, frugal example of this theme, called "Jail Bait" (1972)—a translation of a slang phrase meaning "game-crossing"—from a play by Franz Kroetz. A fourteen-year-old girl called Hanni (Eva Mattes) is made pregnant by a nineteen-year-old boy called Franz (Harry Baer) with fifties-era hair. The father, who dotes on her incestuously, asks what sort of government it is that can't defend fourteen-year-olds. Under the Nazis, the boy would have been properly got rid of. "But," says the mother, "the Nazis weren't *all* good." Hanni persuades the boy to murder her father, saying they'll go to the cinema afterward. The child is born deformed and dies. One generation poisons another.

Fassbinder is fascinated by a particular kind of lolling hypocrisy that he finds in our times. "Jail Bait" is a painful statement about the ways the sins of a wartime generation can be visited on its offspring. The director, as ever, is beset by the determinist notion that the young are at the mercy of their glands. He sees them as being quite without will, like the headless chickens whirling around in the slaughter room where Franz hoses down the dangling poultry. It is this determinist philosophy that leads Fassbinder to his obsession with power—sadomasochistic, parental, economic—and to films of calculated mannerism, like "Chinese Roulette" (1976), in which a despotic teen-ager whose legs are paralyzed has vicious sport with her parents, who have both planned to have affairs in their castle over a weekend in the delusion that their spouses will be elsewhere. The dislocated family have politely nervy feasts together. Gestures seem patterned; even faces look choreographed. Exaggeration is one of Fassbinder's ways of underlining the ersatz quality and the loneliness that he finds everywhere. In "Jail Bait," the family house is cluttered with the artifice of sanctimony. Replicas of saints and of the Madonna abound, china ducks make a dreadful aviary. Nothing seems real. Not even some of the people.

Fassbinder's typical shot is like a stare. The camera hardly budges. People are apparently trapped in doorways or between other vertical edges, unable to move. The style is a reflection of Fassbinder's pity for his characters. We are all immobilized nomads, talismanic objects, he says. Many of his films are about foreigners; there is the Moroccan in "Ali: Fear Eats the Soul" (1973), the Greek worker he himself plays in "Katzelmacher" (slang for "troublemaker": 1969). We are all from somewhere else. When we find it so difficult to be alone, we ought to consider living together rather than parting: this is the undertow of what he is saying. His long, static takes lead to unease, not to boredom. Solitude lays its dark hand even on his moments of drollness.

In "Ali," a thirty-year-old immigrant laborer (El Hedi Ben Salem) in Munich marries a sixty-year-old cleaning woman (Brigitte Mira). There is much petulance from her grasping family. (Fassbinder plays her brute of a son-in-law.) The neighbors say that they don't want real-estate values on the block brought down. Fassbinder gives ferocity to shots that most directors would make meditative. There is murder in his long, thoughtful gazes, a razor blade hidden in the fist of a trivial insolence.

Fassbinder makes no use of suspense or the maudlin. If Godard has influenced him, the most potent effect on Fassbinder's prolific work has probably come from "Vivre Sa Vie," with its theme of exploitation and prostitution in an inarticulate world of outsiders. As in Fassbinder's elegant "The Bitter Tears of Petra von Kant" (1972), his characters—his scripts are nearly always his own—make demands that are sadistic or wanton. In other, less highbred films of his in the same vein, we are in a world of autocratic landlords, baleful people in launderettes and supermarkets and corner cafés. He is much concerned with the emancipation of women—the heroine of his magnificent "Effi Briest" (1974) is sister to Ibsen's Nora—though there is also a lot of unwitting misogyny in the way he treats his women characters, turning them into mannequins or squalling witches or pretty toys. At his most true-pitched, he shows us both men and women not as sadists or minxes but as objects of humor and pity, living out lives of courage in considerable loneliness. His characters are in the dark, consigned to the crypts of their temperaments. One is moved by the Fassbinder pallor of the lighting of their faces. They inhabit frighteningly empty landscapes. When lyricism comes, it gives the film a subdued moral glow, which floods the screen. Margarethe says in his "The American Soldier" (1970), "Happiness is not always gay."

Fassbinder shows us in his films that people who mix with the aspiring bourgeois are generally cheated by them. He seems to feel that he would prefer to live in a society in which it wasn't necessary to be an artist, though I doubt whether it would be easy, or right, for this prodigy to stop making films. Half of his apparent rebelliousness, like the insolence of his colors, is a gauntlet thrown down. His benignity is concealed, as much as he can manage it. There is unmistakable sweetness in the way the sixty-year-old heroine of "Ali" shows off her lover to her friends. Look at his muscles! What's more, he takes a bath every day! But her innocent wish to flourish him drives him back to his colleagues in a rundown bar.

Fassbinder's films tell us about the entrenched race prejudice of his own middle class. The landlord's son in "Ali" points out that subletting is not allowed. The sixty-year-old woman says staunchly that then the thing is to get married. There is a celebratory wedding breakfast in a restaurant where Hitler used to eat. The waiter turns out to be amiable. But unplaced fear is already devouring the couple's spirit and destroying them from within. It is at moments like these, not at the moments of Fassbinder's nonchalant aggressiveness, that we recognize a cinematic poet, whose topic is the attrition of souls.

MAY 30, 1977

Black and white are the most ravishing colors of all in film. It is not only Truffaut's "Jules and Jim" that has told us this. Now we have in New York another black-and-white masterwork: "Effi

277

Briest," directed by Rainer Werner Fassbinder, who is a German prodigy. At thirty-one, he has made more than twenty films. "Effi Briest" was the first film he wanted to make, but he couldn't raise the money until 1974, by which time he had made nineteen other films. This one comes from the famous German novel of 1893 by Theodor Fontane, and it lives in a literary climate, which is not to say that it is not also altogether cinematic. As with most of Fassbinder's films, its concern is in the sophistry of the powerful; it is kin to his "Chinese Roulette," a mysterious comedy of calculated mannerisms.

Effi Briest, played by Hanna Schygulla, a member of Fassbinder's great acting troupe, is a girl of seventeen who lives with her parents in a small town stamped with the Prussian determinism of the Bismarck period. A man with a face like a knife edge, Baron von Innstetten (Wolfgang Schenck), remotely courts her and asks her parents for her hand. Twenty years ago, he was her mother's suitor. After Effi has been his wife for a while, the general agreement is that he would have done better to marry the mother. Not the most encouraging thing for a daughter to hear. The daughter is a fearful, beautiful creature with a hint of wildness somewhere in her. But the wildness is subdued. The iron ineloquence of the Bismarck attitude that oppresses society also muffles personal temperament, and Fassbinder's way of using a staring, distant camera to photograph scenes and then making them discrete by title cards that bleach to white is like a hand of benediction on the violence of the story. The opening card reads, "Many who have an idea of their possibilities and needs nevertheless accept the prevailing order in the way that they act, and thereby confirm and strengthen it absolutely." Effi is ambitious in paltry ways that run along the tracks of Prussian convention. When she goes to Berlin with her mother to buy her trousseau, she wants a Japanese screen. Her entrancing self seems metaphorically hemmed in by the frame of the film. Title card: "A story of resignation cannot be bad." No? Her spirit of adventure is quenched. In a misleading idyllic sequence, she follows in her mother's footsteps on a walk in high grasses: two graceful figures made awkward by a nervous etiquette between intimates. When she gets married and goes to live in a house by the Baltic, her intelligence is overtaken by her susceptibility to superstition. Innstetten tells her about a family ghost. He says that a Chinese servant who was the victim of an unhappy love affair is buried out in the sand dunes. Effi hears the family ghost above their bedroom; an eerie servant tells her that it is only the brush of the long curtains across the floor. Fear begins to consume Effi's spirit from the inside, like a tapeworm in her imagination. No wonder she fancies herself in love with a debonair Pole, called Major Crampas. She has just had a baby, who is something of an anticlimax, being female. The doctor says, "Pity it's a girl." But there will be other chances, he says. "There are lots of Prussian victories." Effi begins to lose her way. One can become so formal that one can grow formless. Crampas tells her stories about Innstetten. He says the Baron uses ghosts as education. Innstetten's ethic, he says, is that a person need only be upright and unafraid. Effi is hurt by the didact Instetten's puzzling impulse to instruct her.

Fassbinder thinks a great deal about oppressed groups, including women. "Effi Briest" is his masterpiece. (It was shot in fifty-eight days, spread over two and a half years, though he usually spends something like sixteen days on shooting a film.) His Effi, true to Fontane's, is the victim of an education that makes girls beguiling and frivolous objects, and so leads inevitably to a whim on the part of society to inhibit them with taboos. Effi is not only intimidated by the ghost but also fearful of committing crimes against bourgeois society, and terrorized by the possibility of appearing to the respectable to be a tart. Whether or not she actually ever has an affair with Crampas is uncertain. It is enough of a crime that she sits with him so often on a windy beach near their Baltic home while Innstetten is away. When some letters from the Major are discovered under a pile of linen, she feels she deserves to be kicked out, deserves to have her child turned against her, deserves to be gracelessly received back by her parents. The film is full of shots of modest, frightened, pent-up people seen through half-open doors: people scared by Prussian tartars and by primitive women with terrible tales to tell. Effi's maid, Roswitha (Ursula Strätz), who delivered Effi's child, recalls her own youth, and speaks of her father's coming at her with a red-hot poker: "When you're as afraid of your father as I was, you're not afraid of God very much." Life is lived by a system of fear and loneliness. God is not supposed to be a comfort, or society to provide companions. Effi is a naturally congenial and lively being, but Bismarck's Prussia blanches her spirit. Fassbinder's film has to do with the monstrous dictates of others about her life. Innstetten, paying a debt to his self-esteem and to the esteem of a friend in whom he has confided, insists on a duel with Crampas, whom he kills. There is a last flicker of rebellion in Effi. "I am repelled by what I did," she seems to be saying, "but what repels me still more is your virtue. Away with you!" It is a virtue consisting of no pity, in a man with a spine of fused lead bullets. Perhaps Effi's mother would have been better able to cope with him. In the last scene, in the parents' garden, where they are having coffee, the mother wonders whether they married Effi off too young. "It's too vast a subject," says the father. Silence. Autumn leaves fall. A coffee spoon chinks.

This is as fine a film as we have seen in a long time. One stands amazed by the fanatic talent of Fassbinder's faithful acting troupe, the moving elegance of the photography (by Jürgen Jürges and Dietrich Lohmann), the beauty of the art direction (as usual, by Kurt Raab, who has also acted in Fassbinder films). This is one of the few films by Fassbinder that haven't a hint of the melodramatic about them. "Effi Briest" is a vivid story of the dousing of a tonic personality by manners, misleading expectations, misled hopes. It is a fiercely philosophical picture; Fontane, at different times, a war correspondent and a drama critic, was seventy-three when he wrote the novel, which questions whether the sensibility of the individual, however strong, can always give a life the liberty to run counter to social models. This magnificent, inquiring film, though it is an epic in its way, is no spectacle; it is, above all, a spyglass on our consciousnesses. Effi Briest knows very well that she was a child and then a mother without ever being a woman. The bourgeoisie is sleepwalking, says the film, but its victims are only too alert.

JUNE 21, 1977

Rainer Werner Fassbinder's "Satan's Brew," with Kurt Raab as a writer who has stopped writing, is a deliberate slap in the face. Kurt Raab plays a slob called Walter Kranz, who operates from the same feckless, uninhibited, unscrupulous, and unpredictable position that Fassbinder does in hurling this movie at us. The film creates an irritable weather all its own. People behave like cross morons, pretend to less intelligence than they actually have, move with the gestures of wooden puppets on tangled strings. Kranz came from the petite bourgeoisie. He has some success as a writer and then, looking for something irreducibly silly to do, returns to a proto-Fascist petit-bourgeois manner, to the accompaniment of mischievous music. He suddenly writes a line or two, plagiarizing Stefan George, whom he decides to become. This means collecting homosexual listeners to pay homage at readings that he gives from George's work, wearing makeup and a black Edwardian suit.

Fassbinder has made this shock-the-middlebrow picture go at a rattling pace, piling on evil comic details to see how much we will take. Kranz's brother is simpleminded and collects dead flies. Fassbinder plants warts on the face of the beautiful Margit Carstensen and gives her a pair of spectacles that make her eyes look deranged, and when she says how much she hates her sister, it is with a sweet smile that would go more aptly with the opposite statement. Fassbinder forever pits words against physical expressiveness in this film, and throws sense out of joint. A policeman with no shoes on investigates a murder and catechizes the murderer with a look of immovable amiability. Kranz is someone who thinks that to be free may not necessarily mean to be bohemian or libertarian; that it could just as well mean being free to express rigidity, authoritarianism, cruelty. The contrary-minded man realizes that he has very little talent. But he has a gift for selling himself, which he accepts as a sufficient substitute. He assimilates nothing; he will never grow up, because he merely reenacts situations without changing them. Fassbinder has given himself the license to go haywire, perhaps in the interests of testing our endurance while we are having a sadomasochistic charade thrown at us like so much mud. Spattered and spluttering, we must be prepared to roll with the punch. Exceptional talent—and Fassbinder appears to possess it—often has moments of running amok. Better to go too far than not to move; and there may even be a compassionate nut of truth about the fate of the underendowed buried somewhere in this gaudy piece of provocation.

AUGUST 15, 1977

INDEX

285